W9-CFG-330

THE
Chef's Secret
COOK BOOK

THE
Chef's Secret
COOK BOOK
By Louis Szathmáry

ILLUSTRATIONS BY CAROLYN AMUNDSON

Foreword by Jean Hewitt

CHICAGO

QUADRANGLE BOOKS

1972

THE CHEF'S SECRET COOK BOOK. Copyright © 1971 by Louis Szathmáry.
All rights reserved, including the right to reproduce this book
or portions thereof in any form. For information, address:
Quadrangle Books, Inc., 12 East Delaware Place, Chicago 60611.
Manufactured in the United States of America. Published simultaneously
in Canada by Burns and MacEachern Ltd., Toronto.

Library of Congress Catalog Card Number: 78-116088
SBN 8129-0213-0

Typography and Binding Design by The Inkwell Studio

FIFTH PRINTING

Contents

Foreword

by Jean Hewitt

Cook books written by European-trained chefs tend to be esoteric, and the aspiring cook often discovers that it's necessary to search for hard-to-find ingredients, and spend hours in a professionally equipped kitchen, to turn out the exotic concoctions described. An intimate knowledge of cooking techniques is taken for granted.

Louis Szathmáry avoids this approach and offers a wide range of cosmopolitan-style recipes in this book which reflect his European background and wide range of interests. They are presented in a down-to-earth, practical way that can be followed successfully in the average American kitchen. There are dishes with Mexican, Far Eastern, French, Italian, and Hungarian accents, as well as variations of American specialties.

Where an ingredient might be difficult to obtain, or a process require a professional skill, Mr. Szathmáry suggests a substitute or a simpler technique. There is no compromise, however, in the end results. Both simple and elaborate recipes have been tested to ensure a superior food experience whether served at a simple family luncheon or an elaborate formal dinner.

About one-fifth of the recipes are for dishes served occasionally at The Bakery, the well-known Chicago restaurant where Mr. Szathmáry is chef-owner. The majority are from his personal files. Born in Hungary, Mr. Szathmáry, who earned a Ph.D. in psychology from the University of Budapest, lived in Austria and other Western European countries before coming to the United States in 1951.

The recipes here are set out in a clear, easy-to-read style, and drawings help explain the more intricate steps in such operations as boning a leg of lamb or making a pocket in a pork chop. Unlike many chefs who cling passionately to the trade secrets of the profession, Louis Szathmáry goes out of his way to share his secrets. At the end of each recipe, he offers several hints to ensure success, and gives reasons for certain procedures.

These footnotes add up to almost a second book beyond the recipes, and represent the knowledge and experience Mr. Szathmáry acquired during his apprenticeship and work in professional kitchens.

For instance, Chef Louis tells why it's necessary to blanch the veal for a Veal Paprikash and how to retrieve the mayonnaise that curdled. There's at least one Chef's Secret for every recipe, and some have as many as six. It would be hard to pose a culinary question about any of the recipes that Chef Louis hasn't anticipated.

Cooking and serving a suckling pig is a major undertaking and can be fraught with hazards but, with the recipe in this book, and the Chef's Secrets on purchasing, carving, and serving, the mysteries are dispelled.

The range of recipes in the book is extensive and goes from an old-fashioned method for roasting a turkey in a brown paper bag to pigeon pie and preparing homemade, potted goose for a cassoulet. A suggestion for a canned alternate for the involved potted goose is typical of Chef Louis' relaxed approach to cooking. "If you can't get fresh peas, use the frozen," he says succinctly.

He's not against a short-cut here, or the use of pie dough mix there. But for those who care, and are willing to spend the time, there's a two-page recipe for making an "easy galantine."

The book is full of helpful information, including how to kill a lobster and make some of the dishes ahead. Besides Chef Louis' original recipes, there are interesting variations of classic dishes. An unusual Boeuf en Daube recipe, when put to the test in the kitchen, was delicious.

This is not a book with only a classic Escoffier approach to food preparation, though there are recipes for brown sauce and petite marmite, but a practical and personal presentation of good cooking that will appeal to the neophyte and the experienced cook.

Introduction

When I give recipes to ladies in my restaurant, The Bakery, the most frequently asked question is "Did you leave out some secret?"

And, when I tell them, "Of course not," they look at me very suspiciously. They do not believe it. They always feel the chef leaves something out of the recipe—a miraculous secret ingredient, an unobtainable taste catalyst that "makes" the dish.

When I tell the ladies that I am able to give them everything except my long years of experience, they still look suspicious. So once again I launch into my best explanation, an old record played over and over again, which goes something like this: "If you go to a concert and listen to Artur Rubinstein playing the *Mephisto Waltz* of Franz Liszt, and if you go and see him backstage after the performance and ask him for the piano notes, and if through some miracle he gives them to you, and you take them home and sit down at your piano (untouched for years), open up the notes, and play the *Mephisto Waltz,* and your husband says, 'Darling, it doesn't sound like Artur Rubinstein . . .'—what do you tell him?"

Probably this: "Oh, what a selfish artist! He left out something from the notes, I'm sure. Because when I play it, it doesn't sound like when he plays it."

"Well, dear ladies, do you really think Rubinstein left out some of the notes? Or do you think his talent had something to do with it—and his daily practice for years and years and years?

"You see, my dear ladies, cooking is just like playing the piano—it needs talent, training, and practice."

That is the way I tell it to the ladies, and as a rule they understand. For this is the first secret of good cooking, the most important "secret ingredients": constant training, constant practice, devotion, and joy in cooking. Yes, you must love cooking to do it right. If you do not, you just suffer.

So the best-kept secret of the good chef is his long training and daily performance. It is not enough to make a dish once and, when it is not up to standard, to declare, "The recipe is no good."

A good cook book, however, should assure excellent results to any person who tries any recipe for the first time. This is why almost every contemporary cook book has, at the beginning or the end, a section of useful general information. Yet, unfortunately, most people who decide to prepare a dish do not take the time to read forty pages of preliminary explanation. Instead, they open the book at "Z" and start to make Zabaglione.

What I have done in this book—and what I feel is unique—is based on my awareness of this very human behavior. Rather than burden the reader with a long introduction to the art of cooking, I have added a "Chef's Secret" after each recipe. Here I give all the necessary information on techniques, temperatures, small tricks, substitutes, and so forth, so that any dish can be prepared successfully without previously acquired knowledge about cooking practices.

Of course, just as every performing artist wants every member of the audience to stay through the whole performance, so every cook book author hopes his book will be read, and its recipes cooked, from cover to cover. Nevertheless, I strongly feel that a person who wants to start preparing a dish should have every bit of essential information immediately at his fingertips.

For this very same reason, we tested and double-tested, checked and rechecked every recipe, asking ladies with very little or no previous experience to cook the dishes for us. We watched their techniques and their frustrations, noted the shortcomings of recipes whose steps were not precisely explained, and then kept working on each recipe until it became easy and understandable. We were determined that each one would be no hardship to prepare and a delight to eat—not only to the cook who prepared it but to a very critical taste panel.

The task was not easy—it took several years of my life and added several pounds to my weight. But finally here it is, *The Chef's Secret Cook Book!* Our only hope is that it will give as much joy to those who read it, prepare its dishes, and then eat them as it gave me, my able staff, my charming guinea pigs, and my stern critics.

It is customary to thank, by name, the masters from whom one has learned and the helpers who have cooperated, and to say, "Without their assistance . . ." and so forth and so on. May I instead direct my thanks to you, the reader, because—let's face it—without you all our work and toil would be in vain. So . . .

Thank you, reader. Thank you, homemaker, gourmet, chef, or whoever is willing to follow me into the realm of gastronomy. Let's stop the talk and start the action. Light the fire, rinse the pots, and get going. And a good appetite to you!

THE
Chef's Secret
COOK BOOK

$\mathscr{A}PPETIZERS$

COLD

Radishes, Butter, and Black Bread
Sausage Tree
Smoked Oysters and Shallots
    Vinaigrette
Re-pickled Pickles
Shrimp-Avocado Spread
Pâté de Foie en Brioche
Elegant Canapés
Eggs à la Russe

Stuffed Hearts of Artichokes
Easy Galantine
Pâté en Croûte
    Parisian Spice
Jambon Persillé
Artichoke Leaves with Red Caviar
Stuffed Strawberries
Cream Cheese Rolls
Ham and Chopped Meat Pockets

HOT

Saucisson en Croûte
Home-Roasted Nuts
Stuffed Mushrooms
Sardine Crêpes
Pepperoni Pinwheels
Cheesecream Rolls

Oriental Lobster Tail
Lumberjack Pie
Quiche Lorraine
Sauerkraut Balls
Fish en Croûte
Blueburger Balls

---

*E*very good meal must be organized and staged like the production of a grand opera. The overture introduces the musical theme and is the "calling card" of the composer and conductor. It is their first meeting with the audience. Just so, the appetizer, the first thing a company or family meets on the table, is of the utmost importance.

The general rules are that the appetizer should not be too much in itself, or the selection too varied or too complicated. It should not compete with the rest of the dinner, just do what the name indicates—whet the appetite, increase the appetite, and prepare the eaters' gastronomical equipment.

Good food is enjoyed not only through and with the taste buds and the mouth in general, but with the eyes, ears, nose, and fingers of the eater. The color combinations and the shapes are just as important as the correct temperature, textures, aromas, and even the sounds which are connected in our mind with the particular food we talk about. Imagine how awful the best chilled dill pickle would taste if, when you bit into it, the crunchy sound would be missing and the texture like that of a ripe banana! And, vice versa, imagine the horror to your eardrums if, when you bit into a ripe banana, you would hear the crunchy sound of a cucumber!

Cold hors d'oeuvres should be cold, but not frozen. Hot hors d'oeuvres should be hot, but never so hot that they burn the mouth.

The following pages contain recipes selected for their great variety, including some of the most popular appetizers as well as a few strangers. Be careful in selecting the ones you want to serve. They must be in complete harmony with the whole meal in general and the main course in particular. But never forget that, important as they are, their role is always just a supporting one.

Appetizers

COLD

Radishes, Butter, and Black Bread

8 servings

1 bunch (approximately 2 dozen) small, firm, fresh red radishes with the leaves on

16 butter balls or butter patties, unsalted, ½ oz. each

8 slices dark German-type rye bread, the kind you slice yourself

coarse salt (kosher salt)

1. Place the radishes with their leaves on in a colander and wash under cold running water.
2. Place washed radishes in an absorbent kitchen towel and shake or swing them dry.
3. Remove the leaves one by one, but leave the middle core with one or two tiny tender leaves.
4. Remove all but ¼ inch of the root of each radish.
5. Cut through this ¼ inch of root two-thirds into the radish toward the remaining leaves. Turn the radish and make a second cut, forming an "X." Be sure not to cut into the remaining leaf core. (See drawing, page 4.)
6. Place the prepared radishes in a plastic container; fill the container with enough water to cover the radishes; add four to six ice cubes; refrigerate for 1 hour or more.
7. Keep the bread and butter at room temperature.
8. To serve, arrange the radishes on a small silver or glass plate. Serve butter and bread according to your wish.

CHEF'S SECRET: Americans traveling in Europe wonder why this appetizer always appears on menus in the finest restaurants and is ordered by so many great gourmets. The chef's secret lies not in the ingredients or in the preparation, but in explaining to your guests how to eat it. Four ordinary ingredients —bread, butter, salt, and radishes—become a gourmet delight if they are eaten properly. First, spread some unsalted fresh butter on a bite-sized piece of fresh bread which has a crust. The bread and butter should be chewed slowly. The radish must be sprinkled with a little coarse salt, then placed in the mouth along with the green leaf core, and should be chewed slowly and thoroughly together with the bread and butter. If you start with the radish, the effect will be entirely different, as it will be if you proceed by swallowing a bite of bread before taking a bite of radish.

If your guests do not already know how to eat this appetizer, and you cannot tactfully explain the method to them, spread the butter on the bread and slice the radishes, omitting the crosscuts. Place the tiny green leaves and stems on the buttered bread and cover them with ½ inch of slices of radish. Serve, offering the salt at the last minute.

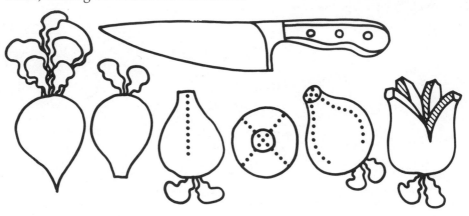

Sausage Tree

At least four kinds of sausages chosen
   from the following:

Italian salami

Hungarian salami

German salami

cervelat

smoked summer sausage

pepperoni

Hungarian style dry sausage

mettwurst

smoked liverwurst (Braunschweiger)

ring bologna

mortadella

The following may be served as ac-
   companiments to the sausage tree:

1 whole loaf rye bread

1 long French bread (flute type)

1 slab unsalted butter

1 or 2 bunches scallions

strips bell pepper

wedges garlic pickle

radishes

olives

1. Tie short strings on one end of the sausages and hang them on a sausage tree (available in many gourmet shops). If you cannot buy a sausage tree, you can make one by screwing two 16-inch pieces of broomstick together to form a T, securing the stem of the T to a 12-inch round carving board, then adding a few hooks across the top of the T.

2. Place two or three very sharp knives next to the sausage tree, and let the guests cut the sausages and eat them with their fingers.

CHEF'S SECRET: The secret of success is in the selection of sausages. Be sure that the four or more chosen offer a real variety. Do not buy all hard or all soft, all highly spiced or all very bland sausages. Be sure that their thickness, color, and texture are different. For instance, Italian salami, ring bologna, cervelat, and mettwurst make a good combination; or Hungarian dry sausage, German salami, mortadella, and liverwurst.

If your guests are real gourmets, you should serve them four kinds of salami: Italian, German, American (summer sausage), and Hungarian. Another secret of success is to offer beers or wines from the same countries from which the sausages come.

Smoked Oysters and Shallots Vinaigrette

4 servings

1 can smoked oysters	1 tbsp. finely chopped shallots
juice of 1 lemon	¼ tsp. sugar
¼ cup vinegar	¼ tsp. salt
½ cup water	black peppercorns

1. Put the oysters carefully into a colander or sieve.
2. Rinse under running lukewarm water, spreading your fingers out under the water stream so that the force of the water will not break the oysters. Rinse off all traces of oil and place the oysters in a plastic bowl.
3. Sprinkle chopped shallots over the top of the oysters.
4. Pour vinegar into a saucepan; add water, sugar, and salt and heat until the mixture comes to a boil.
5. Cool the vinegar mixture for a few minutes, then pour it over the oysters and shallots.
6. Cool to room temperature, then refrigerate for several hours.
7. To serve, drain the oysters, using a fine sieve, and place them with the shallots on a serving dish. Spoon 1 or 2 tbsp. of the vinaigrette sauce back onto the oysters and shallots. Add the lemon juice and grind black pepper coarsely over the top.
8. Serve with buttered dark bread.

CHEF'S SECRET: Most important in making this dish perfect is maintaining the right temperatures. While you are rinsing the oysters, the water must be just a little warmer than your hand. Otherwise, the oil will not come off the oysters and the vinaigrette sauce cannot penetrate them. The vinaigrette sauce itself must be brought to a boil in order to dissolve the salt and sugar completely, but it should be cooled slightly so that it will not toughen the surface of the oysters. The shallots should be cut with a stainless steel knife. They will then release their full flavor but remain raw, adding a crisp texture to the final dish.

Re-pickled Pickles

2 quarts

1 pt. jar tiny white onions
1 pt. jar small dill gherkins
1 pt. jar pickled green tomatoes
1 pt. jar sweet banana peppers or
　sweet finger peppers
1 pt. white vinegar

½ cup sugar
1 qt. water
10 whole black peppercorns
10 whole white peppercorns
1 bay leaf
1 clove garlic

1. Place the white onions in a colander and rinse under cold running water for 15 to 20 minutes. Drain.

2. Drain the pickling liquids from the gherkins, tomatoes, and peppers into a stainless steel or enameled saucepan.

3. Put both the white and the black peppercorns in a piece of cheesecloth and tie it up. Hit the bag with a wooden object until the peppercorns are crushed.

4. Add the vinegar, sugar, water, bay leaf, garlic, and cheesecloth bag of peppercorns to the pickling liquids and bring the liquid to a boil.

5. In a large glass or ceramic jar, alternate the three kinds of pickles and the onions. Slowly ladle the boiling liquid over them. Be sure to set the glass jar on a metal surface or let it stand on a long-bladed knife so that it will not crack from the heat.

6. Let the re-pickled pickles stay at room temperature until they cool, then refrigerate them for 3 to 4 hours or more.

CHEF'S SECRET: After rinsing the small onions, prick them all over with a long thin sewing needle so that they will absorb the pickling liquid faster and more deeply and yet remain crisp and crunchy. If you like hot pickles, add one or two dried pods of chili or pepperoni or use a few "hot sports" peppers in the mixture. You may add canned olives or any other pickle you like to the mixture. If you use canned black or green olives, discard the liquid from them and increase the amount of water and vinegar in the recipe. This mixed re-pickled pickle is served as an appetizer in the finest restaurants in the southern part of France, in Spain and Italy, and throughout North Africa. If you find your own formula and mixture for it, it will be a great success.

Shrimp-Avocado Spread

4 servings

1 ripe avocado
6 to 8 boiled, peeled, deveined, me-
　dium-sized shrimp, or 1 can shrimp
juice of ½ lemon and ½ lime

1 tbsp. corn oil
salt and freshly ground pepper to taste
½ tsp. sugar

1. Blend the shrimp in an electric blender until they are finely cut.

2. Dissolve the sugar in the lemon and lime juice. Add the juice, ripe avo-

cado, oil, salt, and pepper to the blender and continue to blend until completely smooth.

3. Pour the mixture into a small serving dish, preferably glass or china, and chill thoroughly. Serve with crackers or small pieces of toast and fresh, crusty French bread.

CHEF'S SECRET: After peeling the avocado and removing the pit, do not discard the pit. When the mixture is blended, put the pit back in the spread and leave it there until serving time and the spread will remain a vivid green.

You can do this with any avocado dish you prepare. Because the skin of the pit has a chemical which keeps the avocado green, your dish will not turn dark, not even overnight, as long as the pit is in the mixture.

Pâté de Foie en Brioche

8 servings

1 loaf fine, firm-textured, sliced white bread, such as Pepperidge Farm or Brownberry Ovens, a good milk bread, or plain coffee bread from your local baker
1 long round or triangular can pâté imported from France or a good quality smoked liver sausage (Braunschweiger)

1 cup canned chicken broth
1 envelope unflavored gelatin
3 tbsp. warm water
1 tbsp. lemon juice
½ tsp. sugar

1. Slice the pâté to the same thickness as the bread slices.

2. With a cookie cutter the size of the pâté (or with the empty pâté can), carefully cut a hole in the middle of each slice of bread (see drawing, page 8).

3. Lay the sliced bread on cookie sheets or aluminum foil and ease a slice of the pâté or liverwurst into the hole you have cut. Refrigerate for 3 to 4 hours.

4. Bring the chicken broth to a boil. Dissolve the gelatin in the warm water. Pour this into the chicken broth and stir until it comes to a boil. Remove from heat. Add lemon juice and sugar.

5. Keep the mixture in the saucepan in which it was cooked and place the pan in ice water. Gently stir until the mixture becomes syrupy.

6. With a pastry brush, carefully coat the pâté in each bread slice with gelatin so that some of the gelatin trickles down the edges of the pâté and adheres to the bread.

7. Chill the slices again in the refrigerator, then remove them from the cookie sheet or aluminum foil with the help of a spatula. Reassemble the loaf and serve.

CHEF'S SECRET: The whole recipe itself is a secret—not mine, but that of a clever young man who is chef at the world famous Pyramide Restaurant in Vienne, near Lyons, France. The original owner, Chef Point, who died some years ago, took to the grave the secret of a brioche filled with goose liver or just plain liver pâté. He had taught his staff how to prepare all the dishes that made the Pyramid famous—except this one. Because the guests demanded it, the new young chef, who did not know how to make the dish, invented a perfect substitute.

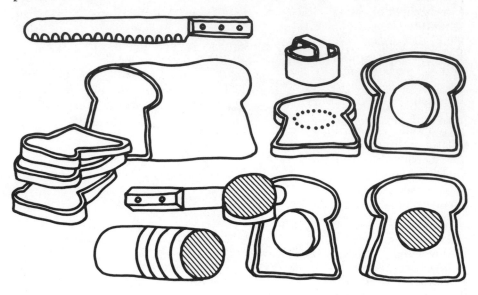

Elegant Canapés

12 servings

½ loaf fine, firm-textured, sliced white bread, such as Pepperidge Farm
½ loaf sliced dark bread
8 oz. butter, whipped with electric beater
1 can small sardines
1 4-oz. package thinly sliced ham
4 hard-boiled eggs
4 oz. Braunschweiger
4 oz. sliced Muenster cheese
1 tsp. prepared mustard
⅛ tsp. cinnamon

1 envelope unflavored gelatin
½ cup cold water
⅔ cup boiling water
1 tsp. vinegar or 2 tsp. lemon juice
salt
sugar
anchovy paste (optional)
sliced carrot
black olives
fresh parsley
catsup

1. Trim the bread and spread all the slices evenly with whipped butter. If you wish, divide the butter into two parts and mix some prepared mustard or anchovy paste into one of the parts, according to your taste.

2. Cover buttered bread slices with a damp towel.

3. Soften the gelatin in ½ cup of cold water. To ⅔ cup of boiling water, add vinegar or lemon juice, salt to taste, and a light sprinkling of sugar. Dissolve the softened gelatin in this mixture, then let it stand at room temperature until it becomes syrupy.

4. Lay out the ham slices side by side, brush them one at a time with

gelatin, and roll them up jelly-roll fashion. When all are rolled, put them in the refrigerator with the lapped edges on the bottom.

5. Carefully remove the sardines from the container. Set them side by side on wax paper or aluminum foil and gently brush them two or three times with thin coats of gelatin. Before the gelatin sets, put a single parsley leaf at the top of the sardine where the head is cut off. Refrigerate.

6. In a small bowl or coffee cup, mash the Braunschweiger with a fork. Add to it the mustard and cinnamon. Now add 1 tbsp. of liquid gelatin. Stir vigorously. Using a pastry bag with a star tube, press ½- to ¾-inch stars onto aluminum foil. Refrigerate.

7. Slice the eggs with an egg slicer. Carefully lay out on aluminum foil the nice middle slices with the yolk and white intact. Brush them gently with gelatin. Refrigerate.

8. Separate the yolk from the white of the remaining pieces of egg. Chop each very fine.

9. After you have come this far, remove from the refrigerator all the ingredients you have been chilling. Uncover the buttered bread slices and place the Muenster cheese, trimmed, on some of the dark slices of bread.

10. From this point on, everything is up to your taste and imagination. The slices of bread can be divided into thirds each way or into halves, depending on the size of canapés desired. The ham rolls can be sliced into one-inch or smaller pieces. The number of possible combinations is larger than you think. You can combine sardines with eggs or with cheese; ham, with eggs and cheese; Braunschweiger, with eggs, ham, or cheese; etc. Decorate the canapés so that the colors of the decorations contrast or match. For example, blanch the carrot slices and, with a small cookie cutter or aspic cutter, cut them into stars or flowers and place these on the egg yolk. Make small dots from the blanched carrot slices, egg white, and black olives, using the cap from a fountain or ball-point pen, and apply them as decorations.

CHEF'S SECRET: Your work will be much easier if you cut out of strong cardboard a perfect square which fits onto a slice of bread, so that you can trim off all the crust by cutting along the cardboard. The slices will then be exactly alike.

If you prepare everything ahead of time and assemble the canapés at the last minute, they will be prettier and look much more professional than if you do all the work haphazardly just before serving.

Some people make the mistake of brushing the whole canapé with gelatin. It is not necessary for the bread to be soaked with gelatin; if it is, the canapés will taste rubbery.

Eggs à la Russe

8 servings

10 hard-boiled medium eggs
2 cups mayonnaise (see page 214)
6 tbsp. sour cream

2 cups boiled potatoes cut into ½-inch
or smaller cubes

1 cup cooked green peas (fresh,
   canned, or frozen)
1 cup cooked carrots cut into ½-inch
   or smaller cubes
2 tbsp. butter

1 tbsp. anchovy paste
salt and pepper to taste
juice of 1 large lemon
fresh parsley

1. Combine the cooked potatoes, carrots, green peas, and chopped white of two eggs. Save the two yolks for later use.

2. Sprinkle the mixed vegetables with salt and pepper according to taste and add the lemon juice.

3. Fold the mayonnaise and sour cream gently together, then fold one-third of this mixture into the vegetables. Let stand at room temperature.

4. Split the remaining eggs lengthwise and remove the yolks. Press the yolks through a sieve. Add soft butter, anchovy paste, and 2 tbsp. of the mayonnaise–sour cream mixture. Beat this with an electric beater until fluffy.

5. Using a pastry bag with a star tube, pipe the egg-yolk mixture into the sixteen egg halves. You will have approximately 1 tsp. for each.

6. Arrange the egg halves and the vegetable-mayonnaise mixture on a serving platter.

7. Gently mash the two remaining egg yolks with a blunt knife or small spatula. Sprinkle over the top of each egg half.

8. Decorate the platter with green parsley. Serve chilled, with the remaining mayonnaise mixture in a side dish.

CHEF'S SECRET: The eggs must be absolutely fresh, and the best method of cooking eggs seems to be the old-fashioned one. Room temperature eggs should go into a stainless steel or enamel pot (not aluminum). Put in enough cold water so that the water level is about 1 inch above the top of the eggs. Add 1 tsp. salt and bring the eggs to a slow boil. Let them boil for 10 minutes, then discard the boiling water and place the pot with the eggs in it under the cold water faucet. Rinse the eggs until they are cool. Cover the pot after discarding the cold water. Hold the lid on with both hands and gently shake the pot up and down so that the egg shells will break. Now fill the pot again with cold water and peel the eggs under the water. This is the fastest, cleanest way.

To split the eggs in half, use the thinnest knife you have.

Stuffed Hearts of Artichokes

4 servings

1 can artichoke hearts
1 cup finely minced or ground leftover
   meat; for example, roast beef, steak,
   roast pork, roast chicken
1 hard-boiled egg
½ cup corn oil

1 cup vinegar
2 cups water
2 cans chicken broth
juice of 1 large lemon
salt and freshly ground pepper to taste
1 cup chopped fresh green parsley

1. Discard the liquid from the can of artichoke hearts.

2. Rinse the artichoke hearts with cold water. Carefully lay them upside down on an absorbent towel.

3. Press the hard-boiled egg through a sieve and mix it with the leftover meat. Add 1 tbsp. oil if the meat is lean. Salt and pepper to taste.

4. Bring the water, chicken broth, and vinegar to a rolling boil and add a little salt. Pour the liquid into a glass dish. One by one, place the artichoke hearts upside down in the hot liquid. Let stand at room temperature until cool, then pour off the liquid.

5. Turn over the artichoke hearts and fill each with the meat mixture.

6. Blend the oil and lemon juice in an electric blender until it becomes opaque. Pour over the artichokes. Sprinkle generously with parsley and serve at once.

CHEF'S SECRET: This excellent, elegant, and inexpensive first course can be prepared a day ahead and assembled at the last minute. In this case, leave the artichoke hearts in the vinegar-water-broth mixture overnight. Keep the meat mixture in a small plastic container and the chopped parsley in a plastic bag. Have the oil at room temperature and the lemon juice chilled. Do not mix them, or add freshly ground pepper, until just before serving time.

Easy Galantine

20 servings

1 3½- to 4-lb. frying chicken	10 to 12 black peppercorns, crushed
1 lb. ham steak	10 to 12 white peppercorns, crushed
1 lb. lean ground veal stew meat	1 cup lukewarm water
1 lb. boneless ground pork shoulder	2 carrots (approximately 4 oz.)
1 lb. ground smoked picnic ham	1 parsley root or parsnip
3 envelopes unflavored gelatin	2 stalks celery
½ cup shelled and cleaned pistachio nuts	1 small onion, unpeeled
3 eggs	1 whole clove
1 cup finely chopped onion sautéed in 3 tbsp. shortening	2 cloves garlic, unpeeled
1 cup coarsely chopped onion	1 tsp. whole black peppercorns
1 tbsp. coarsely chopped garlic	2 tbsp. salt
	1 10½-oz. can chicken broth

1. With a sharp knife, cut through the back of the fryer from the neck down to the tail, or ask the butcher to do so.

2. Remove the bones from the opened fryer, leaving only the wing bones in.

3. Make a surface with a double layer of aluminum foil at least 18 inches wide and 2½ feet long. Lay the boned fryer, skin side down, on the aluminum foil. Sprinkle the flesh with salt and one envelope of dry gelatin.

4. In a small glass or plastic container, mix the coarsely chopped raw onion, garlic, crushed peppercorns, and about ½ to 1 tbsp. salt (depending on how salty the smoked picnic ham is; it varies from brand to brand) and pour the cup of lukewarm water over this mixture. Let stand at room temperature for at least 1 hour, stirring once in a while.

5. Cut the ham steak into equal-sized cubes and then run the trimmings, ends, and fat parts through the blender.

6. Add the blended ham pieces to the other ground meats. Add the sau-

téed onion, including the shortening, and the raw eggs. Add ½ to 1 tbsp. salt and 1 envelope of dry gelatin. Through a strainer, pour into the meat mixture the lukewarm water in which the onions, garlic, and crushed peppers have soaked.

7. Work the mixture together, using both hands. Taste it and add salt and very fine ground black pepper if needed.

8. Purée the meat mixture, bit by bit, in an electric blender. Do not overfill the blender, because this will only delay the work. Collect the blended meat in a large mixing bowl.

9. Spread half of the meat mixture over the inside of the fryer. Gently press the ham cubes into the center of the meat mixture inside the fryer, distributing them evenly. Do the same with the pistachio nuts. Spread the second half of the meat mixture over the top.

10. Bring the two sides of the skin of the chicken together in the middle. With a strong white thread, sew it from the tail to the neck, overlapping the skin. The fryer will then look as it did before being split and boned, the filling being completely enclosed.

11. Sprinkle the third envelope of gelatin evenly over the skin and fold the aluminum foil over the fryer from all sides, securing it on the back.

12. Preheat oven to 400 degrees.

13. Coarsely cut up the carrots, parsnip or parsley root, and celery. Slice the onion and garlic cloves, leaving the skin on. In a large roasting pan, put the cut vegetables, including the onion and garlic, along with the whole clove and black peppercorns. Lay the foil-wrapped fryer, breast down, on top of the vegetables.

14. Put the bones, gizzard, heart, and liver into the pan. Add the chicken broth and enough water to cover the fowl completely. Cover and bake in the preheated oven for 2½ hours.

15. Remove the galantine from the oven; place it on a tray. Strain the liquid, discarding the bones, vegetables, etc., but keeping the liquid.

16. Prepare a surface of double aluminum foil the same size as before. Carefully open up the foil that is covering the fryer and let the liquid run from it onto a tray.

17. Let the galantine cool at room temperature just enough so that you can handle it without burning your hands. Place it on the fresh double aluminum foil and mold the foil firmly around it.

18. Place the galantine back in the roasting pan and pour the strained cooking liquid over it. Let this cool to room temperature and then refrigerate overnight.

19. Remove the galantine from the foil and with a very sharp knife, slice it into ¼-inch slices. Arrange the slices on a large serving platter. Chop up some of the natural gelatin (or aspic) which the liquid has turned into while being refrigerated. Decorate the platter with chopped aspic and serve with Oxford Sauce (see page 213) or Sauce Louis (see page 215).

CHEF'S SECRET: The big secret is the use of three envelopes of gelatin. The first, sprinkled on the surface of the fryer's flesh, is activated as the chicken cooks and causes the ground meat to adhere to the flesh. The second package, mixed into the meat, gives a firmness to the filling and makes it possible to slice it nicely. The third, sprinkled on the skin, catches and absorbs the juices oozing from the chicken during cooking. Eventually, all this gelatin is absorbed into the cooking liquid and turns into a nice aspic.

Pâté en Croûte

12 servings

1 package pie dough mix
½ lb. ground beef
½ lb. ground veal
½ lb. ground lean pork
4-oz. slab bacon cut into ½-oz. cubes or 4 oz. ham from a thick slice cut into ½-oz. cubes
1 cup onion finely minced
3 tbsp. shortening, preferably lard or bacon drippings
½ tsp. freshly ground black pepper

¼ tsp. garlic salt
1 tsp. Parisian Spice (see page 14)
2 eggs
½ cup milk
3 to 4 tbsp. good brandy or cognac
1 tbsp. salt
2 whole bay leaves
3 tbsp. unflavored gelatin
1 egg yolk, beaten with a sprinkling of sugar and 1 tbsp. warm water

1. Preheat oven to 375 degrees.
2. Mix the two raw eggs with the milk and brandy. Beat with a fork, adding all the spices except the bay leaves. Keep the mixture at room temperature.
3. In a large mixing bowl, combine all the meats except the bacon or ham.
4. Sauté the onion in the lard or bacon drippings.
5. If you use bacon, blanch the bacon cubes: Drop them into a small pan filled with cold water and bring to a boil. After 3 minutes, pour off the boiling water and cool the blanched bacon cubes immediately under cold running water.
6. When the ground meats are fairly well mixed, add the cooled sautéed onions. Spreading your hands over the surface, make holes in the meat mixture by pressing all of your fingers into the meat. Beat the egg-spice mixture again with a fork and pour it evenly over the meat so that it runs into the holes.
7. Knead the meat as you would a bread dough until you feel that the mixture is very even. Then sprinkle 2 tbsp. of the dry gelatin over the meat and work the gelatin into the mixture vigorously and thoroughly.
8. Brush a loaf pan with shortening and dust it with flour. Press half of the meat mixture into the loaf pan. Distribute the bacon or ham cubes evenly over the middle of the loaf. Put the remaining meat mixture on top, pressing it down gently.
9. Set the loaf pan in a larger pan containing 2 inches of boiling water. Put bay leaves on top of the meat and bake it for approximately 2 hours.
10. Remove the loaf from the oven and pour off all excess fat. Let it stand for 10 to 15 minutes. Then remove it from the pan, turning it upside down on a rack or tray. If you use a tray, put two or three layers of paper towel under the loaf so that it will absorb all the fat oozing out. Let the loaf cool overnight.
11. Prepare the pie dough according to the directions on the box. Chill it for several hours or overnight in the refrigerator.
12. Roll out the pie dough on a slightly floured surface into an oblong shape,

approximately ¼ inch thick, large enough to enclose the pâté loaf completely. Rinse the pâté loaf under hot water for about 1 minute and then sprinkle the third tablespoon of gelatin evenly on its surface. Place the rinsed, sprinkled loaf on one end of the dough. Fold the rest of the dough over, seal edges, and trim excess.

13. Loosen the bottom with a spatula and lift the pastry-enclosed loaf onto a slightly greased cookie sheet. With a round cookie cutter or a plastic pill container, cut two or three holes ½ inch in diameter in the top of the pâté.

14. Mix the three cutout pieces with the trimmings from the dough and make simple decorations for the top. Beat the egg yolk with a sprinkling of sugar and 1 tbsp. warm water. Brush the entire surface of the dough with this mixture and then bake the loaf at 400 degrees for 10 minutes. Remove the loaf from the oven, brush the top a second time with the egg yolk mixture, and bake the loaf for an additional 15 to 20 minutes. Remove from oven, cool to room temperature, and refrigerate overnight. Serve with Oxford Sauce (see page 213).

CHEF'S SECRET: It used to be a great art to make a pâté en croûte; the best chefs worked many years to learn the secret of making this pâté without having the dough burn while the meat cooked. Problems included the undercrust and side crusts being half raw, gummy, and loaded with aspic. With my method, any housewife can make a perfect pâté without special skill or training. Of course, you can use the same method with any other type of pâté mixture.

The loaf must be rinsed with hot water before the gelatin is sprinkled over it and it is encased in the pastry. Any ground meat always oozes fat when it is cooked, and in this case the fat is undesirable; gelatin will not adhere to fat.

Parisian Spice

1 tbsp. crushed bay leaf	½ tbsp. ground cloves
1 tbsp. dried thyme	½ tsp. nutmeg
1 tbsp. powdered mace	½ tsp. ground allspice
1 tbsp. dried rosemary	1 tsp. white ground pepper
1 tbsp. dried basil	2 tsp. Spanish paprika
2 tbsp. cinnamon	1 cup fine table salt

1. Mix all the ingredients well in a spice mortar or, if you do not have a mortar, crush all together in a deep bowl with the bottom of a cup.

2. Sift through a fine sieve two or three times, crush again all that is left, and sift until everything goes through.

3. Keep in a tightly closed jar.

Jambon Persillé

6 servings

2½ cups beef or chicken stock	3 cups cooked smoked ham, cut in ½-inch cubes
½ cup Madeira wine	
1½ tbsp. unflavored gelatin	1 cup freshly chopped parsley

1. Dissolve the gelatin in ½ cup of warmed stock. Add this to the remaining stock and the wine.

2. Heat the mixture slowly until it is almost boiling.

3. Cool it to room temperature.

4. Add chopped parsley.

5. Place ham in a 2-qt. mold or bowl; pour the gelatin mixture over it. All pieces of ham should be covered. Cover the surface with a piece of plastic wrap.

6. Chill in the refrigerator for several hours or overnight.

7. Run hot tap water around the sides and bottom of the mold and turn it over onto a platter. Cut in ¼-inch slices with a very sharp knife. Serve cold.

CHEF'S SECRET: The cooling time of the aspic can be reduced by placing it in a light aluminum pan or in a bowl in an ice water bath and stirring it constantly.

Chill the mold or bowl in the refrigerator, then pour in some room-temperature gelatin and move it quickly in all directions before adding the ham mixture. This will coat the bottom and walls of the mold with gelatin.

Before running the hot water around the outside of the mold, remove the plastic wrap and ease away the edges of the gelatin with a thin, warm knife. Cover the mold again with the plastic wrap; then run the hot water around the mold. Remove wrap and place the platter over the mold; then invert onto the serving platter. Turn the two together so that the platter is on the bottom and the mold is on the platter. If the aspic still will not move, dip a towel in very hot water, wring it dry, and put it over the mold. By leaving the plastic wrap on when running the hot water around the outside of the mold, you will prevent any water getting into the mold.

Artichoke Leaves with Red Caviar

20 to 30 servings

2 large artichokes	2 tbsp. salt
½ lemon	1 jar red caviar
1 pt. sour cream	salt and pepper to taste

1. Wash and trim the artichokes. Put them in a saucepan and cover with cold water. Add salt and the juice of the ½ lemon (keep the squeezed lemon for later use). Cook the artichokes until they are tender—approximately 30 to 45 minutes, depending on their age and size.

2. Discard the cooking liquid and rinse the artichokes two or three times in cold water, or until they are cool enough to handle.

3. Cut the squeezed ½ lemon into three or four pieces and put these into 1 qt. of cold water. Beginning at the outside, remove the artichoke leaves one by one and drop them into the cold water. (See drawing, page 16.)

4. When you get to the "choker," discard it and remove the fine hair from the inside of the bottom, or heart, of the artichoke. Save the hearts of the artichokes.

5. Lay the leaves on absorbent paper and let them dry.

6. Chop the artichoke hearts very fine and season with a little salt and freshly ground pepper. Fold them into the sour cream.

7. Divide this mixture by the number of leaves you have and put dabs on the stem end of the leaves. Top each dab with a few dots of red caviar. Arrange the leaves on a serving platter and serve them chilled.

CHEF'S SECRET: Before boiling the artichokes, cut off the sharp tips of the outside leaves with sharp scissors and discard them. This will save a lot of trouble in preparing them.

Empty the red caviar into a sieve and dip the sieve into and out of lukewarm water until the water has washed off all the gluey substance covering the caviar. Cold water will not do this, and hot water turns the liquid around the fish eggs into shreds like egg white which are ugly and hard to remove. So be sure that the water is just lukewarm.

The artichoke hearts will turn blue after they are chopped and will make a nice color combination with the white sour cream and red caviar.

Stuffed Strawberries

8 servings—3 strawberries per serving

24 large, not overripe strawberries	1 envelope unflavored gelatin
limes to make 24 wafer-thin slices and	⅓ cup cold water
1 tbsp. juice	⅔ cup boiling water

| salt | 2 tbsp. sour cream |
| sugar | 1 small jar red caviar |

1. Have on hand 3 sculptured egg boxes, one-dozen size. With the lids cut off and the boxes turned upside down, they make convenient temporary holders for the strawberries, the berries fitting into the holes between the egg cups.

2. Wash the strawberries under the cold water faucet very quickly and shake them dry, or dry them carefully on a towel.

3. Gently stir the sour cream with a spoon and fill a small wax-paper cone or a small pastry bag with a plain ⅛-inch opening.

4. With a very sharp knife, slice the limes as thinly as possible. With a sharp cookie cutter, cut off the rind from the slices. You may find it more convenient to peel the lime before slicing it. Keep the slices at hand on a small plate.

5. Cut off the stem end of each strawberry with a sharp knife; with a melon-ball cutter, carefully enlarge the natural hole in each berry. Be sure that you do not go through the flesh. Place each prepared berry cut side up in the egg box.

6. Wash the caviar by the method described in the *Chef's Secret* of the preceding recipe, page 16. Then divide it among the 24 strawberries, partially filling the cavities but leaving room for the sour cream.

7. With the paper cone or pastry bag, fill up the strawberries with sour cream. Be sure that they are not overfilled.

8. Soften the gelatin in the cold water and then add to the boiling water, with a sprinkling of salt, sugar, and the lime juice. Let this mixture stand until it is syrupy.

9. Dip the lime slices one by one in the syrupy gelatin and cover each strawberry with a slice. When all the berries are covered, refrigerate them for ½ hour. Then transfer the berries from the egg boxes to a tray or cookie sheet, turning them over so that they rest on the lime slices. Lightly brush them with the remaining syrupy gelatin. Reheat the gelatin if it becomes stiff.

10. Refrigerate again for 2 to 3 hours. Serve chilled, if possible on some kind of green leaves.

CHEF'S SECRET: Be sure that the strawberries are not overripe. You will not be able to handle them if they are.

If it is necessary to intensify the color of the berries, dye the gelatin which you use on top of them with a very little red food color. The best way to control the amount of food color is to dip a thick kitchen needle into the color and then swirl it in the gelatin until it dissolves. Repeat this procedure two or three times if necessary, but do not try one drop of color, because it will be too much.

If you do not have a good knife, you will have great difficulty slicing the limes. But in your favorite grocery or delicatessen or butcher shop the man who works the electric slicer will slice your limes for a big smile.

Cream Cheese Rolls

40 to 44 servings

| 1 portion of cream cheese dough (see page 20) | 4 tbsp. grated Parmesan or Romano cheese |
| 2 cups finely grated Swiss cheese | |

salt, amount depending on sharpness of
   cheese
¼ tsp. white pepper
2 cups milk
4 tbsp. flour
2 tbsp. butter

2 sticks butter, room temperature
2 eggs
2 tbsp. water
1½ cups Swiss cheese grated into thin
   long strips

1. Preheat oven to 400 degrees.

2. Roll out one-half of the dough into a rectangle 16 by 12 inches. Cut it into strips ¾ inch wide by 12 inches long. You will have twenty to twenty-two strips, depending on how accurately you measure.

3. Have on hand two dozen metal cones, oiled and dusted with flour. With your left thumb, press one end of a 12-inch strip of dough to about the middle of a cone and roll it toward the narrow end, overlapping approximately ¼ inch on each turn (see drawing).

4. Gently press the other end to the narrow end of the cone. Lay the cone on a greased cookie sheet. Repeat until you have used all the cones. Refrigerate them for at least ½ hour.

5. Beat the eggs with the 2 tbsp. of water. Brush the top of the rolls with this mixture. Do not let the mixture run down the sides.

6. Bake for 12 to 15 minutes or until the rolls are golden brown.

7. Let them cool a few minutes. Remove the roll from each cone by gently pushing the thicker end with two fingers.

8. Repeat the process with the other half of the dough.

9. Bring the milk, flour, and 2 tbsp. butter to a boil, stirring constantly. Remove the mixture immediately from the heat and continue stirring until it cools slightly. Scrape it into a mixing bowl and start to mix it with an electric mixer at low speed, adding first the finely grated Swiss cheese and then the Parmesan or Romano. After adding the Parmesan or Romano, when the mixing bowl becomes lukewarm, increase the speed and start to add the sticks of butter, tablespoonful by tablespoonful, until all the butter is blended in. Add the white pepper and salt. Now you will have a fluffy, tangy cheese filling.

10. Fill a pastry bag (see drawing), fitted with a ½-inch plain cone, with the cheese filling. Pipe the cheese mixture into the baked rolls from both ends.

11. Dip both ends of the rolls into the Swiss cheese strips. Serve cold.

CHEF'S SECRET: These little cone forms are available in New York City at Bazaar Français and at Lekvar by the Barrel; in Chicago, at Crate and Barrel, Cooks' Cupboard, Marshall Field and Company, and the Gourmet Shops; and in San Francisco, at Capricorn, Thomas E. Cara Ltd., Williams-Sonoma Kitchenware, and Cost Plus Imports.

You can use them for full-sized rolls or smaller ones. You can fill the rolls with whipped cream or a substitute and serve them as a dessert. These are the famous German pastries called *Schiller Locken*.

As an appetizer, the half size may be filled with salted whipped cream combined with a purée of ham, blended smoked salmon, etc. The rolls freeze well after baking.

The temperature of the white sauce is important. The Swiss cheese must go into it while it is hot and the Parmesan or Romano while it is warm. The butter must go in while it is lukewarm; otherwise, it will ooze out.

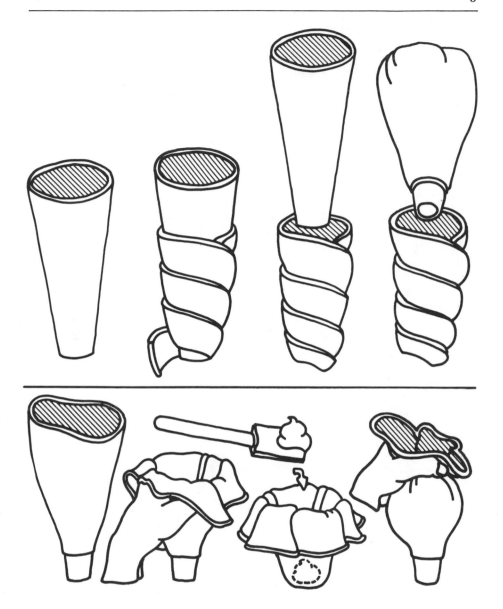

Ham and Chopped Meat Pockets

16 pieces

8 slices ham 5 by 3 inches (cut in half)
    or 16 slices 3½ by 3½ inches
2 tbsp. unflavored gelatin
½ cup cold water
1½ cups canned chicken broth
lemon juice to taste

1 cup finely minced or ground leftover
    meat
1 tbsp. prepared mustard
1 hard-boiled egg
fresh parsley

1. Dilute the gelatin in the cold water. Bring the chicken broth, flavored with lemon juice, to a boil, then dissolve gelatin mixture in it. Let the mixture stand until it is syrupy.

2. Press the hard-boiled egg through a sieve.

3. Lay out all the ham slices and brush them lightly with the syrupy gelatin.

4. Mix the ground meat, mustard, egg, and one-half of the gelatin mixture. Divide into sixteen even portions and place one portion, just off the middle, toward one of the corners, on each ham slice. Fold the opposite corner over the filling and press the edges with your fingers until they stick.

5. Brush the ham pockets with the remaining gelatin and decorate each with a single parsley leaf.

6. Chill and serve.

CHEF'S SECRET: To handle gelatin, you must have on hand a bowl of cold water big enough so that you can dip into it the pot in which the gelatin was cooked. The bowl should contain 2 or 3 handfuls of ice cubes. Gently stir the gelatin with your finger until the temperature is just about the temperature of your finger. Then immediately remove the pan of gelatin from the ice water and start to work with it.

The lemon juice takes away from the blandness of the gelatin. Good chefs always sprinkle a small amount of sugar in it because you can then add more lemon juice without making the gelatine too acidic.

It is advisable to brush a little more gelatin on the edges of the ham slices just before folding and to press the edges together with your finger for 20 to 30 seconds.

HOT

Saucisson en Croûte

12 or more servings

1 lb. sausage, not too dry; for example, thin bologna, Polish sausage
(cooked), not too dry Hungarian
sausage
12 oz. flour (3 cups)

8 oz. butter (2 sticks)
8 oz. cream cheese
1 egg
1 tbsp. water

1. In a large cold bowl, mix the flour, butter, and cream cheese, working very quickly, until the mixture looks like coarse cornmeal. Press into a ball, then divide it into two portions. Wrap each portion in plastic and refrigerate for at least 3 to 4 hours.

2. Remove the casing or skin of the sausage.

3. Roll out enough dough to encase the sausage. If you use one large sausage, combine the two pieces of chilled dough. If you use two sausages, roll out each piece of dough and encase the sausages separately.

4. Beat the egg with the water.

5. Lightly grease a cookie sheet. Brush the top of the dough-wrapped sausage with the egg wash and bake it at 425 degrees for 15 to 25 minutes, according to the size of the sausage.

6. Let the sausage stand at room temperature for a few minutes before slicing. Serve warm but not hot.

CHEF's SECRET: This dough is very versatile; it can be used for at least 100 different dishes once you have mastered its preparation.

You must mix it with your hands, and you must be sure that they are not hot. If they are hot, have on hand some ice water in a tightly closed plastic bag and chill your hands on its surface. Be sure they do not get wet.

When you drop the sticks of butter and slab of cream cheese into the flour, cover their entire surfaces with flour before you touch them. Then break the sticks of butter in two and dip the broken surfaces into the flour. Break the pieces of butter again and dip again in flour. Then start breaking the cream cheese, dipping in flour. Keep repeating this procedure, never touching the same piece of butter or cream cheese twice in succession. When all the pieces are the size of an almond, put both hands on the bottom of the mixing bowl and try to turn the whole mixture over.

From then on, press the mixture together with the fingertips, working quickly, and running your thumbs from the little finger to the index finger in a circular motion. After two or three tries, you will master this dough, and you will find that you can roll it and fold it once, twice, or three times as you would the famous puff paste. This dough, however, is much quicker, easier, and more economical and does not require as much skill.

Home-Roasted Nuts

2 lb. nuts

1 lb. shelled almonds
4 oz. shelled pecans
4 oz. shelled hazelnuts
4 oz. shelled English walnuts
4 oz. shelled cashews

1 tbsp. corn oil
1 egg white
3 to 4 tbsp. coarse salt, according to taste

1. Wipe dry an enamel-coated or iron frying pan large enough for the nuts to be spread out in it. Put the oil into the pan and tilt the pan until it is coated evenly.

2. Add the nuts and put the pan over medium heat. After 2 or 3 minutes, gently shake the pan until you notice a warm nut smell. Then increase the heat and with a metal spatula or large spoon, turn the nuts gently. If they brown too quickly, reduce the heat; if they brown too slowly, increase it.

3. When the nuts are roasted to your liking, remove them from the heat and cool to lukewarm.

4. Beat the egg white into a light froth and add the salt.

5. Put the nuts in a mixing bowl with the egg white–salt froth and gently shake the bowl until all the nuts are evenly coated.

6. Spread them out on aluminum foil, and sprinkle some more coarse salt on them if you wish.

CHEF'S SECRET: Store-bought nuts will never taste as good as the ones you roast at home the morning of the party or the day before. The coating of the egg white dries evenly on the nuts and keeps the salt on them.

If you can, buy kosher salt in the specialty section of your supermarket. Its consistency is entirely different from that of regular kitchen salt.

Stuffed Mushrooms

8 servings

12 oz. fresh mushrooms
2 strips lean bacon
½ cup finely chopped fresh parsley
4 tbsp. bread crumbs
1 tbsp. chopped onions

freshly ground black pepper
salt
1 egg
1 cup sour cream

1. Preheat oven to 350 degrees.
2. Cut off and discard the ends of the mushroom stems.
3. Wipe the mushroom caps with a damp cloth or, if they are very dirty, rinse them quickly under cold water and immediately shake them dry in an absorbent towel.
4. With a sharp knife, cut out the stems and save them.
5. Lightly grease a cookie sheet and on it place the mushroom caps with the cavity up. Cover with a damp towel.
6. Chop up the stems and any broken caps.
7. Chop the bacon into small pieces. Place in a cold frying pan. Add the onions and sauté over medium heat, stirring constantly, until the onions and bacon become translucent.
8. Add chopped parsley and stir.
9. Immediately add the chopped mushroom stems. Increase the heat to high and keep turning the mixture with a metal spatula.
10. As soon as the mushrooms start to ooze liquid, remove from heat and empty frying pan into a mixing bowl.
11. Stir until mixture cools slightly, then add the bread crumbs.
12. Mix the sour cream with the egg. Add freshly ground pepper and salt to taste and spoon half into the mushroom–bread crumb mixture. Mix thoroughly with wet hands; form little balls and place one in each mushroom cap. Bake in preheated oven for 8 to 12 minutes, the time depending on the size of the mushrooms.
13. Remove from the oven, and with a pastry bag fitted with a ½-inch plain tube, press a small dot of the remaining sour cream–egg mixture on top of each mushroom. If you like you may sprinkle some grated cheese or some Spanish or Hungarian paprika on the tops.
14. Bake the mushrooms for an additional 2 to 3 minutes, serve warm.

CHEF'S SECRET: Keep the mushrooms in a brown paper bag in the refrigerator until you use them.

If you have to wash mushrooms in cold water, sprinkle over and mix into the water approximately 2 to 3 tbsp. of all-purpose flour. This will help the mushrooms retain their white color, and they will not absorb the flour-water mixture as fast as they would absorb plain water.

The egg mixed into the sour cream keeps the sour cream from burning, helps it to thicken quickly, and makes it look attractive on the mushrooms.

Sardine Crêpes

8 servings

1 portion crêpe recipe (see page 262), sugar omitted
1 large can imported Portuguese sardines in oil

2 tbsp. soft butter
juice of ½ lemon
freshly ground black pepper
2 lemons

1. Preheat oven to 400 degrees.
2. Make crêpes and keep them warm.
3. Drain and discard the oil from the sardines.
4. Put sardines, butter, and lemon juice in a mixing bowl. Grind in black pepper, then mash all together until the mixture is creamy.
5. Divide the mixture into eight portions and spread over the crêpes.
6. Roll crêpes jelly-roll fashion.
7. Arrange rolled crêpes in an ovenproof dish and heat them in the oven for 8 to 12 minutes, according to how warm the crêpes were at the beginning.
8. If you wish, serve with Sauce Louis (see page 215) or with sour cream. Cut the lemons into 8 wedges. Serve one wedge with each crêpe.

CHEF'S SECRET: You can make the crêpes earlier and reheat them quickly, one by one, over medium heat in a heavy skillet which has been brushed lightly with butter.

Use skinless, boneless sardines if you object to the color of regular sardines, but the taste will never be as good. In the case of skinless, boneless sardines, increase the butter to 3 tbsp.

Pepperoni Pinwheels

approximately 40 slices

1 11- to 12-inch pepperoni or similar thin, dry sausage if pepperoni is not available
1 package pie dough mix

1 cup catsup
1 small egg
1 tsp. finely crushed oregano
2 tbsp. grated Parmesan cheese

1. Prepare the pie dough according to the directions on the box and roll it out to form an oblong shape as long as the pepperoni plus 1 inch.
2. Beat the egg and mix it with the catsup, oregano, and cheese.
3. Spread the catsup mixture over the pie dough, leaving ½ inch of space on three sides and 1 inch on the edge farthest from you.
4. Place the pepperoni on the dough and roll it jelly-roll fashion to the edge farthest from you.
5. Place the roll on a sheet of aluminum foil, being sure that the outside

edge of the foil is on the bottom of the roll; then wrap the roll. Chill overnight or freeze for 4 to 5 hours.

6. Cover a cookie sheet with aluminum foil. Brush lightly with shortening.

7. Preheat oven to 400 degrees.

8. With a very sharp knife, cut the roll into ¼- to ⅜-inch slices. Lay these on the aluminum foil lining the cookie sheet. After the slices reach room temperature, bake for 10 to 12 minutes. Serve hot or cold.

CHEF'S SECRET: The beaten egg in the catsup thickens the catsup and keeps it from running.

If you place two or three thin-bladed sharp knives in hot water and change them after each two to three slices, you can slice the roll while it is still frozen, making even and straight-surfaced slices.

Cheesecream Rolls

8 servings

8 commercial salt sticks, 1 day old	4 tbsp. melted butter
8 tbsp. commercial Cheddar cheese spread	4 tbsp. softened butter
	2 tbsp. grated Parmesan cheese

1. Preheat oven to 400 degrees.

2. Cut each salt stick in half at the middle. With a sharp knife, remove the inside soft part. Brush the salt sticks inside and outside with melted butter.

3. Heat them on a cookie sheet for 5 minutes. Remove and cool.

4. Mix together the cheese spread, softened butter, and grated Parmesan. Spoon the mixture into the cavities of the rolls.

5. Place the rolls on a cookie sheet so that the filled, open end is higher. The easiest way to do this is to wrinkle up a piece of aluminum foil, place it on the cookie sheet, and lean the rolls on the foil.

6. Heat for another 2 to 3 minutes. Serve warm.

CHEF'S SECRET: Salt sticks are rolls made from a dough similar to the dough used for hard rolls. They resemble the shape of a banana, and the top is covered with coarse salt and caraway seed. They are available in most supermarkets and bakeries.

This is a quick, last-minute appetizer. When you remove the inside of the roll, use a knife with a very narrow blade, and instead of trying to cut the insides out, remove them with sawing motions.

Oriental Lobster Tail

8 servings

8 6- to 8-oz. lobster tails	3 tbsp. Japanese or 2 tbsp. Chinese soy sauce
Court Bouillon (see page 131)	½ tsp. black pepper
1 cup finely minced celery	salt to taste
2 cups homemade or high-quality commercial mayonnaise	

½ tsp. garlic salt or a small pinch   1 tsp. sugar
  garlic powder   4 tbsp. melted butter

1. Preheat oven to 350 degrees.

2. Boil the lobster tails in the Court Bouillon. Cool immediately in ice water.

3. With kitchen scissors, cut out the stomach membrane. Remove the meat from the lobster tails and chill. (See drawing.)

4. Clean and rinse the shells. Be sure that you do not break them. Dry them on absorbent towels, then put them in the oven for 3 to 4 minutes.

5. From each tail, slice 3 to 4 nice even crosswise slices. Set aside.

6. Chop up the remaining lobster meat and put it into a mixing bowl. Add the celery, garlic salt, salt, pepper, and sugar.

7. Gently fold the soy sauce into the mayonnaise.

8. Set aside one-third of the mayonnaise mixture and add the remaining two-thirds to the chopped lobster-celery mixture.

9. Mix and let marinate at room temperature for at least 1 hour.

10. Fill the lobster tail shells with this mixture.

11. Arrange the shells on a shallow, ovenproof serving dish; or you may use a cookie sheet if, after baking, you transfer the lobster tails to a serving dish.

12. Pour the melted butter over the top and bake the lobster tails 10 minutes. Remove from oven. Arrange the sliced pieces of lobster meat on top of each shell. Using a paper cone or a pastry bag, pipe the remaining one-third of the mayonnaise mixture across the top of the lobster slices in a long stripe, or zigzag it over the whole surface.

13. Return to oven for an additional 10 minutes. Serve hot.

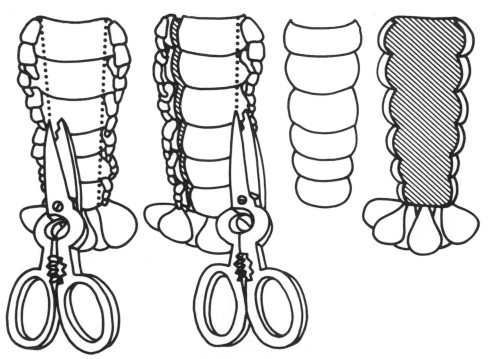

CHEF'S SECRET: The mayonnaise blended with the soy sauce gives a real oriental taste to the lobster tail, and the blend will not separate or run as you might imagine. The best way to cut out the belly membrane so that the flesh remains in one piece and is easily removable is to hold the lobster tail firmly in the left hand with the tail close to you. Insert the scissors in the natural opening by the root of the middle fin of the tail and go along the armor up to the other end. Remove the scissors. Insert the scissors again by the middle fin and go up on the other side. Do not try to cut too much at once, just snip little pieces with the tip of the scissors.

If you can buy Chinese celery instead of regular celery, it will improve the taste.

For a very pungent appetizer, replace the celery with the same amount of finely chopped "Kim Chee," available in most supermarkets. In this case, omit the salt and garlic entirely.

Lumberjack Pie

24 to 36 pieces

1 package pie dough mix
1 egg
1 tbsp. cold water
½ cup boiled potatoes cut into ¼-inch cubes
3 tbsp. finely chopped onions
½ cup finely chopped ham, leftover roast pork, or any other leftover meat
2 strips bacon or 2 tbsp. bacon drippings
freshly ground black pepper
salt

1. Prepare the pie dough according to the directions on the box and place it in the refrigerator to chill.

2. Sauté the onions in the bacon fat or with the two slices of bacon finely chopped. When the onions start to brown, add the chopped leftover meat and stir. Add the potatoes and cook the mixture until the potatoes heat through and absorb some of the fat. Remove from heat; add freshly ground black pepper and salt to taste. Let cool to room temperature.

3. Roll out half of the pie dough to form a square approximately 12 by 12 inches.

4. Gently press a ruler into the dough and divide it into twelve or sixteen equal-sized pieces. Beat the egg and cold water together. Brush the surface of the dough lightly with this egg wash.

5. Repeat with the other half of the dough.

6. Preheat oven to 375 degrees.

7. Place a small dab of the filling on each section of the dough. Cut the dough along the marks into individual pieces and fold over half of each piece so that the filling is completely covered. Gently press the edges together. Bake on a lightly greased cookie sheet for 12 to 15 minutes, the time depending on the size of the pieces. Serve hot.

CHEF'S SECRET: Many people have difficulty measuring equal-sized pieces of dough, even with a ruler, especially if the dough is not rolled to a near-perfect square. The best method is this: Cut a piece of wax paper exactly the size of the dough and carefully fold it to give you equal-sized sections. For example, for twelve equal sections you would fold the wax paper first in thirds in one direction, then in fourths in the other direction. Then place the wax paper over the dough and mark along the folds.

If you do not have boiled potatoes on hand, you can cook potatoes very quickly if you cut them uniformly as follows: Peel a potato and cut it with a thin-bladed knife into even slices but only to 1 inch away from one end, so that the slices do not fall apart. Turn the potato and cut crosswise, being careful that the knife does not run through the whole potato. Then slice in the third direction, and you will have even little cubes which will cook quickly. (See drawing.)

Quiche Lorraine

8 servings

1 package pie dough mix, or your favorite recipe for a 2-crust pie	8 large eggs
	4 cups half-and-half
4 oz. butter	4 tbsp. flour
½ lb. Cheddar cheese	1 tbsp. salt
½ lb. Swiss cheese	nutmeg
2 tbsp. grated Parmesan	½ can luncheon meat (optional)

1. Prepare dough according to directions. Divide in half, roll out, and line two pie dishes.
2. Preheat oven to 375 degrees.
3. Heat the butter until it is dark brown. Let it cool to lukewarm.
4. Grate the Cheddar and Swiss cheese coarsely. Mix them with the grated Parmesan, 1 tbsp. of the flour, and a sprinkling of nutmeg.
5. Divide this mixture evenly and place in the two pies.
6. Beat the eggs together with the salt and 1 tbsp. of flour.
7. Mix the eggs with the half-and-half and the remaining 3 tbsp. of flour. Strain this mixture through a fine sieve into another bowl. This is a very important step.
8. Beating vigorously, add the 4 oz. of browned lukewarm butter. Divide this mixture between the two pies. Place the pie dishes on a cookie sheet and bake at 375 degrees for 30 minutes. Lower the heat to 350 degrees and bake for an additional 15 to 20 minutes.
9. Cut in wedges, small diamonds, or triangles. Serve lukewarm.

CHEF'S SECRET: This recipe for Quiche Lorraine freezes extremely well and can be easily reheated in aluminum foil. If you bake it in an aluminum foil pie pan, you can freeze it in the pan. Add finely chopped luncheon meat to this Quiche Lorraine if you desire.

You can also bake the quiche in square pans. Then, of course, the oven temperature should be a little lower, beginning at 350 degrees, and the baking time should be shorter because the filling will be thinner.

With this basic Quiche Lorraine recipe, your imagination is the only limit in developing your own hors d'oeuvres.

Sauerkraut Balls

40 to 50 balls

1 15½-oz. can corned beef hash	2 tbsp. water
1 1-lb. can sauerkraut	2 cups fine bread crumbs
3 eggs	shortening
2 tbsp. bread crumbs	

1. Drain and chop the sauerkraut and mix it with the canned hash, 2 tbsp. of bread crumbs, and 2 of the eggs. Let stand at room temperature for ½ hour.

2. With wet hands, form balls ½ inch in diameter. Freeze the balls for 2 hours or longer.

3. After the balls are frozen, beat the third egg with the water. Roll the balls in the egg wash and then in the bread crumbs. Shake off excess crumbs.

4. Fry the balls in shortening until golden brown. Put them on absorbent paper to drain, then transfer them to a serving dish. Serve warm.

CHEF'S SECRET: After pressing out the sauerkraut juice through a sieve or colander, chop up the sauerkraut on a wooden board. Place it in a kitchen towel. Fold the towel over the sauerkraut, forming a ball. Wring the ball out so that all the juice is squeezed out, and only then add it to the hash. Otherwise, the balls will not be firm, and you will not be able to fry them.

The best and fastest way to make the balls the same size is to spread the mixture on a cutting board in an even layer and divide it with a long, wet knife into equal-sized cubes. Then, with wet palms, roll each cube into a ball.

If you freeze the balls beforehand, you may bread them easily without ruining their shape.

Fish en Croûte

10 to 12 servings

1 package pie dough mix, enough for a double crust	4 oz. chopped or cubed ham
	3 tbsp. flour
2 tbsp. oil or shortening	1 cup white wine
2 tbsp. butter	1 lb. lake trout fillets
½ lb. medium-sized fresh mushrooms	1 cup half-and-half or cream

1 egg   fresh parsley
1 lemon   white wine for swirling pan
salt and pepper to taste

1. Prepare pie dough according to the directions on the package and chill.

2. Cut the trout fillets into 2-inch pieces. Season them with salt and pepper.

3. Remove the stems from 10 to 12 nice mushrooms, the number depending on the number of servings you desire. Chop up the stems and the remaining mushrooms, and sauté all the mushrooms in the oil and butter for 3 minutes. Set aside the nice mushroom caps to use as a garnish later.

4. Add the chopped ham to the pan and sprinkle the ham and mushrooms with the flour. Stir for 2 to 3 more minutes over low heat.

5. Add the white wine and the pieces of trout. Simmer 3 to 4 minutes.

6. Add half-and-half or cream. Stir until it reaches a slow boil.

7. Remove from fire. Put a strainer over a saucepan, empty the mixture into the strainer, and let it drip through to the second pan.

8. Swirl the sauté pan clean with some white wine and pour this over the mixture in the other pan.

9. Roll out the pie dough to a rectangle 11 by 10 inches. Beat the egg and brush the entire surface of the dough with it.

10. Preheat oven to 350 degrees.

11. Carefully spoon the fish, ham, and mushroom mixture, without any sauce, onto the side of the dough near you, leaving 1 to 2 inches of the opposite ends empty.

12. Starting at the edge near you, roll the dough over the filling and keep rolling it until you have reached the far side. Form the left end into the shape of a fish head and the right end into the shape of a fish tail. Make an eye out of a small piece of dough. Gently lift the whole fish roll onto a well-greased baking sheet. Brush it with the remainder of the egg. Take ordinary scissors and cut some scales in the dough.

13. Bake the fish at 350 to 375 degrees for 5 minutes. Brush with egg again and bake for another 10 to 14 minutes, according to the size of the fish and the temperature of your oven.

14. If necessary, reduce the sauce by simmering, or thicken it with a mixture of butter and flour. Correct the seasoning with sugar and salt if necessary.

15. Serve the fish decorated with green parsley and lemon slices and pour the sauce over each serving. Place one of the mushroom caps on each serving.

CHEF'S SECRET: Any kind of smoked pork or ham cooked together with seafood improves the flavor. Chinese chefs consider this the secret of their success. Their fish dishes are so popular because they always put pork bones or ham in Court Bouillon.

It is easier to make the scales if you dip the tip of the scissors in flour before snipping the little pieces. If you hold the scissors at about a 45-degree angle, the tips of the scales will turn up, and since the dough is thin, they will brown faster than the other parts and will make the fish look very attractive.

The dough expands somewhat in the first 5 minutes of baking and in so doing absorbs a part of the egg wash. Therefore, a second brushing on the already hot surface will immediately bake onto it and keep the fish shiny.

Blueburger Balls

36 to 40 1-inch balls

1 lb. good-quality ground beef
4 oz. blue cheese, crumbled
2 tbsp. finely minced raw onion
2 tbsp. finely minced fresh green parsley

freshly ground black pepper
1 egg
½ cup ice water
1 bowl ice water to wet your hands

1. Combine all the ingredients in a mixing bowl. Let stand at room temperature for ½ hour.

2. Divide the mixture into 36 to 40 portions.

3. Form balls from the portions and chill.

4. Just before serving, fry the blueburgers in a preheated, slightly greased large frying pan. Constantly shake the pan while cooking, and only cook until the blueburgers are medium rare.

CHEF'S SECRET: The success of this dish depends on two things. First, crumble the blue cheese with a fork on a metal pie plate and freeze the crumbs for at least 1 hour, keeping them in the freezer until you add them to the meat. Second, work the mixture quickly with wet hands, then spread it on an even surface and divide it with a sharp knife, first in halves, then in quarters, and so on until you have 36 equal portions. By following this procedure, you will be able to make balls of equal size. Dip your hands in ice water often while you are forming the balls.

You can use this method on any meatball mixture.

SOUPS

BEEF

Old-Fashioned Beef Soup
Beef Goulash Soup with Tiny
    Dumplings
Real Double Consommé

Mexican Beef Soup
Beef and Barley Soup
Beef Dumpling Soup

CHICKEN

Old-Fashioned Chicken Soup
Cream of Chicken Soup with Rice
Chicken Consommé with
    Mousselines

Oriental Chicken Soup in Winter
    Melon
Petite Marmite, Henry IV

VEGETABLE

Clear Tomato Soup
Cauliflower Soup
Mushroom-Barley Soup
Real Bean Soup

Cream of Green Bean Soup
Beet Borscht
Lentil Soup with Franks
Mixed Vegetable Soup

FISH

Bouillabaisse
Fish Chowder

Lobster Bisque

FRUIT

Cold Cherry Soup
Apple Cream Soup

Avocado Soup with Champagne
Swedish Fruit Soup

*F*or thousands of years, up to just a very short while ago, it was unimaginable to have a noon or evening meal without soup. Among canned foods, for decades soup was unquestionably the most popular. It is still worthwhile to learn how to prepare good soups because they are coming back in style again and getting very popular in today's home entertainment.

With soup, probably more than with any other food, the proper cooking equipment is just as organic a part of your success as the ingredients used and the skill, attention, and love applied. The proper pot is large and heavy, its lid closes tight, and it retains the heat for a long time. If you feel that your equipment is light and tinny, stick to soups which need a shorter cooking time, and wait until the heavy pot arrives before trying the heartier ones.

Many of the soups in this chapter could serve as meals in themselves, especially at lunch or supper, and some of them could be the main attraction on a party table.

Crackers are fine and an ideal accompaniment to soups. Still, a cheese stick, salt stick, crusty French bread, freshly made toast rounds or triangles, or buttered, toasted bread cubes can lift the ordinary into the special and the special into the exceptional.

Soups

BEEF

Old-Fashioned Beef Soup

8 generous servings

1 lb. soup bones
1 lb. lean beef, preferably marbled
½ lb. fat beef
1 onion, unpeeled
1 clove
2 medium carrots, peeled and split in two
1 parsnip or parsley root
2 stalks celery or piece of celery root
1 small turnip or slice of larger one
2 cloves garlic, unpeeled
1 tsp. black peppercorns, slightly bruised
1 whole bay leaf
3 tbsp. salt
3 qt. water

1. Place all ingredients in a large pot in their listed order, the 3 qt. of water last.

2. Cover, place over medium heat, and bring to a boil. Immediately reduce the heat to low, and simmer the soup for 2 hours or more.

3. One hour before serving, remove from the heat and strain through a large colander into another pot. Place the meat and vegetables on a tray and cool until you can handle them. Discard all spices and bones.

4. Peel the onion and discard the peeling. Cut the onion into small pieces. Cut up the carrot, parsnip or parsley root, celery, and turnip. Cut up the lean meat into ½-inch cubes. Trim the fat meat, discard the fat, and cut the edible parts into cubes.

5. Place all meat and vegetables in a large soup tureen. Remove the fat from the soup. About 10 minutes before serving time, cover and heat the soup over medium heat until it begins to boil. Pour it over the warm vegetables and meat and serve it at once.

CHEF'S SECRET: The best way to handle the clove is to make a cross-cut at the root end of the onion with a sharp knife and press the clove into the onion.

The skin of the onion adds a reddish hue to the beef soup. Without it, the soup will be light yellow, like chicken soup.

If you have only a large onion and want to use just half of it, cut it crosswise, dividing the root end from the leaf end. Lightly brush the cut surface of the onion with shortening and press it to the hot surface of the stove top for 30 seconds. Or in a small frying pan heat a little shortening until it is smoking and press the cut surface of the onion into it. With this method, the natural sugar in the onion will caramelize and will darken the color of the soup.

If you skim the fat from the soup and want to remove the last particles, dip a towel into cold water, wring it dry, place three to four ice cubes in the towel, and, holding the ice cubes tightly, dip the towel about ½ inch into the soup and move it slowly. All the fat particles will adhere to the surface of the towel, and you can remove them at once.

Beef Goulash Soup with Tiny Dumplings

8 servings

For the soup:

2 lb. cubed boneless beef, chuck or similar cut

2 cups finely minced onion

6 tbsp. lard or bacon drippings

1 qt. ¾- to 1-inch potato cubes

1 small carrot, sliced

1 bell pepper, cut in pieces

1 large ripe tomato, peeled and chopped, or 4 tbsp. canned tomato purée or 2 tbsp. canned tomato paste

¼ cup flour

2 tbsp. Hungarian paprika

2 tbsp. salt

½ tsp. ground black pepper

¼ tsp. garlic salt or 1 small pinch garlic powder

1 tsp. caraway seeds

1 small bunch green parsley

1 whole bay leaf

For the tiny dumplings:

1 small egg

2 tbsp. water

¾ cup flour

1 pinch salt

1. Mix the ¼ cup of flour with 1 tbsp. of the Hungarian paprika, 2 tbsp. of salt, the black pepper, garlic salt or powder, and the caraway seeds.

2. Tie the parsley and bay leaf securely together.

3. Sauté the onions over medium heat in a heavy skillet in 4 tbsp. of the lard or bacon drippings. When they become glossy, pour in a cup of water and add the carrot and bell pepper. Cover and simmer over low heat for 15 to 20 minutes.

4. Spread out the meat on a cookie sheet and sprinkle half of the spice-flour mixture over it. Turn over the pieces of meat and try to coat them evenly.

5. Increase the heat to high. Lift the lid and let the water evaporate, so that the onions start to fry.

6. Quickly add the meat to the onions, one-fourth at a time. Keep turning the meat with a spatula after each addition, waiting until the red color leaves before adding more meat.

7. When all the meat is added, decrease the heat to low. Cover the pot tightly and let it simmer for 5 minutes. Add ½ cup of water and scrape the

bottom of the pan. Cover again and let simmer for 45 minutes to 1 hour, stirring once in a while.

8. From the remaining flour and spice, make a slurry by adding a little water. Be sure that it is completely smooth and without lumps. Keep it at room temperature.

9. Pour 2 qt. of water over the meat and increase the heat to medium. Add the fresh or canned tomato, parsley, and bay leaf. Once the liquid comes to a boil, stir in the slurry, pouring it in a slow even stream.

10. Cover and again bring the mixture to a boil. Add the potatoes and simmer over low heat until the meat is tender and the potatoes are cooked.

11. Just before serving, remove the parsley and, in a small saucepan, warm up the remaining 2 tbsp. of lard or bacon drippings. Add the remaining 1 tbsp. paprika and stir constantly until it warms and turns a vivid red. Put this in the soup.

12. To prepare the tiny dumplings: Mix the egg, water, pinch of salt, and flour in a small bowl with your hands, or you can use the paddle of an electric mixer. When these ingredients are thoroughly mixed, bring to a boil 1 qt. of water with 1 tsp. of salt. Dip the tip of a spoon into the boiling water. With the wet spoon, take a piece of dough no bigger than a hazelnut and drop it into the boiling water by gently hitting the side of the pot with the spoon handle.

13. Dip the spoon into the water again, and repeat the process until all the dough is used. Decrease the heat and cook the dumplings for 3 to 4 minutes. With a colander, drain the dumplings and rinse them with cold water. Shake off all the water and then add the dumplings to the soup.

CHEF'S SECRET: Be careful with the onions. Their preparation is the most important part in making the soup. Cold onions should go into a cold pot with the lard or bacon drippings, then they are heated together. This is important because if the pot and the shortening are hot, the onions will start to fry, brown, and evaporate instead of turning into a thick soft substance.

The slurry (this is an expression from the food-manufacturing industry) is the safest and fastest way to secure a lump-free soup without making a roux.

The melted shortening and paprika mixture gives the color to the soup that housewives try for but seldom achieve.

Real Double Consommé

8 servings

1 lb. lean ground beef	1 cup cold water
2 egg whites	1 2-inch carrot, finely grated
4 cans beef consommé, 10½ oz. each	1 tbsp. unsalted butter
4 cans cold water	dry sherry or Marsala wine
1 tsp. cornstarch	

1. Pour the consommé and the 4 cans of water into a large pot.
2. Beat the egg whites and thoroughly mix them with the meat. Add this

mixture, spoonful by spoonful, to the cold liquid, and stir after each addition, so that the meat particles separate.

3. Sauté the grated carrot in the unsalted butter. Drain off any remaining fat and add to the meat mixture .

4. Mix the cornstarch with the cup of cold water.

5. Bring the soup to a boil over medium heat, stirring with a wire whip every 4 or 5 minutes.

6. Slowly add the water and cornstarch mixture, stirring constantly. Bring the soup to a boil again, decrease the heat, and let it bubble slowly for 1 hour. Turn off the heat, cover the pot, and let it stand for at least another hour.

7. Skim off as much fat as possible and, without stirring, pour the warm soup into another pot through a wet kitchen towel or several layers of cheesecloth. Do not try to pour the bottom part with the meat in it.

8. When ready to serve, reheat the soup but be careful not to bring it to a boil. Add a few tablespoons of the wine.

CHEF'S SECRET: Having been served various misrepresentations of this soup by overworked personnel in understaffed hotel kitchens, people often have a wrong idea about this most delightful of all soups. Once you try to prepare it and discover how simple it is, you will want to serve it often to your guests and family. The cornstarch gives the delightful syrupy texture, and the grated carrot heated in the butter adds the beautiful deep golden color.

The beef adds the extra beefy flavor, and the egg whites capture all the particles which would make the soup cloudy or break its brilliant transparency.

The ground beef mixed with the egg white makes an excellent meat pudding. Combine it with the yolks of 2 eggs, 4 slices of white bread soaked in milk and pressed, plus salt, pepper, and freshly chopped parsley. Steam in a shallow dish in a water bath.

Mexican Beef Soup

4 servings

2 10½-oz. cans beef consommé
1 can water
1 small young ear of corn, cut into 4 pieces
4 pieces bell pepper, cut into 1-inch squares
4 chunks tomato
1 4- to 5-inch young zucchini, peeled and cut into 4 pieces
4 chunks boiled potato

2 strips leftover steak, 4 by 1 inches each, or 4 to 6 cubes raw tenderloin or sirloin, approximately 1 inch each
2 tbsp. butter
1 clove garlic
sprinkling of cumin
salt to taste
1 tsp. cilantro (Mexican parsley), finely chopped
grated Parmesan cheese

1. Bring the consommé and the water to a boil. Drop in the pieces of corn. Cover and cook over medium heat.

2. In another, heavy pan, melt the butter over low heat. Cut the clove of garlic in half and add it to the butter, cut side down. Keep stirring, gently pressing the garlic with the back of a spoon until the butter has a garlicky scent.

3. If you use the sirloin or tenderloin cubes, quickly sauté them in the butter and remove.

4. Add the zucchini, pepper squares, tomato chunks, cumin, salt, and cilantro to the butter and garlic. Cover and simmer over very low heat until the vegetables are tender.

5. Add the strips of leftover steak or the meat cubes and the boiled potato chunks to the sautéed vegetables. Cover until all heats through.

6. Remove the two garlic halves and then put the mixture into the consommé.

7. Evenly divide all the vegetables and meat into four soup plates. Ladle the liquid into the plates. Sprinkle with grated cheese and serve with Mexican hard rolls or any similar crusty hard roll.

CHEF'S SECRET: In a Mexican restaurant in Mexico City, I watched the chef prepare this dish. It took him about fifteen minutes from beginning to end, and it was one of the best beef soups I ever tasted.

The zucchini must be very young. If you cannot get a zucchini, you can use a small peeled fresh cucumber instead.

To sauté the vegetables so that they keep their shape, color, and flavor, you need a frying pan or sauté pan 8 to 9 inches in diameter with a well-fitting lid. With a large pan, you can keep the vegetables separated as you sauté them.

A light sprinkling of sugar on the cooking vegetables will not make them sweet but will add a fresh taste.

Mushrooms, asparagus tips, young green peas, or pieces of celery heart may be used instead of, or in addition to, the vegetables mentioned; however, the young corn is a must.

Beef and Barley Soup

8 servings

1 lb. boneless beef cut in ½-inch cubes	½ cup barley, washed and drained
1 lb. beef bones	2 tbsp. chopped parsley
½ cup minced onions	½ tsp. black pepper
2 tbsp. shortening	1 bay leaf
1 4-inch carrot cut in ½-inch cubes	1 tbsp. salt
1 4-inch celery stalk cut in ½-inch cubes	3 qt. water
½ cup turnip, rutabaga, or parsnip cut in ½-inch cubes	

1. In a large, heavy soup pot, sauté the onions and the beef in the shortening, stirring constantly, until the onions turn glossy.

2. Add the barley and parsley. Keep stirring for 5 minutes, then add all the other ingredients, cover, and cook over very low heat for at least 2 hours.

3. Discard the bones and serve.

CHEF'S SECRET: When you add the barley with the chopped parsley after the meat has cooked, the barley picks up some of the meat juices and therefore has an added flavor.

Beef Dumpling Soup

8 servings

For the soup:
1 lb. soup meat
2 lb. soup bones
2 carrots
1 parsley root or parsnip
1 piece celery root or turnip
2 stalks celery
1 small bunch green parsley
1 leek
1 small onion, unpeeled
1 clove garlic
1 bay leaf

12 black peppercorns, slightly bruised
1 tbsp. salt
For the dumplings:
½ lb. ground beef
1 cup cooked rice
3 tbsp. finely minced onion sautéed in
   1 tbsp. shortening
1 egg, slightly beaten
1 tsp. salt
½ tsp. finely crushed marjoram or
   oregano
¼ tsp. black pepper

1. Put all the soup ingredients except the meat in a large soup pot. Add 3 qt. water or enough to cover.

2. Cut the soup meat into three to four pieces and place on top of the other ingredients. Over high heat, bring the soup to a boil; reduce the heat to low and cook for 1½ hours.

3. Remove the soup meat and continue cooking the rest of the soup.

4. When the soup meat is cool enough for you to handle, cut it into small pieces and run them through a blender.

5. In a large mixing bowl, combine all the dumpling ingredients with the blended soup meat. With wet palms, form dumplings about the size of a walnut.

6. Place the dumplings in a large pot. Using a fine sieve, pour in enough liquid from the soup to cover them. Bring to a boil over medium heat.

7. Strain the rest of the soup. Add the clear liquid to the dumplings. Put the carrots into a soup tureen. Discard the other ingredients.

8. When the dumplings are cooked, place the soup with the dumplings in the tureen and serve at once.

CHEF'S SECRET: Adding the blended, boiled meat to the raw ground beef and rice gives an interesting texture to the beef dumplings and is an economical use of the soup meat.

In forming the dumplings, if you have difficulty with "portion control," use a metal ¼-cup measuring cup or a small ice cream scoop. In either case, dip the device into cold water before dipping it into the meat mixture.

The marjoram or oregano will give a distinctive taste to the dumplings. If you wish, mix together 3 tbsp. cream, 1 egg yolk, and the juice of ½ lemon, dilute with 2 to 3 tbsp. of the hot soup, and add this mixture to the soup tureen before pouring the hot soup into it. This will make the soup into a Balkan-style soup, as it would be served in Greece, Bulgaria, Rumania, and Yugoslavia.

CHICKEN

Old-Fashioned Chicken Soup

8 servings

1 3½- to 4-lb. stewing hen, split in
   half or cut in quarters
2 cups coarsely chopped carrots
4 celery stalks, cut up
1 small onion, unpeeled, studded with
   1 clove in the root end
1 parsley root or parsnip
1 piece celery root or turnip
1 clove garlic
1 tbsp. salt
12 black peppercorns

1 pinch mace
1 pinch nutmeg
1 or 2 blades saffron
½ lb. beef or veal bones
1 gallon water
1 tbsp. chopped parsley
1 piece chicken belly fat
1 tbsp. finely grated carrots
2 tbsp. butter
1 tbsp. sugar

1. Place all ingredients except the last five in a large soup pot. Bring to a boil over medium heat.

2. Reduce the heat and simmer for at least 4 hours.

3. Remove from the heat and let the soup stand for 30 minutes. Skim off the fat and pour the soup carefully through a sieve into another pot.

4. Let the meat and vegetables cool on a cookie sheet.

5. Sauté the chopped parsley for 1 to 2 minutes in the chicken belly fat. Then add the cooked carrots, celery, and parsnip or parsley root; cover the sauté pan with a lid.

6. Reduce the heat as much as possible and cook for 10 minutes.

7. In a small frying pan, heat the sugar slowly until it starts to turn brown. Add the butter and the grated carrot.

8. Stir this mixture for 10 to 15 seconds, then remove from heat and dilute it with ½ cup chicken soup. Bring it to a rapid boil and then strain it through a fine sieve into the soup. This will give color to the soup.

9. Remove the chicken skin and bones; cut the meat into chunks.

10. Put the meat and the vegetables sautéed with the parsley into a serving dish. Pour the soup over them and serve at once.

CHEF'S SECRET: The belly fat of the chicken is at the end of the breast and around the upper part of the thigh. The parsley sautéed with this fat will give an intense chicken flavor that people look for in vain in most modern chicken soups. The vegetables sautéed with this parsley will taste as vegetables should.

The carotene, released from the grated carrot by the heat, combined with the browned sugar, gives the color that Grandma's chicken soup used to have.

Although the soup is called chicken soup, do not try to make it with a young chicken; only a soup hen will give the taste you want.

Cream of Chicken Soup with Rice

8 servings

1 3½- to 4-lb. stewing hen, cut in 4
    pieces
2 carrots, scraped and split
2 stalks celery
1 tbsp. salt
1 small whole onion, peeled and
    studded with a clove
1 clove garlic
3 to 4 mushrooms or ½ tsp. mushroom
    powder
1 bay leaf

¼ tsp. nutmeg
2 qt. water
3 tbsp. butter
3 tbsp. other shortening, such as
    chicken fat or lard
3 tbsp. flour
2 tbsp. starch (preferably rice starch)
2 cups half-and-half or milk
2 egg yolks
2 cups cooked rice

1. Place the first ten ingredients in a large soup pot. Bring to a boil, reduce heat, and simmer for at least 2 hours.

2. Remove from heat and let stand for ½ hour. Strain the liquid through a fine sieve. Reserve the pieces of chicken; discard the vegetables and seasonings.

3. In a small saucepan, melt the butter and the shortening.

4. Mix the flour and rice starch in the half-and-half or milk.

5. Slowly pour the milk-flour-starch mixture in a thin stream into the melted shortening, stirring constantly with a wire whip.

6. Add 2 to 3 ladles of chicken soup to this mixture and keep stirring it. Be sure that during this time you keep the mixture at a slow boil.

7. Now add this mixture to the soup. Add the rice, cover, and let it simmer over low heat. If your soup pot is not very heavy, it is advisable to put an asbestos pad under it.

8. Remove the breast and thigh meat. Cut it into ½-inch pieces.

9. Beat the 2 egg yolks with a fork in a small mixing bowl. Slowly add 2 to 3 tbsp. of the cream soup to the egg yolks. Stir and then pour it into a soup tureen.

10. Add the cut-up chicken meat to the soup. Correct the seasoning with a little salt, ground white pepper, and nutmeg if you like. If you wish, you may add finely chopped mushrooms to the soup.

11. Pour the soup into the tureen. Serve at once.

CHEF'S SECRET: By cooking the rice separately, you can control the degree of doneness and not have to fish for it among the bones and vegetables.

By pouring the milk-flour-starch mixture into the hot shortening, you will achieve an excellent white sauce more quickly than with the old method of heating flour or starch and shortening first and then adding the liquid.

Chicken Consommé with Mousselines

8 servings

4 10½-oz. cans chicken broth, diluted according to directions, or 2 qt. chicken stock
8 oz. raw chicken breast, skinless and boneless

4 egg whites
approximately 1 pt. heavy cream or whipping cream
⅛ tsp. nutmeg
½ tsp. salt or more according to taste

1. Cut the chicken breast into ½-inch cubes. Grind it twice with the finest blade of a meat grinder. Add the nutmeg and salt and then purée the mixture in an electric blender until it turns into a frothy pale substance. Place the mixture in a bowl in which you can mix it with an electric mixer.

2. Chill the blended chicken meat in the coldest part of your refrigerator for at least ½ hour. Also, chill the wire whip of the mixer. Approximately ½ hour before serving time, start to whip the chilled puréed chicken, using the chilled wire whip. Gradually add some of the cream and some of the egg white. Be sure that all ingredients are well chilled. When all of the egg whites and heavy cream have been added, you will have a substance resembling overwhipped whipping cream.

3. In a shallow pan, bring to a gentle boil approximately 1 qt. of lightly salted water. Dip a tablespoon into the boiling water, and then take from the mousseline preparation, using the warmed spoon, an amount about the size of an unshelled almond. Gently slide it into the water. Repeat until you have eight to ten mousselines.

4. Increase the heat slightly, until the mousselines puff. They will grow to double their original size.

5. Just before serving, put one mousseline into each soup bowl and pour the hot chicken broth or stock over it. Serve immediately.

CHEF'S SECRET: It is advisable to cook one mousseline and then taste it for saltiness before proceeding to cook more. You can then correct the seasoning by adding more salt if needed.

If you want to make the mousselines beforehand, they must be kept submerged in warm water at approximately 160 to 170 degrees until serving time. Do not try to keep them in the stock, because they will lose their beautiful snow-white color. For a variation you can add thin slivers of tender ham to the mousseline preparation before poaching.

Oriental Chicken Soup in Winter Melon

12 servings

1 winter melon, approximately 1 foot in diameter and 1 foot high (if you cannot purchase one, a firm yellow pumpkin will do very well)

1 lb. raw chicken breasts, boneless and
  skinless, cut in 1½- by ½-inch strips
1 lb. peeled, deveined, frozen shrimp
  or 10 oz. peeled, deveined, cooked
  shrimp
2 cups crosscut Chinese celery stalks
  or, if these are not available, crosscut
  stalks of ordinary celery
6 oz. sliced mushrooms
8 oz. fresh bean sprouts or 1 can bean
  sprouts, drained
1 cup frozen green peas or 1 package
  frozen Chinese snow peas

1 cup peanut oil
4 10½-oz. cans chicken broth (diluted
  as directed) or equivalent amount
  of homemade chicken broth
1 tbsp. salt
4 tbsp. soy sauce
½ tsp. ground white pepper
½ tsp. freshly chopped ginger or ¼
  tsp. ground ginger
¼ tsp. Tabasco sauce
1 tbsp. sugar
4 tbsp. rice starch or cornstarch

1. Select a pot which is large enough to hold the whole winter melon or pumpkin.

2. Cover the bottom of the pot with a towel which is large enough so that you can tie its ends diagonally above the top of the winter melon or pumpkin.

3. At two points about 1½ to 2 inches from the top, make sharp horizontal marks on the skin of the melon. Cut through the marks while cutting off a top slice. Scrape out and discard the seedy, soft parts. Put the melon in the pot.

4. Bring two cans of chicken soup to a rolling boil. Pour the boiling soup into the cavity of the melon.

5. In ½ cup of the peanut oil, sauté the pieces of chicken over high heat. Remove the chicken from the oil with a slotted spoon and put it in the winter melon or pumpkin. Sauté the mushrooms, then the celery, in the same oil and pan. Add both to the soup.

6. Now add the other ½ cup of oil to the pan. Quickly sauté the shrimp, the raw or canned bean sprouts, and the snow peas or green peas and add all to the winter melon or pumpkin.

7. In a heavy pot, bring the other two cans of chicken soup to a boil. Blend the starch, salt, pepper, ginger, and sugar together in a bowl and add the soy sauce and Tabasco. Slowly stir this mixture into the boiling chicken soup. Keep stirring. Be sure that no lumps remain.

8. Pour this mixture into the winter melon or pumpkin, straining it through a very fine sieve if you have used chopped ginger.

9. Carefully pour boiling water around the melon or pumpkin so that the top of the water is about 2 inches below the cut surface.

10. Replace the top of the melon, fitting it by the marks you made before cutting off the top. Tightly tie the four corners of the towel diagonally over the top of the melon. Cover the pot and boil gently for 5 to 6 hours. Replace the boiling water around the melon if necessary.

11. Pour ice water on the knots made in the towel. This will cool the towel immediately so that you can remove it without burning your hands.

12. Place the winter melon or pumpkin on a serving dish. Add salt if necessary. Serve the soup at once.

CHEF'S SECRET: This is an impressive soup but is definitely not as complicated as it sounds. By first pouring the boiling chicken soup into the winter melon and then adding every ingredient hot from the sauté pan, you will keep all the ingredients at a high temperature while you complete the recipe. All the tastes will blend, but the thick walls of the melon will prevent the ingredients from overcooking.

Petite Marmite, Henry IV

8 servings

8 4-oz. pieces lean beef; for example, shank or the lean part of chuck
2 lb. beef bones
1 large stewing hen, cut into 8 serving pieces (2 drumsticks, 2 thighs split in half along the bone, 1 breast cut in half)
2 lb. chicken backs and necks or wing tips
2 carrots, coarsely chopped
2 celery stalks, cut up
3 to 4 sprigs parsley tied with a bay leaf
1 medium onion, studded with a clove

8 pieces turnip the size of a walnut, shaped like a walnut
8 pieces carrot, same size, same shape
8 pieces potato, same size, same shape
8 pieces beet root, same size, same shape
8 small boiling onions, peeled
8 fresh mushrooms, slightly trimmed on the stem end
2 cans beef consommé, 10½ oz. each
2 cans chicken broth, 10½ oz. each
1 tbsp. Worcestershire sauce
salt and freshly ground black pepper to taste

1. Sprinkle the beef pieces lightly with salt and grind some fresh pepper over them. Let stand at room temperature.

2. Sprinkle the pieces of stewing hen with salt. Place the beef and hen pieces in a large soup pan. Add the coarsely chopped carrots, cut-up celery stalks, parsley with the bay leaf, and onion. Pour in the beef consommé and chicken broth. Add the backs and necks of chicken and the beef bones. Add the Worcestershire sauce. Cover with water and bring to a slow boil over medium heat. Let simmer for at least 3 hours.

3. In the meantime, bring a second pot of salted water to a vigorous boil. Cook the shaped carrots until tender. Remove and cook the turnips in the same water, then the onions, the potatoes, the mushrooms for only 30 seconds, and, finally, the beets.

4. Except for the beets, you can keep all the cooked vegetables together in a pot of lukewarm water. The beets must be kept separate, also in lukewarm water.

5. After the soup has simmered for at least 3 hours, pour it through a fine sieve into another pot. Put the bones, vegetables, and meat on a tray. Place in individual bowls (*petites marmites*) one portion of beef, one of chicken, and one piece each of the separately cooked vegetables. Fill up the bowl with soup. Serve with grated cheese and dry thin toast.

CHEF'S SECRET: A petite marmite is an individual-sized earthenware pot. Of course, if you do not have any petite marmites, this soup can be served in any ordinary soup bowls.

To do a proper job on the vegetables, first cut the turnip or other vegetables into eight cubes, then round the cubes by cutting off first the upper four corners, then the bottom four corners, and then all twelve edges.

Cut the carrots first into small cylinders and then round off the top and bottom edges of each cylinder. This is not as complicated as it sounds.

VEGETABLE

Clear Tomato Soup

12 servings

2 lb. veal bones
1 coarsely chopped carrot
1 chopped parsley root or parsnip
1 cut-up celery stalk
½ onion, unpeeled
5 to 6 black peppercorns
1 tbsp. salt
1 bay leaf
1 clove garlic
3 tbsp. sugar

1 tsp. butter
1 6-oz. can tomato paste
1 46-oz. can tomato juice
2 tbsp. dried tarragon
2 tbsp. dried dill weed
6 tbsp. cornstarch
liquid from 2 ripe tomatoes, chopped
    up and run through a blender
fresh lemon juice to taste
fresh dill weed if available

1. In a large soup pan, place the veal bones, carrot, parsley root or parsnip, celery, onion, peppercorns, salt, bay leaf, and garlic. Add about 3 qt. of water. Cover and cook slowly for at least 4 hours. The amount of stock should then be approximately 2 qt.

2. Strain the stock into another pot; skim the top if necessary.

3. Dissolve the sugar in the butter, heating until it starts to caramelize. Pour 1 qt. of stock over the butter-sugar mixture. Add to this the tomato paste and tomato juice. Bring to a boil, reduce heat, and simmer.

4. In the meanwhile, cool 1 pt. of stock and bring another pint to a boil.

5. Sprinkle into the boiling stock the tarragon and dried dill weed. Let boil for 2 minutes. Strain this stock, removing the herbs, into the simmering tomato soup.

6. Stir the cornstarch into the cold pint of stock and slowly pour the starch-stock mixture into the simmering soup. This will make the soup syrupy-thick and clear.

7. Add chopped dill weed if you have fresh dill. Correct the seasoning of the soup with lemon juice, sugar, and salt. Pour the liquid from the ripe tomatoes into the soup tureen and ladle the hot soup over it. Serve immediately.

CHEF'S SECRET: Adding sugar to the tomato juice and tomato paste brings out a fresh tomato flavor and reduces some of the acidity.

The addition of fresh lemon juice before serving adds a tang, and using cornstarch instead of flour as a thickening agent makes a translucent and syrupy soup which is very different from other tomato soups.

Cauliflower Soup

8 servings

1 head (about 1 qt. cut up) firm white
  cauliflower
1 small carrot, scraped
½ cup chopped onions
1 cup chopped celery
½ tsp. peppercorns, ½ bay leaf, and 1
  tsp. dried tarragon tied in a cheesecloth bag
2 qt. veal stock or chicken stock, or
  enough canned chicken broth, diluted, to make 2 qt.

2 cups milk
1 cup half-and-half
2 tbsp. shortening, preferably lard
4 tbsp. butter
6 tbsp. flour
1 tbsp. salt
2 tbsp. chopped fresh parsley
1 cup sour cream at room temperature

1. In a large soup pot, melt the 2 tbsp. of shortening. Add the chopped onion and cook, stirring constantly, over medium heat until the onion starts to turn yellow. Add carrot and celery and cook for another 2 minutes, continuing to stir. Add cauliflower and 1 tbsp. of the chopped parsley. Cover the soup pot and turn the heat to very low.

2. Stir the mixture once in a while. Be sure that it does not stick to the bottom of the pot. After 15 minutes, add the stock of your choice and the cheesecloth bag of herbs.

3. Bring the soup to a boil over medium heat. Reduce the heat and let it simmer.

4. In a small saucepan, melt the butter. Mix the flour into the milk with a wire whip, and slowly, stirring constantly with the wire whip, add the flour-milk mixture to the butter. If you add it slowly enough, it will thicken immediately, and when you finish you will have a white sauce of medium consistency. Remove from heat and dilute with the half-and-half. Pour this mixture into the simmering soup. Stir gently with a wooden spoon and let it simmer for another 15 to 20 minutes.

5. Check for seasoning and add a little more salt if necessary. (The amount will depend on the saltiness of the stock used.)

6. Just before serving, place the sour cream in the soup tureen. Mix in the remaining chopped fresh parsley. Put two to three ladles of hot soup into the tureen and stir it into the sour cream. Remove the cheesecloth bag from the soup, pour all of the soup into the tureen, and serve immediately.

CHEF's SECRET: If you make your own veal or chicken stock for cauliflower soup, be sure that the green leaves, white stalks, and hard white core of the cauliflower are all cooked with the soup bones. The stock itself will then have a cauliflower flavor.

If you use canned chicken broth, chop up the cauliflower trimmings and boil them in the water which you will use to dilute the canned broth.

Sautéing the celery, onion, carrot, and cauliflower over low heat, without adding any water, intensifies and blends the aromas.

If you wish, you can remove a cupful of the cauliflowerets from the soup, purée them in a blender, and add this purée to the soup. This will also intensify the cauliflower taste.

Mushroom-Barley Soup

8 servings

1 lb. beef bones, in small pieces if possible
1 carrot, coarsely cut up
2 stalks celery, cut in pieces
1 lb. chicken backs and necks or wing tips
1 cup barley
4 tbsp. shortening
1 cup finely chopped onion

2 cups thinly sliced fresh mushrooms
2 tbsp. chopped parsley
1 tbsp. salt
½ tsp. freshly ground black pepper
½ tsp. mushroom powder or 2 to 3 dried mushrooms broken into small pieces (approximately 1 tbsp.)
3 qt. water

1. Place the bones, carrot, celery, and chicken backs and necks or wing tips in a soup pot. Add the water and the salt and pepper. Bring to a boil, reduce heat, and simmer for 2 to 3 hours.

2. In 2 tbsp. of the shortening, sauté half of the barley (do not sauté the second half) until it starts to give a crackling sound and begins to turn yellow. Add the chopped onion and continue cooking, stirring constantly, until the onion becomes limp and turns glossy.

3. In the other 2 tbsp. of shortening, quickly sauté the sliced mushrooms with the green parsley. Set aside.

4. Strain the broth through a sieve. Discard the bones and vegetables.

5. Add to the stock the barley which was not sautéed. Add the mushroom powder or dried mushrooms and let this cook for 30 minutes.

6. Add the sautéed barley-onion mixture and cook for 30 minutes more.

7. Add the mushroom-parsley mixture and simmer for 10 additional minutes. Let soup stand under cover for at least 30 minutes before serving.

CHEF'S SECRET: Half of the barley, because it was sautéed in hot shortening, will keep its shape. The other half will cook to a pulp, and this will give thickness to the soup.

Adding the slightly sautéed mushrooms at the end, combined with the cooked-in flavor of the mushroom powder or dried mushrooms, intensifies the mushroom taste of this popular soup.

Real Bean Soup

8 servings

2 cups dry white navy beans or other small white beans, soaked overnight in 1 qt. of cold water in a 2-qt. pan
½ lb. smoked ham shank or 1 lb. smoked neck bones or a ham bone
2 carrots, scraped and split

1 parsley root or parsnip, scraped and split
1 whole bay leaf
1 to 1½ tbsp. salt, the amount depending on saltiness of the smoked pork product used

2 tbsp. shortening
2 cups milk mixed with 4 tbsp. all-
    purpose flour

1 small clove garlic
1 small, finely minced onion
2 qt. water

1. Rinse the soaked beans; discard the water. Place the carrot, parsley root, and smoked shank, neck bones, or ham bone in a soup pot. Add the beans, water, salt, and bay leaf. Cover the pot and bring to a gentle boil.

2. When beans are done, melt the shortening in a frying pan. Add garlic and onion and cook over medium heat, stirring constantly. Do not let onion or garlic burn.

3. When onions are cooked, remove garlic. Increase the heat and stir in the milk-flour mixture. Keep stirring, using a wire whip, until it comes to a boil.

4. Remove from fire and stir in two to three ladles of the soup. Stir until completely smooth. Remove the carrot, parsnip or parsley root, and bay leaf from the soup. Pour the milk-flour mixture into the bean soup and continue cooking over low heat for 30 minutes. Serve at once.

CHEF'S SECRET: To test the beans for doneness, remove a few with a slotted spoon and blow on the beans. When the skin pops on the beans and turns away from the air, the beans are done.

Cream of Green Bean Soup

8 servings

1½ lb. fresh green beans or wax beans,
    cleaned and diagonally cut into 1- to
    1½-inch pieces
1 tsp. granulated sugar
1 clove garlic, mashed
1 tsp. salt
¼ tsp. black pepper
2 qt. chicken stock, or enough canned
    chicken broth, diluted according to
    directions, to make 2 qt.
1 tbsp. chopped parsley

1 tbsp. finely minced onions
½ tsp. dried or 1 tsp. fresh tarragon
½ cup 4% white vinegar
2 cups milk
1 tbsp. cornstarch
4 tbsp. all-purpose flour
2 tbsp. freshly chopped parsley for
    garnish
1 cup sour cream
salt and pepper to taste

1. Mash the garlic with the 1 tsp. salt. In a large soup pot, place the beans, sugar, mashed garlic, black pepper, and just enough stock from the 2 qt. to cover the beans. Cover the pot and bring to a vigorous boil.

2. Add the balance of the stock, cup by cup, so that the soup continues boiling and is just under the boiling point after all the stock has been added.

3. Mix the milk with the flour and cornstarch.

4. Add the minced onions and the 1 tbsp. of chopped parsley and, using a wooden spoon, stir in the milk-flour-starch mixture.

5. In a small saucepan, bring the vinegar to a boil. Drop in the tarragon and immediately remove the pan from the heat. Let the tarragon steep in the vinegar until cool. Then pour the liquid through a fine sieve into the soup and discard the tarragon particles.

6. Keep the soup gently boiling until the beans are tender but still firm. Correct the seasoning with salt and pepper.

7. Just before serving, place the soup in a tureen and dot the surface with teaspoonfuls of sour cream sprinkled with the freshly chopped parsley.

CHEF'S SECRET: Cooking the beans with the mashed garlic and sugar in very little liquid intensifies the green bean taste.

Tarragon would never taste the way it should if it were simply sprinkled into the soup; steeping it in hot vinegar releases all its flavor and fragrance.

It is desirable to have small lumps of sour cream in this soup. Therefore, you do not stir the sour cream into the liquid, but simply add it to the hot soup. In this way you get a third texture, in addition to the liquid part of the soup and the beans.

Beet Borscht

8 servings

1 lb. lean beef, suitable for boiling
2½ cups canned sauerkraut, drained, rinsed, and pressed (keep the drained liquid)
2½ cups canned sliced beets, rinsed (discard the liquid from the can)

1 cup firmly packed, thinly sliced white cabbage or Savoy cabbage
8 oz. bacon, cut in small pieces
1 tsp. whole black peppercorns, slightly bruised
10 cups water

1. Chop the sauerkraut and place it in a soup pot. Add the fresh sliced white or Savoy cabbage and the peppercorns.

2. Cut the beef into small pieces and place them in the pot.

3. Pour in half of the water. Cover, bring to a boil, then reduce heat and simmer for 45 minutes.

4. Fry the bacon in a saucepan until the pieces are glossy and start to turn yellow. Pour off the fat. Drain the half-fried bacon on absorbent paper.

5. Add the beets, the rest of the water, and the bacon to the soup. Cook for another fifteen minutes. Serve with sour cream.

CHEF'S SECRET: Different brands of canned sauerkraut differ greatly in salt content. That is why it is good to keep the original liquid from the can and add it to the soup at the end if it isn't sour enough.

Cutting the beef into small pieces helps flavor the soup and reduces the cooking time.

This soup is very good cooked slowly in a preheated 250-degree oven in a tightly covered pot for 6 to 8 hours. In this case, you can leave the beef in one piece.

Lentil Soup with Franks

8 servings

1 cup dried lentils
1 small carrot cut into 1-inch cubes
2 cups potatoes cut into 1-inch cubes
1 large onion, finely chopped (about ¾ cup)

4 tbsp. bacon drippings or lard
1 bay leaf
1 clove garlic
1 tsp. salt

1 ham bone, or some small pork ribs or neck bones, or 1 or 2 smoked pork shanks
salt and pepper to taste

3 qt. cold water
1 frankfurter per person
1 cup yogurt or 1 cup sour cream

1. Mash the garlic with the 1 tsp. salt. Melt lard or bacon drippings in a large soup pot. Sauté the onion until glossy. Add lentils, garlic, bay leaf, salt, and a generous amount of coarsely ground black pepper.

2. Stir with a wooden spoon until the onion turns yellow and the frying lentils begin to make a noise.

3. Add the ham bone, ribs, neck bones, or pork shanks, the carrot, and the cold water. Bring to a gentle boil, covered, and cook for approximately 30 minutes, keeping the soup just at the boiling point.

4. Add the potatoes; stir. Add more salt if necessary and more water if too much evaporates.

5. Just before serving, add the franks, sliced or whole. When serving, offer yogurt or sour cream to be stirred into the soup by your guests. Also serve vinegar in a small jar if you wish.

CHIEF'S SECRET: The potatoes are the thickening agent of this old German soup, and the vinegar offered with it on the table counterbalances the heaviness of the soup.

The color of the lentils will change according to the type of cooking pot used. An enamel-coated or cast iron pot is best. Lentils will have a completely different color if cooked in heavy aluminum. Discoloration does not mean any change in quality; nevertheless, if possible do not use an aluminum pot.

Mixed Vegetable Soup

8 servings

1 cup medium-chopped carrots
1 cup chopped celery
1 cup green peas
1 cup cubed raw potatoes
1 parsley root, scraped and chopped
1 cup cubed turnip
approximately 3 leeks
1 tbsp. chopped fresh parsley

1 tbsp. sugar
4 tbsp. shortening
small bunch green parsley
1 bay leaf
10 cups water, or canned chicken or beef broth diluted according to directions to make 10 cups
salt and pepper to taste

1. Slice the white parts of the leek crosswise, to make 1 cup. Tie the green part with the bunch of parsley and the bay leaf.

2. Melt the shortening in a large soup pot. Add sugar, chopped parsley, and green peas. Cover the pot and let the mixture cook for 3 to 4 minutes.

3. Remove the lid, raise the heat as high as possible, and add the carrots, celery, parsley root, turnips, and chopped white parts of leeks.

4. Stir the vegetables rapidly until they heat through, their own liquid evaporates, and they start to brown on the edges. Immediately lower the heat. Add all the water or broth at once. Salt and pepper to taste.

5. Add the green part of the leek tied with the bay leaf and parsley.

Simmer slowly for about 30 minutes. Add the potatoes and simmer for an additional 10 minutes. Correct the seasoning and serve.

CHEF'S SECRET: The special preparation of these vegetables gives the soup an excellent taste and helps each vegetable retain its own unique flavor.

This soup is one of the few soups which taste good made from water, because the preparation turns the water into a vegetable stock.

FISH

Bouillabaisse

8 servings

For the liquid:
1 lb. onions, chopped very fine
2 bell peppers, chopped very fine
2 stalks celery, thinly sliced
1 cup tomato pepper sauce, Italian style
2 fresh tomatoes, chopped
3 to 4 sprigs parsley
1 clove garlic, crushed
1 tsp. salt
1 bay leaf, crushed
1 cup oil
2 lb. fish bones and fish heads or 1 lb. inexpensive fish, such as smelt, perch, or pike
12 cups water
2 blades saffron
1 tbsp. Spanish or Hungarian paprika
½ tsp. dried fennel

For the fish:
2 lb. red snapper fillet with the skin on

1 lb. perch fillet
1 lb. pike fillet
1 lb. striped bass or black bass fillet
1 lb. whitefish fillet or lake trout fillet
1 lb. shrimp in the shells

Optional:
lobster or lobster tail, fresh, frozen, or canned
clams (littleneck or cherrystone) or oysters

For hot sauce:
1 cup cold mashed potatoes
½ cup oil
½ cup strained cooking liquid from the fish stock
1 tsp. or more Tabasco sauce
1 to 2 cloves garlic
1 tbsp. prepared mustard
1 tbsp. Spanish or Hungarian paprika
salt to taste

1. Mash the garlic with the salt. In a large kettle, sauté the onions in the oil for approximately 10 minutes, stirring constantly. Add the green pepper, celery, garlic, and crushed bay leaf. Pour in 2 cups of water, cover, and cook over very low heat, stirring occasionally so that the mixture does not stick to the bottom of the pan. Cook until it turns into a pulp.

2. Add the fish bones and the rest of the ingredients for the liquid. Bring to a slow rolling boil. Boil for at least 2 hours. Strain, discarding everything from the strainer. Boil the strained liquid, covered, for another 30 minutes over very low heat.

3. Cut the fillets of fish into bite-size or serving pieces. Twenty minutes before serving, place the cut fillets in a low casserole-type pot. If you use clams or oysters, before adding them wash off all the sand and then wash them again three times in a sieve under running cold water. If you use lobster, cut it up into chunks. Do the same with lobster tail.

4. Make the sauce by mixing together all the ingredients and then pressing them through a fine sieve.

5. Pour the boiling fish stock over the fish. Over high heat, bring to a rolling boil. Check the thickest piece of fillet to see if the fish is done. Serve at once, offering the sauce on the side. Also serve thin, freshly made, buttered garlic toast.

CHEF'S SECRET: Probably the most controversial of all soups in the world, this is simple to make and delightful to eat.

The onions cooked into a pulp add a thickness to the broth which cannot be achieved any other way. If you brown or fry the onions, they will not work as a thickener. Be sure to add the water as soon as they begin to get limp.

Not all the fish mentioned can be purchased fresh at all times. It is possible to use some frozen fish, but, of course, if all are frozen, the taste will not be the same.

The hot sauce made with mashed potatoes enables everyone to add as much spice to his own dish as he desires or can tolerate, without forcing the others to eat the Bouillabaisse too hot or too mild.

In some restaurants in Marseilles, they omit the paprika and overload the broth with saffron. However, having watched many American tourists' faces after they have eaten this version, I would not recommend it.

Fish Chowder

8·servings

2 tbsp. oil	1 bay leaf
2 tbsp. butter	5 or 6 whole peppercorns, crushed
2 cups finely chopped celery	2 cups milk
1 cup finely chopped onion	4 tbsp. flour
2 cups potatoes, cut into ½-inch cubes	8 cups water
1 lb. skinless haddock fillet, cut into 1-inch pieces	1 tbsp. salt
	¼ tsp. garlic salt
1 lb. skinless, boneless flounder, cut the same	¼ tsp. celery salt
	2 tbsp. freshly chopped parsley
1 4-oz. can minced clams	cream (optional)
1 can clam juice	

1. Mix the milk with the flour.

2. Melt the butter with the oil in a large soup kettle. Add the onion and celery. Cover the pot and cook over medium heat for approximately 10 minutes, stirring two or three times.

3. Add the clam juice and the juice from the minced clams. Add 2 cups of water and bring to a slow boil. Add the potatoes and cook for 15 minutes.

4. Add the remaining water, the salt, crushed peppercorns, bay leaf, garlic

salt, celery salt, and fish. Bring to a boil. Using a wooden spoon to stir, add the milk-flour mixture. Bring to a boil. Remove from heat and let stand in a warm place, under cover, for at least 30 minutes.

5. Add the minced clams and heat through. Serve immediately, with or without the addition of cream. Sprinkle the chopped parsley on top of the chowder before serving.

CHEF'S SECRET: Cooking the potatoes in the concentrated clam juice gives the potatoes a strong clam taste, so that when you eat them, you think you are eating clams. Also, if you add the clams at the last minute, they will not become rubbery.

Lobster Bisque

8 servings

1 live chicken lobster, 1 to 1¼ lb.	1 qt. water
1 10½-oz. can lobster meat	2 cups milk
1 large leek, white part only	3 tbsp. flour
8 tbsp. butter	1 tbsp. cornstarch
2 oz. good brandy or cognac	2 cups light cream or half-and-half
2 to 3 parsley sprigs, 1 celery stalk, and 1 bay leaf, tied together with a string	1 tsp. Spanish or Hungarian paprika
	salt and pepper to taste

1. Mix the milk, flour, and cornstarch together.
2. Using a cleaver, chop the live lobster into small chunks, leaving the shell on (see drawing). Be sure that you cut the claws into at least three pieces. Discard the stomach bag.
3. Sauté the leek and the raw lobster pieces in 4 tbsp. of the butter, under cover, over medium heat, for about 5 minutes, stirring occasionally.
4. As soon as the pieces of shell turn red, pour in the liquid from the canned lobster meat. Add the water, parsley sprigs, celery stalk, and bay leaf. Bring to a boil.
5. Once the mixture boils, strain it into a soup pot. Keep the pot in a warm place.
6. Remove all the meat from the chopped-up lobster and add this meat to the canned lobster meat. Crush the lobster shell into very small pieces.
7. Melt the other 4 tbsp. of butter in a heavy skillet. Add the crushed shell pieces. Over high heat, keep stirring the shells in the butter until they turn the butter pink and the shells become pale. Remove and transfer to a metal mixing bowl. Add paprika and pound the mixture with a wooden object or, if you have an old-fashioned mortar, pound it in the mortar.
8. After pounding, add 1 cup of water and transfer the mixture to a small saucepan. Bring to a boil, then strain through cheesecloth or a wet kitchen towel into a small plastic dish. Put the dish in the freezer.
9. Select the nicest pieces of the lobster meat, using both the canned and the fresh lobster. Put the rest in your blender. Add a small amount of the liquid from the soup pot and blend the mixture to a pulp.
10. Heat the brandy in a small saucepan. Ignite it with a match, then pour

it over the choice lobster chunks. Add this to the liquid in the soup pot. Add the lobster pulp.

11. Bring to a boil, then stir in the milk-flour-starch mixture. As soon as the soup starts to boil again, remove it from the heat. Spoon a small amount of the soup into the light cream, to warm it up, then pour the cream-soup mixture into the bisque.

12. Remove the chilled red lobster butter from the freezer and spoon the top part of it onto the bisque. Discard the bottom part, where there may be small pieces of shell. Serve with croûtons.

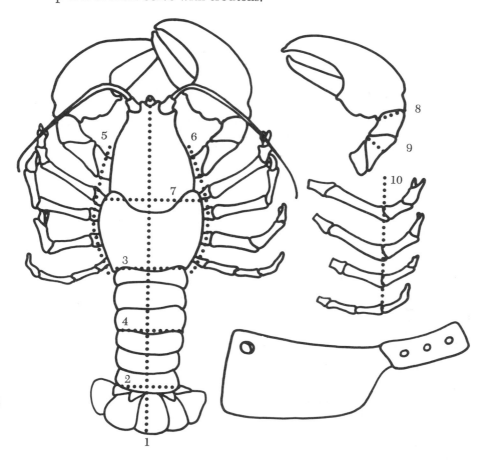

CHEF's SECRET: Frying the crushed lobster shell in butter releases the red dye and turns the lobster butter an attractive pink. During certain times of the year, you may find inside the lobster a red substance called the "coral." This, mixed with butter, is used in Europe to decorate canapés. At other times you may find a vivid green substance called the "emerald." This, mixed with butter, gives a pleasant taste and provides a beautiful green color when used for decoration. It is possible to freeze either one and use at a later date.

The flaming brandy or cognac poured over the lobster meat gives the bisque its mysterious taste.

Sometimes Lobster Bisque is served with a generous dab of firmly beaten whipped cream flavored with salt and brandy.

FRUIT

Cold Cherry Soup

8 servings

2 cans water-pack pitted sour cherries
6 cups water
1 2-inch piece cinnamon stick
6 to 8 whole cloves
¼ tsp. nutmeg
small pinch mace
1 cup granulated sugar

2 1-inch squares lemon rind
juice of ½ lemon
½ lemon, sliced wafer thin
1 or 2 drops red food coloring
1 cup sour cream
1 cup buttermilk

1. Place a large sieve over a soup pot. Pour the canned cherries into the sieve, straining the juice into the pot. Add the 6 cups of water to the pot, pouring it over the cherries. Remove the cherries from the sieve and refrigerate them. Add all spices, sugar, and lemon rind (not the lemon juice or wafer-thin slices of lemon) to the pot and bring to a boil.

2. Boil the mixture for 2 to 3 minutes. Remove from the heat; let it stand, covered, in a warm place for 1 hour. Strain the liquid and discard the spices and lemon rind. Cool to room temperature. Add the cherries and refrigerate.

3. Gently fold the sour cream into the buttermilk. To serve, put the sour cream–buttermilk mixture into the soup tureen and, using a wire whip, gently whip the soup, cup by cup, into it. Float lemon slices on top of the soup. Serve very cold as a first course.

CHEF'S SECRET: Keeping the pitted sour cherries in the refrigerator keeps them firm and prevents overcooking.

Letting the soup stand for 1 hour slowly dilutes the spice oils, which flavor the soup after the spices themselves have been discarded.

Mixing the sour cream with the buttermilk makes the sour cream lighter and tastier, and it mixes more easily with the soup.

Apple Cream Soup

8 servings

2 lb. chicken wings, each cut at the
    joints into 3 pieces
1 tbsp. finely minced shallot or onion
2 tbsp. butter

8 medium-sized tart apples, cored but
    not peeled
6 cups water
2 cups milk

4 tbsp. flour

1 cup sugar

1 2-inch cinnamon stick

1 tbsp. grated lemon rind, yellow part only

2 cups half-and-half or light cream

8 ¼-inch-thick slices lemon, each studded in the middle with a clove

salt to taste

1. Sauté the chicken wings with the shallot or onion in the butter over very low heat for about 5 minutes, stirring occasionally. Add 2 cups of the water, cover, and cook for 30 minutes.

2. Cut the unpeeled, cored apples into thin wedges. Add them to the above mixture along with the remaining water, sugar, grated lemon rind, and spices and cook for 10 minutes.

3. Mix the milk with the flour. Using a wooden spoon to stir, add this mixture to the chicken-apple mixture. Bring to a boil and simmer over very low heat for about 15 minutes.

4. Pour the half-and-half or cream into a soup tureen. Slowly add 1 cup of the hot soup, stirring constantly. Then add the rest of the soup, being careful not to break the apples.

5. Float the clove-studded lemon slices on the top and serve hot or cold.

CHEF'S SECRET: This soup is very tart and it should be, but if you would like to add sweetness, you may increase the sugar.

If, on the other hand, the apples are not sour enough, add 2 to 3 tbsp. vinegar immediately after adding the apples.

To keep the apples from turning brown, use a stainless steel knife and quickly slice the apples, one by one, into the soup pot.

If you wish, you may stop the preparation after cooking the wings for 30 minutes. Let it stand until cool enough to handle. Remove the bones and discard the wing tips, then proceed with the preparation of the soup.

Avocado Soup with Champagne

8 to 12 servings

2 cups milk

1 cup fine white bread crumbs

4 large avocados

4 cups champagne

juice of 1 lemon

1 tbsp. sugar

¼ tsp. mace

2 cups whipped cream

1. Soak bread crumbs in milk for 2 hours at room temperature, stirring occasionally. Pour into a blender, add one cut-up avocado, and blend. Pour the blended mixture into a soup tureen.

2. Run the other three avocados through the blender. After each avocado add 1 cup champagne. Rinse the blender with the fourth cup.

3. Add the mace, lemon juice, and sugar. Place in the tureen. Just before serving, fold in the whipped cream. Serve chilled.

CHEF'S SECRET: The avocado meat right under the skin has a very bitter taste so you should be sure to trim this completely off.

Avocados will not turn dark but will stay a vivid green as long as the pit is not removed. If you have to peel the avocados in advance, simply leave the pit in.

Swedish Fruit Soup

8 servings

1 lb. mixed dried fruit or dried apricots   3 tbsp. cornstarch
11 cups water   5 tbsp. cold water
4 tbsp. sugar

1. Wash the fruit and if possible soak it in the water for several hours.
2. Add the sugar to the fruit and boil until tender.
3. Mix the cornstarch with the cold water and pour into the fruit, stirring constantly. Bring to a boil again.
4. Serve the soup lukewarm or cold as a first or last course.

CHEF'S SECRET: Soaking the fruit before cooking is the best method, but you should remove the prunes and soak them in a separate container of water. When you boil the fruits, use the water in which they were soaked.

In most places it is possible to buy pitted prunes, which are especially good for this type of soup. The taste of the fruit is enhanced if the soup is served lukewarm.

MEATS

BEEF

Roast Beef
  Chef's Salt
Boiled Tafelspitz (Boiled Beef
  Brisket)
Steaks
  Broiling
  Pan Frying
Boeuf en Daube

Good Hamburger
Roast Tenderloin
Tender Pot Roast
Braised Oxtails
Sauerbraten
Hungarian Goulash
Viennese Roastbraten
Beef Ragout

PORK

Roast Pork Stuffed with Hungarian
  Sausage
Roast Suckling Pig

Gypsy Grill
Quick Tenderloin
Stuffed Pork Chops

VEAL

Scaloppine (3 ways)
  Veal Scaloppine Natural
  Scaloppine à la Riccadonna
  Scaloppine à la Milanese

Veal Paprikash
Veal Birds
Old-Fashioned Blanket of Veal
Roast Veal

LAMB

Roast Lamb—Different Cuts
  Roast Leg of Lamb
    Stuffing
  Roast Rack of Lamb

Cassoulet
  Potted Goose
Irish Stew
Braised Lamb Shanks

*A*ccording to the nutritionists, meats are our main source of protein, according to home economists the main part of our food expenditures, and according to most chefs and most eaters the main source of the joy of eating.

The general rules for preparing meats are very simple—but this is no wonder. Through the ages, beef cooking, especially roasting, broiling, and grilling, has seen few changes.

Probably due to its popularity, and to its high price, meat is the subject of more fallacies, heresies, legends, and misrepresentations than any other food.

One of the biggest and most common myths is about the aging of meat. Once a lady showed me a two-inch-thick porterhouse steak with great pride. She had kept it for ten days in her refrigerator to age it. The top was crusty, jet black, with light greenish spots of mold, the bottom was smelly from a pink glue oozing out around the edges—and how proud she was! Then I told her that to age beef, first of all you need a so-called *primal cut*, such as a front quarter, hind quarter, whole loin, short loin, or in very special cases even a whole tenderloin. You also need a special room equipped with constant moisture and temperature controls, proper lighting, carefully designed ventilation, and constant bacteriological surveillance. Those who like aged meat should buy it aged and never attempt to age it at home. Of course this pertains only to beef; pork, veal, or lamb should never be aged.

Meats

BEEF

Roast Beef

8 servings

1 7–8 lb. U.S. Choice 4-rib roast or a
  standing rib roast
1 cup Chef's Salt (see page 60)
1 carrot, scraped and coarsely chopped
1 large onion, unpeeled and coarsely
  chopped

1 small clove garlic
4 tbsp. Kitchen Bouquet
4 tbsp. corn oil

1. Preheat oven to 375 degrees.
2. Mix the Kitchen Bouquet with the corn oil and rub the whole surface of the roast, especially the two cut ends and the surface of the bony part, with the mixture. Score the fat on the top if you wish.
3. Crush the garlic to a pulp with some of the Chef's Salt. Rub the entire amount of Chef's Salt and garlic into the surface, including the fat, covering completely.
4. Pour water to a depth of 1 inch in the bottom of a roasting pan, and add the coarsely chopped onion and carrot.
5. Place the meat on top of the vegetables, fat side up.
6. Roast the meat in the oven, uncovered, for 30 minutes. Cover the pan and continue roasting until a meat thermometer registers the temperature you wish: 100 degrees for rare, 115 degrees for medium rare, or 140 degrees for medium. Remove roast from the oven and let it stand on a board for at least 1 hour.
7. Ten minutes before serving, bring the oven temperature as high as the control allows. Put the roast on a cookie sheet and place in the oven for 10 minutes. If you like a dark crusty surface, heat 4 to 6 tbsp. shortening to the smoking point and pour this hot fat over the beef before putting it back into the oven.

59

Chef's Salt

Mix well and use instead of salt:

1 cup salt   ¼ tsp. ground white pepper
1 tbsp. Spanish paprika   ¼ tsp. celery salt
1 tsp. ground black pepper   ¼ tsp. garlic salt

Be careful to use garlic *salt,* not garlic *powder.* If you use garlic powder a small pinch is enough.

CHEF'S SECRET: The beef will not be salty. The salt will not penetrate the meat and it will not "draw" the juices as some people believe. In fact, the British cover their roast beef completely with salt and bake it in a crust. It is never salty.

Rubbing the surface with the Kitchen Bouquet and oil will close the pores and give a caramelized color. This may also be achieved through searing, but searing is very cumbersome in a household kitchen, takes lots of time, is wasteful, and needs high skill. Kitchen Bouquet gives the same results in a few seconds.

Definitely invest in a good food thermometer which registers from o to 200 degrees—one that you never leave in the meat like ordinary meat thermometers, but just insert for registering temperature, then remove. These are expensive in comparison with ordinary thermometers, but if properly used, they save their price at least 20 times in the first year. If you are unable to find such a thermometer, you may write me for an order form and price list:

Chef Louis
Thermometer
2218 North Lincoln
Chicago, Illinois 60614

Boiled Tafelspitz (Boiled Beef Brisket)

8 servings

1 whole beef brisket, not too closely trimmed
water to cover meat in the pot
1 tbsp. salt for each quart of water used
12 black peppercorns, slightly bruised
1 bay leaf
1 clove garlic, crushed
1 small bunch parsley tied with two celery stalks, each stuck with 1 clove, and 1 leek

4 to 6 medium carrots, scraped and cut into 2-inch pieces
1 celery root or celeriac, peeled and quartered, or 2 parsley roots, scraped and coarsely chopped, or 2 parsnips, scraped and chopped
2 large onions with skin left on, split crosswise in half
3 tbsp. Chef's Salt (see recipe above)

1. Place all the vegetables in a large soup pot. Add the spices, and the parsley tied with the celery and leek. Rub the meat with the Chef's Salt and place it in the pot on top of the vegetables. Add enough water to cover, then add another inch of water on top. Cover the pot and bring to a boil over

medium heat. Check every ten minutes or so, and as soon as it starts to boil, reduce the heat and simmer.

2. Simmer for about 2 hours, being sure that the liquid does not boil. Remove from the heat after two hours and let the brisket stay in the pot, covered, for another hour.

3. Remove the meat to a carving board. Let it stand for 10 minutes. Remove all the fat and discard. Slice the meat against the grain.

4. Place the sliced brisket in a roasting pan. Strain enough of the cooking liquid over it to barely cover. Cover the roasting pan and keep the brisket in the oven at 200 degrees until serving time (15 to 45 minutes).

CHEF'S SECRET: Boiled brisket is the tastiest beef dish in the world if it is prepared correctly. It is tender, juicy, full of flavors, and, cut against the grain, is not at all stringy.

If you allow the water to continue to boil instead of simmering, the boiling will dry out the meat and it will take a much longer time for the fibers to get tender.

If you want to use the cooking liquid as a beef broth or as a soup, add 2 or 3 marrow bones to the pot before cooking. After removing the beef, strain all the liquid. Use only as much as you need to cover the brisket in the roasting pan and make a soup from the rest.

Steaks

4 servings

4 strip steaks, or equivalent, 12 to 16   2 to 3 tbsp. corn oil
  oz. each   salt and pepper to taste

Broiling

1. Set the oven control to broil. Brush the steaks with oil and sprinkle with salt and pepper. As soon as the broiler is ready, place the steaks very close to the source of heat for a few seconds. As soon as the surface starts to brown, turn and repeat.

2. After the second side is slightly browned, move the steaks 5 to 6 inches away from the heat and continue broiling, turning once or twice, until an inserted meat thermometer registers the desired doneness.

Pan Frying

1. Place a large skillet over medium heat and melt a small amount of shortening. A combination of two shortenings—lard, butter, or oil—is preferred. Increase the heat under the skillet and continue heating until the shortening reaches the smoking point. Brush the steaks with corn oil and sprinkle with salt and pepper. Gently lower the steaks into the fat in the skillet.

2. After 10 to 15 seconds, turn the steaks. Decrease the heat to medium and fry the steaks for 2 to 3 minutes, shaking the pan once in a while.

3. Turn them again and continue frying, shaking the pan, until the steaks reach the required doneness.

CHEF'S SECRET: The greatest part of the success in preparing steak is the shopping. Buy only in a reliable store, and select U.S. Government–graded, cherry red, well marbled, evenly cut steaks with a firm white fat cover.

If the steaks are fresh, have them at room temperature for broiling or frying. If the steaks are frozen, do not defrost. Rub the frozen steak surface with oil and spices and proceed according to directions, using either method, but increase the cooking time.

Don't serve the steaks immediately after they are done. Start the preparation in advance so the steaks can rest in a warm place, after being broiled or pan fried, for 10 to 15 minutes before serving.

Boeuf en Daube

8 servings

2 lb. beef tenderloin, tail or head, well trimmed
2 lb. beef shank with the bone in
2 large onions, with skin left on
4 large carrots
1 lb. button mushrooms
2 stalks celery
1 bay leaf
3 sprigs parsley
1 large ripe tomato or 4 tbsp. tomato purée
1 lb. raw pork rinds or 2 lb. pigs' feet or pigs' tails

2 cups dry red wine
2 cubes beef bouillon or 2 tsp. beef extract
10 black peppercorns
2 cloves garlic
2 tsp. salt
4 oz. bacon
1 package frozen green peas or 1 cup fresh shelled green peas
salt and freshly ground black pepper to taste
2 tbsp. butter
2 tbsp. oil

1. Preheat oven to 350 degrees. Trim tenderloin very closely; reserve trimmings. Roll trimmed tenderloin pieces very tightly in aluminum foil and place in freezer.

2. Mash one of the garlic cloves with the 1 tsp. salt. Bruise the other garlic clove and split it in half. Dissolve the beef extract or bouillon in 2 cups of boiling water.

3. In a large roasting pan or Dutch oven, put the skin of the two onions; the celery stalks; the stems of the mushrooms; the parsley, garlic, peppercorns, and bay leaf; two of the carrots, coarsely cut; the bacon rind or pig's feet; the beef shank with bone; the red wine; the tomato; and the dissolved beef bouillon or extract. Add the trimmings from the tenderloin. Cover the pot or Dutch oven tightly and place it in the oven. After 1 hour, reduce the temperature to 250 degrees and bake for another 4 to 5 hours without lifting the lid.

4. Turn off the oven and leave the roasting pan in the oven for another 2 hours. Remove from the oven and let it stand without removing the lid.

5. In the meantime, mince the 2 onions very fine. Render all the fat from the bacon. Transfer the crisp bacon to an absorbent paper and gently sauté the minced onions in the bacon fat under cover for 15 to 20 minutes, stirring

once in a while and being sure that they don't burn or even turn brown. The onions must cook to a pulp.

6. Cut the remaining 2 carrots into even pieces, approximately 1 inch in length. Gently simmer the carrots in lightly salted water until they are half cooked. Discard the water.

7. After the Dutch oven has been out of the oven for at least 1 hour, lift the lid. Remove the shank. Pour the liquid through a fine sieve. Discard vegetables, pork rinds, and so forth.

8. Skim all the fat from the liquid. Pour the liquid over the onion pulp and bring to a boil. As soon as it starts to boil, reduce the heat and simmer for a few minutes. Then, add the half-cooked carrots, the trimmed, washed mushroom caps, and the frozen or fresh green peas. Cover and simmer.

9. Remove the trimmed tenderloins from the freezer. Discard the aluminum foil and cut the tenderloins into approximately 1-inch cubes. Sprinkle lightly with salt and freshly ground black pepper. In a large skillet, heat the butter and oil. Add the tenderloin cubes and brown them quickly over very high heat, turning with a spatula. Don't overcook.

10. Pour the sauce with the vegetables over the meat. Scrape the bottom of the pan and, after 1 minute, put the Boeuf en Daube into a deep serving dish, with a cover if possible. Serve with plain boiled potatoes, whole or cubed, plain boiled rice, or noodles.

CHEF'S SECRET: This is a new version of a very old French dish. In the old times, they used to bake the dish overnight, and then they ate the shank and eliminated the tenderloin. Our version is much more expensive but much more elegant and easier to prepare.

The main secret is that the roasting pan should be very tightly closed so that the steam generated through cooking cannot escape but must recirculate into the cooking liquid. Long ago, a firm paste of flour and water was smeared on the outside edge of the pot and lid to seal it. Today you don't have to do this. Buy 2-inch–wide masking tape. After you place all ingredients in the Dutch oven or roasting pan, put the lid on, wipe around the edges with a kitchen towel dipped in vinegar to get rid of all the grease; then tape all around with the masking tape so that one edge sticks to the lid and the other to the pot.

The best way to remove all the fat is to pour the cooking liquid into a tall, narrow container, refrigerate until the fat coagulates, and then simply remove it.

Chill the shank. Remove the bone and slice the meat crosswise against the grain. It will make the best cold beef sandwiches you ever tasted.

In France, they eat the leftover Boeuf en Daube as a cold luncheon dish with potato salad or cucumber salad. If you have any leftovers, try it. It's terrific.

Good Hamburger

4 servings

1 lb. ground chuck or other ground beef	4 tbsp. ice cold water salt and pepper to taste

1. Dissolve salt and pepper in the water. Use at least ½ tsp. salt for 1 lb. meat.

2. Add the spiced water to the meat. Form four patties. Broil, grill, or pan fry.

CHEF'S SECRET: Dissolving the salt in the water assures you that the spice will be evenly distributed throughout the meat. This is how sausage makers add spices to sausage.

Adding the water to the beef loosens up the consistency and replaces the amount of natural juice which evaporates through the cooking process.

If you want to add a little onion or garlic flavor, add to the water along with the salt and pepper. If using garlic, mash a clove with the salt. Chop onion and put in water. Let water stand at room temperature for 30 minutes, then chill it. Pour the water through a sieve or strainer into the meat and discard the garlic or onion.

Roast Tenderloin

8 servings

5 to 6 lb. untrimmed tenderloin or 3 to 3½ lb. trimmed tenderloin
1 tbsp. Chef's Salt (see page 60)
1 tsp. coarse black pepper or ½ tsp. fine black pepper
½ tsp. sugar

2 to 3 tbsp. Kitchen Bouquet
½ cup corn oil
1 cup lard, bacon drippings, shortening, or oil
1 cup red wine or canned consommé

1. Rub the whole surface of the tenderloin with the sugar, salt, and pepper. Mix the Kitchen Bouquet with the ½ cup corn oil, pour the mixture onto the beef, and massage it in. Let stand at room temperature.

2. Preheat the broiler. Line the broiling pan with aluminum foil. Place the tenderloin on it and bring it as close to the source of heat as possible. Turn it every 2 to 3 minutes until the whole surface is seared. Let the tenderloin cool at room temperature.

3. Wrap the tenderloin in heavy-duty aluminum foil, pouring the wine or consommé over the meat before closing the foil on top.

4. Roast the foil-wrapped tenderloin at 350 degrees for 40 minutes. Remove. Let it cool at room temperature. This can be done in the morning and the meat can stay at room temperature all day long (except on hot summer days, when you would refrigerate it if it were to stand longer than 2 hours at room temperature).

5. Half an hour before serving, heat the 1 cup of shortening in a small saucepan until it reaches the smoking point. Place the tenderloin on a cookie sheet covered with aluminum foil. Pour the smoking hot fat over the surface of the meat and roast, uncovered, at 450 to 500 degrees for 10 to 15 minutes. Let it sit for 10 minutes before slicing.

CHEF'S SECRET: I have been called "crazy" and "a nut" for this method by just about every "expert" in the country—until they try it once. After you try it, you will find that it is not as complicated as it sounds when you first read it, it takes very little work, and it will produce the greatest yield, with pink, juicy, tasty roast tenderloin throughout.

Tenderloin is the most expensive cut of beef. Therefore, it is worthwhile to take very good care of it. Rubbing the sugar into the surface with the salt and pepper will not make the beef sweet at all but, together with the Kitchen Bouquet and oil, will give a very desirable surface that will never burn or overcook.

The Kitchen Bouquet and oil should be rubbed or massaged into the surface by hand. No brush would give the necessary pressure to penetrate the surface.

The wine or consommé used in the first 40 minutes of roasting, mixed with the natural juices oozing out of the beef, will serve as an excellent *au jus* or it can be used as the stock for any sauce you plan to serve with the roast tenderloin.

Exactly the same method can be used for roasting boneless, well-trimmed sirloin strip or whole rib eye. Of course, the moist roasting time is longer for a 6-lb. (completely trimmed) sirloin strip. In this case, 1½ hours would be required for a medium rare roast; approximately the same time would be needed for a rib eye of the same weight.

If you let the completely finished meat cool to room temperature and then refrigerate it overnight, you will have the world's best-tasting and best-looking cold beef. With a good knife, a roast tenderloin which would serve 8 people as a hot main course can be sliced into 24 to 30 beautiful cold slices, depending on your skill. (To have the most even slices, see the drawing below.)

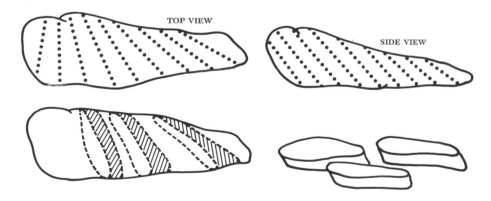

TOP VIEW

SIDE VIEW

Tender Pot Roast

6 servings

3 to 4 lb. beef for pot roast—blade, arm, chuck, boned rump, eye of round, boned and rolled sirloin tip, or brisket
Chef's Salt (see page 60)
2 tbsp. lard, chicken fat, or oil
water or beef stock

1 medium onion, peeled and sliced
¼ cup sliced celery
½ cup diced turnip
½ cup diced carrot
2 tbsp. freshly chopped parsley
1 package frozen peas

1. Sprinkle salt on all sides of the meat.

2. Over high heat, in a heavy pot or Dutch oven, heat the fat to the smoking point.

3. Brown the meat on all sides in the hot fat, adjusting heat if necessary. Remove the meat and add the onions; brown slightly.

4. Return the meat to the pot and add enough water or stock to cover half the beef.

5. Preheat the oven to 325 degrees.

6. Bring the liquid in the pot to a boil. Cover with a tight-fitting lid and place in the oven. Do not disturb for one hour.

7. After 1 hour, add the celery, turnips, and carrots. If liquid level is low, adjust. Replace lid and cook for another hour.

8. Check to see if the roast is done by piercing it with a fork in its thickest part. It should give very little resistance and the juice should run clear.

9. Add the parsley and peas. Replace lid and cook 20 minutes longer.

10. Place the meat on a cutting board or platter. Strain the liquid from the vegetables and place the vegetables on the platter around the meat.

11. Boil the liquid until it is reduced to half the original amount and serve it hot with the beef. Taste for salt.

CHEF'S SECRET: If you start to preheat the oven as you start to bring the cooking liquid to a boil, the oven will reach the desired temperature at just about the same time as the liquid begins to boil.

If you don't have a really tight-fitting lid, you can first cover the pot with aluminum foil, using a piece somewhat larger than the top of the pan, then put the lid on. Or use wide masking tape and tape the lid to the pan in two or three places. It is very important that the lid fit tightly, because the liquid must not evaporate.

If you like gravy that is a little thicker instead of the thin reduced juice which will result from the recipe, you can make a slurry from 1 or 2 tbsp. flour mixed with ¼ cup water and stir it into the juice before returning it to the heat to reduce it. If you like a richer color, brush the meat with 1 to 2 tbsp. Kitchen Bouquet before browning it.

If you like a garlic flavor, add 1 clove, slightly bruised, together with the carrot and turnip.

Braised Oxtails

4 servings

2 lb. oxtails, cut in 2-inch pieces
1 cup coarsely chopped onions
1 carrot, scraped and chopped
1 clove garlic
1 tsp. salt
6 whole black peppercorns
1 bay leaf
1 ripe tomato, or 2 to 3 tbsp. tomato purée, or 1 cup tomato juice

1 cup red wine and 1 cup canned consommé, or 2 cups consommé
½ cup shortening
4 tbsp. flour
2 cups mixed fresh vegetables (green peas, green beans, carrots) or 1 package frozen mixed vegetables

1. In a heavy, large casserole or skillet, bring ¼ cup of the shortening to the smoking point.

2. Add the oxtails and keep turning them, browning on all sides. When they are all nicely browned, remove and discard the shortening.

3. Place the other ¼ cup of the shortening in the pot and add the onions while the shortening is still cold. Stir over medium heat until the shortening dissolves and warms up. Cover and cook over medium heat for 30 minutes, stirring every 5 minutes.

4. Mash the garlic with the salt.

5. Add the oxtails, garlic-salt mixture, peppercorns, bay leaf, and carrots. Cover and cook over medium heat for 30 minutes, stirring every 5 minutes.

6. Sprinkle the flour over the meat, then add all the remaining ingredients except for the fresh or frozen mixed vegetables.

7. Cover and cook over low heat for 3 to 3½ hours, stirring once in a while. Check the larger oxtails to see if they are tender. If not, you can remove the smaller ones and continue cooking the larger.

8. If you use fresh vegetables, add them 20 minutes before serving time. If you use frozen ones, add 15 minutes before serving time.

9. Remove the bay leaf and serve. If you like a thicker, darker gravy, dissolve an additional 4 tbsp. flour in ½ cup water. Add 1 tsp. Kitchen Bouquet. About 10 minutes before you add the mixed vegetables, slowly stir this mixture into the braised oxtails.

CHEF'S SECRET: Many chefs prefer to blanch the oxtails before cooking them. This results in a milder taste. The blanching is done by bringing to a boil 2 qt. water with 2 tbsp. salt and 1 bay leaf; when the water reaches the boiling point, pour it over the oxtails in another pan. Bring the oxtails and liquid to a boil, then discard the blanching liquid and proceed with recipe.

Try to talk as nicely as possible to your butcher so that you can get a mixture of large-, medium-, and small-diameter oxtails. The big ones provide the meat, the medium ones enhance the taste, and the small ones provide the gelatin substance necessary for the excellent gravy.

In France, chefs always put a 5-by-5–inch piece of bacon rind or pork skin in the pot when cooking oxtails. You can do the same.

Sauerbraten

8 servings

1 cup sliced onions	1 3- to 4-lb. piece of beef—any cut suitable for pot roast, but preferably flank or eye of round
½ cup sliced carrot	
1 parsley root or parsnip, sliced	
1 clove garlic	10 to 12 black peppercorns, slightly bruised
2 tbsp. salt	
3 tbsp. sugar	1 or 2 cloves
3 qt. water	1 bay leaf
2 cups vinegar	1 tsp. tarragon
juice and rind of ½ lemon	¼ tsp. dry mustard

4 to 6 tbsp. shortening
4 tbsp. flour
4 tbsp. sugar

4 to 6 gingersnaps, or a light sprinkling
of ginger, or 2 cups sour cream
mixed with 1 cup buttermilk

1. Combine all ingredients up to the beef in a large pot and bring to a boil. Place the beef in a container (preferably not aluminum; the best is a roasting pan with an enamel surface). Pour the boiling pickling liquid over the meat and let it stand in a cool place overnight.

2. Remove the meat and again bring the liquid to a boil, then pour it back over the cold meat. Repeat this 2 or 3 times during the next 48 hours.

3. When you bring the pickling liquid to a boil for the last time, add the peppercorns, cloves, bay leaf, tarragon, and dry mustard, then pour it over the meat and let it stand just until it cools to lukewarm.

4. Remove the meat; strain the liquid and set aside.

5. Place all the vegetables and spices in the bottom of a roasting pan and place the meat on top.

6. Heat the shortening to the smoking point in a small saucepan. Pour the smoking hot fat over the meat.

7. Add 4 cups of the pickling liquid to the pan and cover. Place in a preheated 350- to 375-degree oven and cook for 1 hour, turning 1 or 2 times.

8. Add 4 more cups of the pickling liquid and cook for another hour.

9. Remove the meat from the pan. Strain the liquid from the vegetables. Skim the fat from the top of the liquid, then pour the liquid back over the meat.

10. Reduce the oven temperature to 300 degrees. Cover the roasting pan and return it to the oven for 35 to 45 additional minutes, or until meat is fork tender. Remove and let stand at room temperature for at least 30 minutes.

11. Meanwhile, discard the spice from the vegetable mixture and press the vegetables through a sieve or food grinder, or chop them up and purée them in small amounts in a blender, on low speed (just purée, don't liquify).

12. Increase the amount of purée to 6 cups by adding some of the pickling liquid.

13. In a dry frying pan, heat the sugar over medium heat until it starts to caramelize. Remove from the heat and add ½ cup of the purée. Place the pan back over the heat and stir until the mixture turns into a brown syrup. Mix the flour with 1 cup of the pickling liquid and stir this into the syrup, then add the remaining vegetable purée.

14. The gravy can be finished two ways: (a) Add the ginger or crush the gingersnaps and stir them into the sauce with 1 to 1½ cups of the pickling liquid. Or (b) mix the sour cream–buttermilk mixture into the sauce.

15. Using a sharp knife, slice the Sauerbraten into thin slices after it has been standing at room temperature. Arrange the slices in the center of a serving platter and pour over the slices just enough sauce to coat them. Serve the balance of the sauce in a gravy boat on the side.

CHEF'S SECRET: The mild but tasty pickling liquid slowly penetrates the meat; if the spices were added in the beginning, they would "overact" and overpower the taste of the meat.

The caramelized sugar adds color and a little sweetness to the Sauerbraten. If you like the sauce darker, add a few drops of Kitchen Bouquet.

Some German chefs crush the gingersnaps into ½ cup or more red wine and then stir the mixture into the sauce for added flavor.

Hungarian Goulash

6 servings

2 lb. beef, from the chuck, cut into
    1-inch cubes
Chef's Salt (see page 60)
black pepper
¼ lb. lard or chicken fat
1 lb. onions, peeled and finely chopped

2 tbsp. sweet Hungarian paprika
2 tbsp. flour
3 cups water or beef stock
2 tbsp. tomato paste
1 tsp. caraway seeds
2 cups sour cream

1. Season meat with Chef's Salt and additional black pepper.
2. In a large heavy saucepan, heat the lard to the smoking point.
3. Brown the meat in the lard, turning with a spatula so that it browns on all sides.
4. Add onions; cook until they become limp.
5. Sprinkle the paprika and flour over the meat and onions. Cook for 2 minutes on low heat, stirring to keep the mixture from sticking.
6. Add the liquid, tomato paste, and caraway seeds. Stir.
7. Simmer, covered, over low heat for 1½ hours or until meat is tender. Check occasionally to see if there is enough liquid; if necessary add more.
8. Serve from a large casserole with the sour cream on the side in a sauce boat.

CHEF'S SECRET: Whenever available, add ½ bell pepper, cut into strips, or 1 whole Hungarian pepper together with the liquid and tomato paste. Definitely use imported Hungarian or Spanish paprika; no other will give the flavor. But, if you can't get either, add ¼ tsp. sugar to the paprika you are using.

If you double this recipe, by all means buy a piece of shank, with the marrow bone in it if possible, and add this to the goulash. It will greatly improve the taste. Some of the goulash may be frozen for later use.

Viennese Roastbraten

8 servings

8 boneless strip sirloin steaks, 6 to 8 oz.
    each
Chef's Salt (see page 60)
black pepper
1 tbsp. prepared mustard
4 tbsp. oil

1 tsp. Kitchen Bouquet
2 lb. onions, peeled and sliced into ¼
    inch slices
approximately 2 qt. shortening, pref-
    erably a mixture of lard and oil or
    oil and margarine

1. Preheat shortening in a deep fryer to about 360 degrees. Fry the onions until they get limp and the edges start to brown. Remove them from the

shortening and spread them out on absorbent paper. Keep warm. (They will be refried later.)

2. With a tenderizing mallet, pound the steaks until they have doubled in size. Spread each with a little mustard, then sprinkle with Chef's Salt and pepper.

3. When all 8 steaks are pounded and seasoned, mix the Kitchen Bouquet with the 4 tbsp. oil and brush each steak on both sides.

4. Place the steaks in a container, stacking one on top of the other. Let stand at room temperature at least 2 hours.

5. Just before serving, heat the deep fryer to 380 to 390 degrees and fry the onions in small amounts until they turn dark brown and are crisp. Spread out on absorbent paper and keep them warm in a preheated 250-degree oven.

6. In a large frying pan, preheated until a small drop of water will immediately evaporate when dropped on it, fry the steaks on both sides for about 2 minutes per side.

7. Place the steaks on a serving platter and pile the crisp onions on top. Serve immediately.

CHEF'S SECRET: This Viennese Roastbraten is a very elegant and unusual way of serving sirloin steak. Because of the way it is treated and the accompaniment of the crisp, rich onions, 6 to 8 oz. makes an ample serving, even for a man with a good appetite.

To make the onions very crisp, no salt or shortening should be sprinkled over them. When you fry them the second time, the great secret is to avoid hurrying. Have the shortening hot and add only a small amount of the onions. After they are brown and crisp, remove and let the shortening regain its heat before adding more. This is the fastest way; if you try to hurry by frying too much at once or adding more before the fat is hot enough, it will take much longer and the onions will never be crisp.

The typical Viennese taste comes from the mustard, so don't forget it.

Beef Ragout

8 servings

The French are so proud of their Beef Ragout
To me it is nothing more than a drunken stew.
OGDEN NASH

3 to 4 lb. cubed beef, preferably a lean, tender cut such as sirloin, tenderloin tip, or tenderloin head
½ cup onion, finely chopped
2 tbsp. butter
2 tbsp. oil
2 tbsp. flour
1 tbsp. Chef's Salt (see page 60)

1 clove garlic, crushed
1 cup canned consommé
1 cup red wine
5 oz. button mushrooms
1 small can tiny onions, drained
1 cup sliced or cubed precooked carrots
1 tsp. Kitchen Bouquet (optional)

1. Melt the butter and oil; add the onion and sauté until onion turns glossy. Dust the meat with a mixture of the flour and Chef's Salt, and add to the hot

oil. Increase the heat and sear the cubes on all sides, turning constantly with a spatula and scraping the pan so the onion and bits of flour won't burn.

2. When all the meat is seared, add the consommé, the red wine, and the garlic clove. Cover the pot and simmer over low heat for about 2 hours, stirring once in a while.

3. Add the precooked carrots and the canned onions and continue cooking for another 10 to 15 minutes over low heat.

4. Add the mushrooms and adjust the liquid by adding more consommé or red wine, or both, to barely cover the meat. Bring the liquid to a boil again, remove from heat, and let stand for about 25 to 30 minutes, covered, without stirring or lifting the lid.

5. Serve with noodles, rice, or potatoes. For richer color add Kitchen Bouquet.

CHEF'S SECRET: If possible, use the same wine for cooking and for serving with the ragout. A cheap cooking wine will spoil the dish.

Rinse the canned onions with cold running water. Bring 1 qt. water with 1 tbsp. salt to a boil. Pour the boiling water over the rinsed onions and let stand for 10 minutes. Discard water; then add the onions to the ragout. The onions will lose their canned taste.

Don't cook the mushrooms at all. It is enough to put them into the boiling ragout just before you shut off the fire. This way they will remain firm and tasty.

PORK

Roast Pork Stuffed with Hungarian Sausage

8 servings

1 3- to 4-lb. pork loin, center cut, all bones except rib removed	2 cloves garlic
	1 stalk celery
1 piece Hungarian or Polish sausage, approximately ⅔ inch in diameter and as long as the pork loin	1 small carrot
	2 tbsp. Chef's Salt (see page 60)
	1 tsp. caraway seeds
1 medium-sized onion, with skin left on	1 qt. water

1. Place the sausage in the freezer.

2. Ask the butcher to remove all the bones except the rib bones. Cut off the fat part from the top of the loin (see drawing, page 72). Reserve fat.

3. With a long, thin-bladed knife, carefully make a hole throughout the entire length of the pork loin, keeping to the middle as much as possible (or ask the butcher to do this for you).

4. Slice the onion (including the skin), the carrot, and the celery and place in the bottom of a roasting pan. Pour the water over the vegetables and add the caraway seed and garlic.

5. Cut the fat which was trimmed from the pork loin into ¼-inch cubes. Fry the cubes of fat in a frying pan until they turn dark brown.

6. Rub the Chef's Salt into the surface of the whole roast—top, bottom of ribs, and the two sides. Carefully insert the stiffly frozen sausage into the pork loin by starting at one end of the roast and gently pushing it in, turning side to side. It will help if you first insert the handle of a wooden spoon, or similar object, slightly smaller than the diameter of the sausage.

7. Place the pork, rib side down, on the vegetables and pour the smoking hot fat over the top. Cover the pan and roast it in a preheated 350-degree oven, basting once every 15 to 20 minutes, for approximately 1 hour and 30 minutes to 1 hour and 45 minutes, or until a thermometer inserted into the thickest part registers 165 to 170 degrees.

8. Remove the roast from the oven and place it on a serving platter. Let it stand in a warm place for at least 30 minutes.

9. Strain the liquid from the vegetables. Skim the fat from the juice, place the juice over medium heat, and reduce it to one-third the quantity. Serve as a clear sauce.

10. If you prefer a country pork gravy, reduce the liquid only to one-half. Combine 1 cup milk and 2 tbsp. flour and add 4 or 5 drops of Kitchen Bouquet. Stir this mixture into the simmering pan juice. If you wish you can purée the vegetables and add all or part of the purée to the sauce; otherwise, discard the vegetables.

CHEF'S SECRET: Freezing the sausage makes it rigid enough to be inserted in the roast. The best way to cut the hole in the roast is to make a cross-cut using a very thin-bladed knife. First push the knife in, cutting vertically; then cut horizontally.

To increase the very pleasant taste of the sausage throughout the pork, press holes in the casing with a fine needle before freezing.

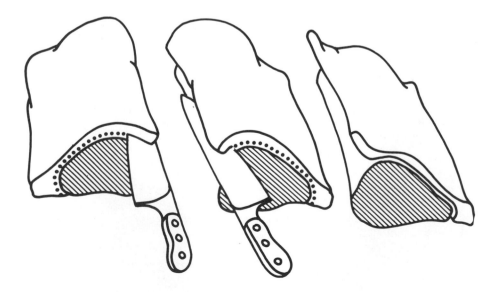

This dish is very elegant and inexpensive for a buffet table. You never have to worry about the sausage falling out; as the pork cooks, the muscles contract and grip the sausage. Also, there is a natural gelatin present in the meat which acts as a glue to hold the meat and sausage together.

Roast Suckling Pig

8 to 12 servings, depending on size

1 small suckling pig, approximately 16 to 22 lb., inspected and government stamped
4 to 6 tbsp. Chef's Salt (see page 60)
1 qt. beer

2 lb. pure lard
1 10½-oz. can chicken broth
3 tbsp. flour
½ cup cold water

1. Prepare a cookie sheet, large flat pan, or other cooking utensil which is large enough to hold the suckling pig in a sitting position (lying on the belly with hind legs pulled up under the body and head resting stretched out on the forelegs) by brushing the pan with shortening, lining it with aluminum foil, then brushing the foil with shortening.

2. Wash and dry the suckling pig inside and outside and rub the surface completely dry with towels. Rub the inside with Chef's Salt, being careful to avoid getting any salt on the outside on the skin.

3. Tie the two hind legs together under the belly, leaving enough room between them so that the belly can lie flat. Tie the front legs together and insert a piece of wood in the mouth so the pig will roast with its mouth open. This will make it easier to insert an apple or lemon in the mouth before serving.

4. Thickly spread the 2 lb. of lard over the entire surface of the skin, covering the back especially well.

5. Preheat the oven to 375 degrees.

6. Place the suckling pig in the oven to roast. After approximately 1 hour, dip a towel in the beer and wipe the entire skin with the beer-soaked towel. Continue to repeat this every 15 minutes; toward the end of the cooking time, which is approximately 3½ to 4 hours, wipe every ten minutes.

7. Remove the suckling pig from the oven when a thermometer inserted into the thickest part of the hind leg registers 175 to 180 degrees. Let it rest until cool enough to be handled.

8. Remove the wood from the mouth. Replace with an apple or lemon. Place the suckling pig on a serving platter and surround it with green parsley or other greens of your choice, or surround it with shoestring potatoes to resemble hay or straw.

9. Serve the suckling pig with a sauce made by scraping all of the beer and fat mixture from the foil-lined pan and diluting it with the can of chicken broth, then thickening it with the flour dissolved in the cold water.

CHEF'S SECRET: Don't ever buy a noninspected suckling pig; you never know. . . . Where to buy? Simply look in the Yellow Pages for a Greek, Mexican, or German butcher and ask him. If he doesn't have a suckling pig, he will be able to tell you where one can be purchased.

If you plan to have the suckling pig for Christmas, New Year's Eve, or New Year's Day, it is advisable to place your order around Thanksgiving. Suckling pigs are always in high demand and short supply at this time of year.

When serving, present the whole suckling pig at the table; then take it back to the kitchen to carve. Don't try to carve it at the dining table.

To carve, first cut off the head by inserting a sharp knife about 1½ to 2 inches below the ears, in the middle, trying to hit in the center of a joint between the neck bones. Split the suckling pig on either the right or left side of the backbone, cutting from the neck along the backbone to the tail. Lay down one half. Cut off the whole hind leg, then the front leg, using a shorter-bladed knife (see drawing). Now cut the rib part into serving-size pieces. Slice or cut up the hind and front legs. Repeat with the other half.

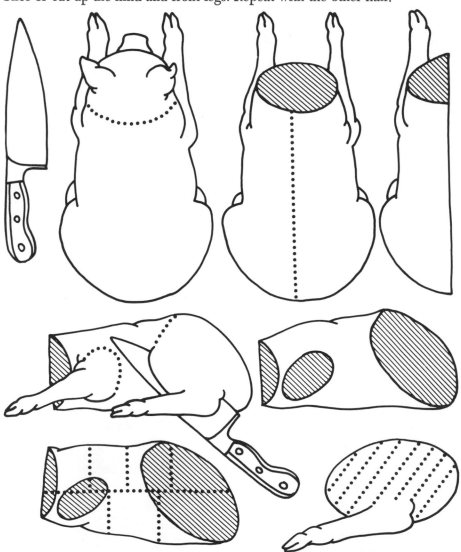

Reheat the pieces in a 425-degree oven for 10 to 15 minutes. Serve piping hot.

Gypsy Grill

8 servings

8 boneless, center-cut pork chops, approximately 5 oz. each
8 slices ranch style bacon
8 mushroom caps
8 thick slices ring bologna, knockwurst, or similar sausage
3 tbsp. flour

2 tbsp. cornstarch
4 tbsp. Hungarian paprika
1 tbsp. granulated sugar
½ tsp. salt
¼ tsp. black pepper
approximately ½ cup white wine

1. Cut each pork chop into 4 even pieces. Gently pound each piece until almost double in size.
2. Mix the flour with the cornstarch. Dip the flattened pieces of pork in the flour-cornstarch mixture.
3. Wash and dry each mushroom. Dip first in water, then in the flour mixture.
4. Cut each slice of bacon in half. Starting with a cold skillet, slowly fry the bacon until it is almost crisp. Remove.
5. In the bacon fat, quickly fry the pork chop pieces on one side until they turn a nice brownish color, then turn and fry on the other side. Remove and keep hot.
6. Now fry, together, the sausage and mushrooms. (If necessary, adjust the amount of shortening by adding more, preferably bacon fat or lard.) Place on absorbent paper to drain.
7. In a small bowl, combine the paprika, sugar, salt, and pepper. Drop by drop, stir in the wine until the mixture reaches a consistency similar to that of ketchup or mustard.
8. Put the pork chops, sausage, mushrooms, and bacon on skewers. Serve each person one skewer and offer the paprika-wine sauce instead of mustard.

CHEF'S SECRET: This is a very quick and tasty authentic Gypsy dish, liked by the Gypsies of Spain, England, and France as well as those of Rumania, Hungary, and Poland. The paprika-wine sauce is an unusual complement which adds a pleasant and mysterious flavor.

Dipping the meat and mushrooms in the flour mixture gives them a beautiful surface and helps them retain their juices.

Quick Tenderloin

4 servings

1 pork tenderloin, 1½ to 2 lb., well trimmed
Chef's Salt (see page 60)

2 tbsp. butter
2 tbsp. lard
1 clove garlic

2 tbsp. flour
1½ cups chicken broth and ½ cup
white wine, or 2 cups chicken broth

½ cup light or whipping cream
freshly chopped parsley (optional)

1. Trim every bit of fat from the tenderloin. Cut the fat into small pieces; render, then discard.

2. Slice the tenderloin into ¼-inch slices according to the drawing.

3. Add butter and shortening to the lard rendered from the fat. Cut the garlic clove horizontally, through the middle, two-thirds from one end, and vertically two-thirds from the other end (see drawing).

4. Fry the garlic in the fat until its edges start to turn brown. Discard garlic.

5. Dust the slices of pork with the Chef's Salt and flour. Add to the pan at once and fry over very high heat, stirring with a spatula, until pieces brown.

6. Pour off excess fat from the skillet. Add the broth and the white wine. Stir, cover, and let simmer over low heat or place in a preheated 250- to 275-degree oven for 10 minutes, or until tender. Blend in cream.

7. Transfer pieces of meat to a serving dish, ladle sauce over the top, and sprinkle with chopped parsley if desired. Serve at once with rice or mashed potatoes.

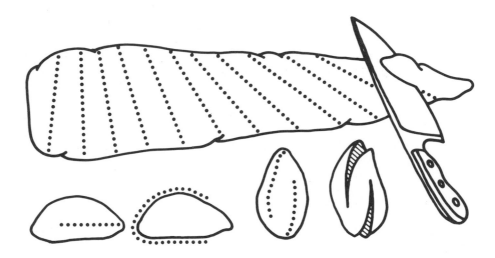

CHEF'S SECRET: This is one of the most popular quick supper dishes in Europe. Here in the United States, where pork tenderloin is so inexpensive and accessible, it is an ideal dish for the working housewife.

You can make many exciting variations of the basic theme. For instance, you can substitute sour cream for the light or whipping cream, or add some catsup to make a red piquant sauce, or add 1 tbsp. mustard. You can also eliminate the white wine and cream, and slice 1 apple and 1 banana into the sauce before simmering; then flavor with a good teaspoonful of curry. Or create your own variations.

If you cut the tenderloin according to the drawing, every slice will be approximately the same size; therefore, cooking time will be uniform.

Stuffed Pork Chops

8 servings

8 center-cut pork chops with bone in, 1 to 1½ inches thick

16 to 24 pitted prunes, depending on size

1 tbsp. orange marmalade or red currant jelly

light sprinkling of cinnamon and ground cloves

1 whole egg

½ envelope unflavored gelatin

1 tsp. Chef's Salt (see page 60)

½ tsp. caraway seed

2 tbsp. flour

1 to 1½ tsp. salt, to taste

1 small onion, thinly sliced

2 tbsp. shortening

1. Soak the washed, pitted prunes for at least 2 hours or more in just enough lukewarm water to cover.

2. Trim fat from the pork chops. Mince it finely and render. Save 2 to 4 tbsp. of this fat, depending on the size of the skillet which you will use, to use in frying the pork chops.

3. With a sharp, small knife, cut a pocket in the pork chops, somewhat larger than the prunes you use. Stick the knife into the pork chop close to the bone and, moving your knife clockwise if you are right-handed or counter-clockwise if left-handed, try to enlarge the inside pocket without cutting through the sides (see drawing, page 78).

4. With a spoon, mix the marmalade or jelly, cinnamon, cloves, and the water from the soaked prunes. Add the whole egg and mix thoroughly. Let stand for 10 to 15 minutes.

5. Put in each chop 2 or 3 of the prunes with a little of the liquid. Lightly sprinkle gelatin on the opening, press together, and secure with 1 or 2 toothpicks. Save the leftover marmalade–prune juice mixture for later use.

6. Mix the Chef's Salt with the caraway seeds, extra salt, and flour. Sprinkle both sides of the pork chops with this mixture and fry pork chops on both sides in very little shortening, over high heat, just until they get a nice color.

7. Lay the chops in a baking dish, add the onion and about 1 cup or more of water, depending on the size of the dish, to cover just the bottom of the dish. Cover and bake in a preheated 350-degree oven for 45 to 60 minutes, basting once in a while with the cooking liquid in the bottom of the dish.

8. When done, arrange the chops on a serving platter and brush with prune juice–marmalade mixture to glaze. Remove toothpicks and serve with fluffy rice or mashed potatoes.

CHEF'S SECRET: If you follow the drawing carefully, you won't have difficulty cutting the pocket in the pork chops. It is important that the knife be very sharp.

Don't attempt to pit the prunes yourself; buy the pitted variety. They are much more moist and less trouble to handle.

The dry gelatin sprinkled on the opening will mix with the juice oozing from the meat and will act as a sealer, so that you can remove the toothpicks before serving.

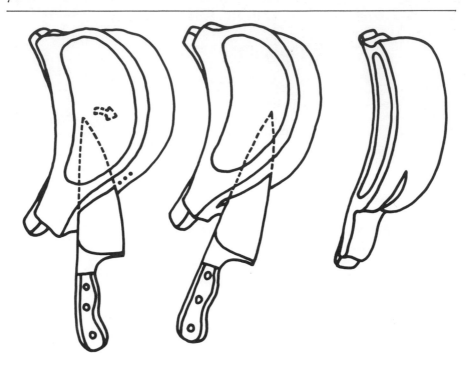

VEAL

Scaloppine (3 ways)

8 servings

The word scaloppine actually means nothing more than thin slice, so veal scaloppine is just thin slices of veal. The great advantage of this dish is the extremely short time in which it may be prepared. Scaloppine Natural makes a very elegant party dish, it is relatively inexpensive, and it is easy to learn how to fix.

Veal Scaloppine Natural

8 5- to 6-oz. thin slices veal, cut across   2 tbsp. flour
     the grain, or 16 2- to 3-oz. slices   1 tsp. Chef's Salt (see page 60)
4 tbsp. butter   2 lemons
2 tbsp. oil   ⅓ cup water

1. With a mallet, gently pound each piece of meat, moving the mallet downward and at the same time outward, until the scaloppine tissues are broken

down. Be careful not to overdo the pounding; it is not necessary to tear the meat (see drawing, page 80).

2. Mix the Chef's Salt with the flour. Sprinkle each scaloppine sparingly with this mixture. Preheat half of the oil and butter to the smoking point, in a large heavy skillet. Brown half the scaloppine quickly on both sides. Remove. Add the other half of the shortening, bring it to the smoking point, and brown the remaining scaloppine on both sides. Remove them and add to the frying pan ⅓ cup water. Scrape all the brown bits from the bottom of the pan. Squeeze the juice of ½ lemon into the pan. Keep stirring this mixture, scraping the bottom, for 1 more minute.

3. Return all the scaloppine to the pan and cook over medium heat for another 2 to 3 minutes.

4. Serve the scaloppine at once with round slices of lemon cut from the remaining 1½ lemons.

Scaloppine à la Riccadonna

16 to 24 small slices of veal
1 tbsp. very finely minced shallot or finely minced scallion (white part only)
1 pinch oregano
1 tsp. finely minced Italian parsley
½ cup mixed red and white vermouth, preferably Riccadonna

2 tbsp. butter and 2 tbsp. oil, or 4 tbsp. oil
1½ tsp. Chef's Salt (see page 60)
2 tbsp. flour
½ tsp. sugar

1. Mix the Chef's Salt, flour, and sugar. Dredge the meat with the flour-spice mixture. Lay meat slices next to each other on absorbent paper, but don't overlap.

2. In a large heavy skillet, sauté the shallots with the shortening until the shallots are limp and translucent. Increase the heat and add the scaloppine, all at once. Keep turning very fast with a spatula. As the color changes, pour the vermouth on the side of the meat (not over it). Using the spatula, lift the pieces slightly to let the vermouth flow under the scaloppine. Reduce the heat to medium. Carefully turn all pieces of meat over. Sprinkle them with oregano and parsley. Turn the meat once more. Serve immediately.

Scaloppine à la Milanese

8 5- to 6-oz. thin slices veal, or 16 2- to 3-oz. slices, cut across the grain
4 tbsp. butter
2 tbsp. oil
2 tbsp. flour
1 tsp. Chef's Salt (see page 60)

½ tsp. sugar
1 No. 2 can Italian-style tomato sauce
sprinkling of oregano
3 to 4 tbsp. grated Italian-style cheese
⅓ cup water

1. With a mallet, gently pound each piece of meat, moving the mallet downward and at the same time outward, until the scaloppine tissues are broken down. Be careful not to overdo the pounding; it is not necessary to tear the meat (see drawing, page 80).

2. Mix together the flour, Chef's Salt, and sugar. Sprinkle each scaloppine

sparingly with the flour mixture. Preheat half of the oil and butter in a large heavy skillet until it reaches the smoking point. Brown half the scaloppine quickly on both sides. Remove. Add the other half of the shortening, bring it to the smoking point, then brown the remaining scaloppine on both sides.

3. Remove the scaloppine and add to the frying pan ⅓ cup water. Loosen all the brown bits from the pan. Return the scaloppine to the pan and pour in the tomato sauce. Let it heat through, turning the meat once in a while. Sprinkle on some oregano to taste.

4. Place in a serving dish, scraping all sauce over the scaloppine. Sprinkle cheese over the top. Serve with pasta or rice.

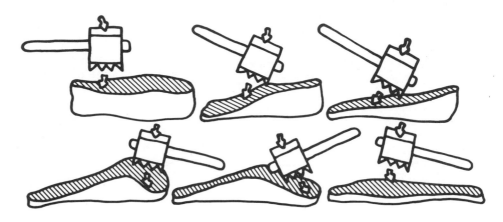

CHEF'S SECRET: The great secret of making a good scaloppine is having a large heavy pot—an enamel frying pan, if possible—and slowly heating it through.

High heat and great speed are very important. Don't give up if the scaloppine doesn't turn out perfectly the first time.

The small amount of sugar is not to make the meat sweet. It won't, but it hastens and heightens the browning and this improves the eye appeal.

If you cannot get scaloppine at your butcher's, buy a nice solid piece of veal hind leg. Look carefully to determine which way the grain is running in it. Wrap in aluminum foil and place in the freezer until it becomes very firm to the touch. Remove from the freezer and, with a very sharp knife, cut your own scaloppine against the grain. If the grain turns, which happens in certain parts of the leg, keep turning the meat.

Veal Paprikash

8 servings

2 to 2½ lb. cubed veal
2 cups finely minced onion
6 tbsp. shortening, preferably lard
2 cups chicken broth or a little veal stock (cooked from veal bones, 1

2-inch piece celery, 1 2-inch piece carrot, 1 small onion, 4 to 5 peppercorns, 1 tbsp. salt, and barely enough water to cover)

4 tbsp. Hungarian or Spanish paprika
2 tbsp. flour
1 cup sour cream
1 cup buttermilk

1 clove garlic
1 tbsp. Chef's Salt (see page 60)
4 to 5 black peppercorns

1. Blanch the veal cubes by bringing to a boil 2 qt. water and pouring the boiling water over the veal cubes. Stir, bring to a boil again, and remove from the fire immediately. Discard the liquid and set the meat aside.

2. Melt the shortening in a heavy pot, add the onion, and, over the high heat, stir in half of the paprika. Cook, stirring, until the onion becomes limp and the edges start to turn brown. Immediately pour in ½ cup chicken or veal stock. Adjust heat to low, cover pot, and let onions cook 10 to 15 minutes. Meanwhile, crush the garlic with the Chef's Salt.

3. Increase the heat and add the blanched veal cubes all at once. Stir, then add the rest of the broth or stock, black peppercorns, garlic crushed with the salt, and remaining paprika. Cover and simmer over low heat, stirring once in a while and scraping the bottom of the pan to avoid scorching, until tender (45 to 60 minutes, depending on the quality of the meat).

4. Sprinkle the flour slowly over the surface of the meat, folding the top meat pieces into the rest with a wooden spoon or spatula until all flour is incorporated. Simmer for an additional 5 to 10 minutes.

5. Mix the sour cream with the buttermilk. Take some of the liquid from the pot and blend it into the sour cream–buttermilk mixture. Then, stir the mixture into the Veal Paprikash.

6. Remove from heat, cover pot, and let it stand for at least 15 minutes. Ladle into a serving dish; garnish the top with additional sour cream or serve sour cream in a sauce bowl on the side and let the guests serve themselves.

CHEF'S SECRET: Blanching the veal will keep the pieces firm; even though they will be tender, the veal won't fall apart.

The best way to sprinkle the flour into the simmering liquid is by shaking it from a sieve into the pan with one hand and stirring with the other hand.

Veal Birds

4 servings

1 lb. very thinly sliced veal cutlets, cut
  into 3-inch squares
¼ lb. mushrooms, chopped fine
1 small onion, finely minced
6 tbsp. melted butter
salt
white pepper

3 tbsp. fresh bread crumbs
flour
½ cup veal or chicken stock
¼ cup dry sherry
2 tbsp. unsalted butter
2 tbsp. chopped parsley

1. Sauté the mushrooms and onion in 2 tbsp. of the melted butter for about 5 minutes.

2. Add salt, pepper, and bread crumbs; mix.

3. Spread the mixture on each piece of veal. Roll from end to end and tie with a piece of heavy thread or secure with a toothpick.

4. Dust the birds lightly with flour.

5. Preheat oven to 375 degrees.

6. In the remaining melted butter, lightly brown the veal birds.

7. Transfer the veal birds to a baking casserole which has a lid. Pour a little stock in the pan in which the birds were browned to loosen any remaining particles, then pour over the birds in the casserole. Add the balance of the stock and the sherry to the casserole.

8. Cover and place in the oven for 45 to 60 minutes. Add more stock as it evaporates.

9. Transfer the birds to a serving platter.

10. Reduce pan juices to half the amount over high heat. Remove from heat.

11. Swirl in the unsalted butter. Immediately strain through a sieve over the veal birds. Sprinkle with parsley. Serve while hot.

CHEF'S SECRET: Try to get the butcher to cut the veal against the grain. If veal birds must be made from meat cut on the grain, cut incisions at ½-inch intervals over the surface with a very fine point of a sharp knife.

If you like a thicker sauce, stir 1 tbsp. flour into ⅓ cup water or stock and stir this mixture into the rest of the liquid. If you like a cream-type sauce, use cream or milk instead of veal or chicken stock.

Old-Fashioned Blanket of Veal

8 servings

1 3- to 3½-lb. breast of veal, cut into ½-inch pieces
salt
6 cups veal or chicken stock
3 stalks celery, cut into 2-inch pieces
3 sprigs parsley
1 bay leaf
1 No. 2 can tiny white onions
12 oz. fresh small whole mushrooms

4 tbsp. flour
6 tbsp. soft butter
3 to 4 egg yolks combined with enough cream to make 2 cups liquid
salt
lemon juice
white pepper
chopped parsley

1. Blanch the veal in boiling water for 5 minutes. Drain.

2. Combine the veal with the stock, parsley, celery, salt, and bay leaf in a large stock pot. Cover and simmer for one hour.

3. Rinse the canned onions under cold running water. Do the same with the mushrooms.

4. Remove the celery, parsley, and bay leaf. Add the onions and the mushrooms. Simmer for 15 minutes longer.

5. Blend the flour and butter in a small cup. Add a few spoonfuls of the hot liquid to the butter-flour mixture. Then, using a wire whip, blend the butter-flour mixture into the veal liquid. Try not to break the pieces of veal. Cook on low heat until thickened. Remove from heat.

6. Blend the egg yolks with the cream. Stir into the sauce, and heat on low heat for one minute.

7. Season with salt, lemon juice, and pepper.

8. Ladle into a casserole and sprinkle with chopped parsley.

CHEF'S SECRET: Be careful when mixing the softened butter-flour mixture and the hot liquid. It is best to wait for the cooking liquid to lose some of its heat, then add to the butter-flour mixture, teaspoonful by teaspoonful.

With a slotted spoon, move the meat away from the part of the pot where you will stir the butter-flour mixture in. This will help to prevent breaking the meat.

When you make this for the first time, it is probably advisable to first remove all the meat to a serving dish, then stir the egg yolk and cream into the thickened liquid to finish the dish. Do this very quickly over very low heat.

Roast Veal

8 servings

1 5- to 6-lb. leg of veal, boned, rolled, and tied	1 clove garlic, crushed
	veal or chicken stock
3 tbsp. Chef's Salt (see page 60)	1 bay leaf
2 tbsp. butter	1 pinch thyme
2 tbsp. oil	1 cup light cream
paprika	1 cup dry white wine
2 medium-sized onions, sliced	2 tsp. cornstarch
1 medium-sized carrot, sliced	2 tbsp. water
2 stalks celery, chopped	

1. Preheat oven to 350 degrees.

2. Rub the roast with 2 tbsp. oil, then with the crushed garlic and Chef's Salt. Spread surface with softened butter and sprinkle with paprika.

3. Place the onions, carrots, and celery in the bottom of a roasting pan. Place the roast on top.

4. Add bay leaf, thyme, and enough stock to cover the vegetables.

5. Cover with lid and place in oven. Cook for approximately 1 hour. Remove cover. Continue to cook until a meat thermometer registers 160 degrees when inserted in the thickest part.

6. Remove from oven, untie roast, and place it on a carving platter. Keep warm.

7. Remove vegetables from the pan, discard bay leaf, and place the vegetables in a blender with a little of the pan juices. Blend into a fine purée.

8. Place purée in a saucepan with the strained pan juices. Add light cream and wine and bring to a boil, stirring constantly.

9. Dissolve the cornstarch in the water and stir into the sauce. Whip over low heat until sauce is thick and smooth. Season with additional salt if necessary. Strain through a sieve into a sauce boat. Serve hot with the carved veal.

CHEF'S SECRET: The butter spread on the roast will give an exceptionally good flavor and, with the paprika sprinkled over the top, a nice brown color. Rubbing the veal first with oil prevents evaporation of inside juices during cooking and helps the spices to adhere to the surface.

Be sure to let the veal leg stay at least 30 minutes in a warm place, covered, before attempting to slice. Otherwise, it will fall apart.

LAMB

Roast Lamb—Different Cuts

8 servings

Roast Leg of Lamb

1 5- to 6-lb. leg of lamb
Chef's Salt (see page 60)
3 cloves garlic
2 cups carrots, coarsely chopped
2 cups onions, coarsely chopped

3 to 4 celery stalks, cut in 1-inch pieces
4 tbsp. shortening
2 tsp. dry tarragon
stuffing (optional—recipe follows)

1. Ask the butcher to remove the bones from the leg, or remove them yourself by proceeding as follows, with the help of the accompanying drawing.

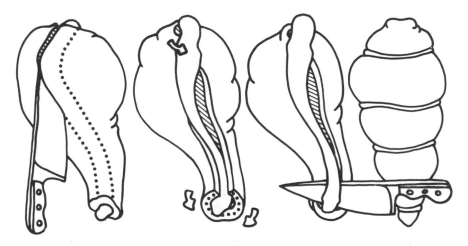

Lay the leg in front of you with the slightly rounded outside part on the cutting board and the inside part upwards. You will see the round head of the joint where the leg was attached to the hip or, probably, part of the back bone with the joint casing of the hip still on. In either case, cut with a sharp knife from the hip joint toward the shank, cutting right along the bone. The ideal way to do it is to let the point of the knife run on the bone. Do this until you get to another big rounded joint. Then, again starting at the hip end, repeat the cut on the other side of the bone. Loosen all the flesh under the bone until you are able to move the freed leg bone in the knee joint. Cut the skin on both sides of the knee joint and then the whole bone will come out easily. Save the bones.

2. Sprinkle the whole inside surface generously with Chef's Salt and rub

the flesh with 1 clove of the garlic, crushed. If you wish to serve in the French way, fill with a stuffing (recipe follows).

3. Reshape the leg and tie with a string. Then rub the outside surface with Chef's Salt.

4. Split the remaining 2 cloves of garlic crosswise, two-thirds of the way down. Over the bottom of a roasting pan, evenly distribute the carrots, onions, pieces of celery, the garlic cloves, and just enough water to almost cover the vegetables. Place the leg of lamb on the vegetables. Put in the bones you removed.

5. Heat the shortening to the smoking point and pour it over the surface of the leg of lamb. Roast covered in a preheated 350-degree oven for 1 hour. Remove cover, turn the leg so the bottom side is up, sprinkle it with 1 tsp. of the dry tarragon, and return it to the oven with the lid off for about 30 minutes. Then turn the leg over again and sprinkle the top with the remaining tarragon. Cover and finish cooking to the desired degree of doneness. A thermometer, when inserted in the thickest part, should register 125 degrees for medium rare, 135 to 140 degrees for medium, and 165 to 170 degrees for well done.

Stuffing

5 oz. fresh mushrooms	1 egg
1 tbsp. coarsely-chopped green parsley	½ cup cream
2 tbsp. shortening	salt and pepper to taste
1 cup firmly-packed soft bread crumbs	

1. Quickly wash the mushrooms under cold running water. Chop them coarsely. Sauté the mushrooms with the parsley in the shortening. Sprinkle with salt and pepper.

2. Beat the cream and the egg together.

3. Place the soft bread crumbs in a mixing bowl and pour the cream-egg mixture over them. Add the slightly sautéed mushrooms and parsley. Mix gently.

4. Stuff the leg where the bones were removed.

Roast Rack of Lamb

1 rack of lamb	tarragon
2 cloves garlic	2 to 3 tbsp. soft butter
1 tbsp. Chef's Salt (see page 60)	

1. Ask the butcher to prepare a rack of lamb, figuring approximately 2 to 3 rib widths per person.

2. Preheat oven to 475 to 500 degrees. Rub the surface of the lamb with a mixture of the garlic crushed with the Chef's Salt. Then rub it with dried tarragon to taste, combined with the soft butter.

3. Place the rack in an open roasting pan and place in the preheated oven for 15 minutes. Baste with its own drippings, tilting the pan and adding a few tablespoons hot water if necessary.

4. Reduce the heat to 375 to 400 degrees and roast the lamb for about 20 to 25 additional minutes, or until a meat thermometer inserted into the thickest part registers 110 to 120 degrees.

5. Carving: It is a sin to carve a rack of lamb, prepared like this, crosswise,

so that it resembles lamb or pork chops. The proper way to carve this is in ribbon-like slices. First, cut down from the top of the back bone to the beginning of the ribs; then slice on a 90-degree angle from the first cut into thin long ribbons (see drawing).

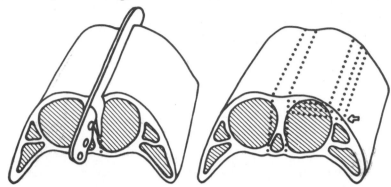

CHEF'S SECRET: Lamb should be eaten pink or not at all. If you don't have a meat thermometer, which is a shame, you can test the doneness by sticking a long needle into the lamb. If a pink liquid starts to run through the hole, the lamb is just about right. Before it is cooked, nothing will come out; if overdone, the liquid will be colorless.

It is probably more important for a leg of lamb or a rack of lamb to stand before being carved than for any other type of meat. Before you start the roasting preparation, secure a warm place where the lamb can stay (the leg about 20 to 30 minutes, the rack 10 to 15 minutes) before being carved for serving.

If the lamb happens to have a stronger lamb odor than you like, this can be remedied before cooking. Boil 2 gallons of water; after it begins to boil, add 2 to 3 cups vinegar and continue to boil for 2 to 3 minutes. Pour this hot vinegar-water over the lamb. Let stand for about 4 minutes; drain, then start the roasting preparation.

Cassoulet

8 servings

For each village in France, there is a different recipe for cassoulet. How to decide which is more authentic than the other? We simply decided on the recipe which we serve at The Bakery and which people like very much.

1 lb. small white dried beans
1 tbsp. salt
1 jar or tin potted goose or goose confiture (or homemade potted goose —recipe follows)
1 lb. assorted French- or German-type sausages, such as French garlic sausage, blood sausage, knockwurst, frankfurters, ring bologna, or Polish sausage

1 lb. lamb front, cubed
1 No. 2 can tomato sauce
1 tsp. mixed dried tarragon, chervil, marjoram, and parsley flakes, to taste
2 cloves garlic
1 small onion, finely minced
1 cup bread crumbs
2 cups tomato juice
1 tbsp. sugar

1. Soak the beans in lukewarm water overnight. Discard the water, and add new water to cover, plus the salt. Over low fire, gently cook the beans until tender.

2. Remove from the fire and place the whole sausages in the cooked beans. Let stand until cool.

3. Remove some of the fat from the potted goose and, in a skillet, sauté the 2 cloves of garlic in the fat until they start to turn brown. Discard garlic or set aside for use in the sauce (see *Chef's Secret*).

4. Place the onion in the skillet and, stirring, sauté until limp. Add the lamb cubes, increase the heat, and, stirring constantly, sear the surface of the cubes.

5. Pour about 2 cups water over the lamb, add the dried herbs, cover, and simmer for about 30 minutes, or until the lamb cubes are tender.

6. Pour off the cooking liquid from the lamb and combine the liquid with the tomato sauce.

7. On the bottom of a heavy casserole, make an even layer of beans, using one-third of them. Skin the sausages and then slice them and distribute half over the beans. Add the lamb cubes and ladle on some of the sauce. Add another layer of beans, distribute the potted goose over it, add the rest of the sausage, and cover with the remaining beans. Pour the remaining sauce evenly over the top. Sprinkle the top with bread crumbs. Cover and bake in a preheated 300-degree oven for at least 2 hours. During the last 15 minutes of cooking, add the tomato juice with the sugar.

CHEF'S SECRET: If you like a very moist cassoulet, add an extra 1 to 1½ cups water to the cooking liquid from the lamb when you are mixing it with the tomato sauce.

The best way to test the beans for doneness is to remove approximately 1 tbsp. of them and gently blow on them. If the skins break and start to curl back, the beans are done.

If you like a good garlicky taste, which is very desirable to certain people, don't throw away the cooked garlic. Mash it and mix it into the tomato sauce.

Potted Goose

If you like this cassoulet enough to make it 3 or 4 times during the winter season, it is worthwhile to make your own potted goose as follows:

1 8- to 10-lb. goose
1 tbsp. Chef's Salt (see page 60)
2 10½-oz. cans clear chicken broth
1 cup sliced carrot
2 cups sliced onion
2 cloves garlic, thinly sliced

1 or 2 sprigs green parsley
10 to 12 black peppercorns, slightly bruised
4 tbsp. shortening, preferably lard, duck fat, or goose fat

1. Ask the butcher to cut the goose into four pieces. Don't attempt to cut the goose yourself, as the bones are extra hard and dangerous. If you buy a frozen goose, the butcher can simply saw it into four sections. In this case, defrost the goose before you start the recipe by leaving it in the refrigerator overnight or placing it in the sink and running body-temperature water over it.

2. In the bottom of a roasting pan, place the chicken broth, carrot slices, onion slices, garlic cloves, parsley sprigs, and peppercorns. Rub the goose parts

with Chef's Salt and smear 1 tbsp. cold shortening over each piece. Place in the roasting pan. Cover and roast the goose for 4 to 5 hours in a preheated 325-degree oven, adding about 2 to 3 cups of warm water during the cooking time.

3. The goose must be cooked until it falls off the bones when touched with a fork. Then remove it from the oven, lift it from the vegetables, and let it cool until it can be handled.

4. Pour the liquid from the roasting pan through a sieve. Press the vegetables through the sieve, leaving only the fibers in the sieve. Discard the fibers.

5. Remove all flesh and skin from the goose. Discard the bones. Distribute the meat and skin into 6 or 8 plastic containers, pressing well down to the bottom. Carefully skim all fat from the cooking liquid and distribute the liquid over the goose flesh. Refrigerate, leaving the fat at room temperature.

6. In about 3 to 4 hours, when the goose with the liquid starts to gel, distribute the fat evenly over the top of the plastic containers. Cool, then freeze. This confiture of goose may be kept refrigerated for 4 to 6 weeks, or frozen up to 3 or 4 months. It is also an ideal gift.

Irish Stew

8 servings

4- to 4½-lb. boneless lamb shoulder, cut into 1-inch cubes
2 to 3 tbsp. Chef's Salt (see page 60)
1 bay leaf
2 large onions, sliced
1 medium head of cabbage, diced
3 or 4 leeks, approximately 1 inch in diameter, white part only, sliced

1 to 1½ cups grated raw potato
Worcestershire sauce to taste
3 tbsp. freshly chopped green parsley
2 cups chopped carrots, green peas, green beans, or any mixture of vegetables you care to use (optional)

1. Blanch the lamb cubes by bringing to a boil approximately 2 qt. water, pouring the boiling liquid over the meat cubes, letting it stand for 5 minutes, then pouring off the water.

2. Place the blanched lamb cubes in a large pot and sprinkle with Chef's Salt. Add the bay leaf, onion, and enough cold water to cover. Bring to a boil, then reduce the heat and simmer for approximately 1 to 1½ hours, or until meat is tender. Add more liquid during cooking if necessary.

3. Remove the meat cubes and place in the bottom of a shallow casserole dish. Keep warm.

4. Add the cabbage and leeks to the cooking liquid and cook over medium heat for 10 to 15 minutes, or until vegetables are tender. If you use any of the optional vegetables, they should also be added at this time.

5. Strain the liquid from the vegetables. Place them over the top of the meat in the casserole.

6. Skim the fat from the top of the cooking liquid. Add the grated potatoes and cook until liquid is thickened.

7. Season with Worcestershire sauce and pour over the meat and vegetables. Sprinkle parsley over the top and serve.

CHEF'S SECRET: As you can see from the recipe, Irish food is very basic and very bland. The secret of the good stew is not so much in the ingredients, but in the cooking time and proper temperatures. If you cook the vegetables separately as the recipe requires, they won't get mushy and will keep their identity.

As we've mentioned before, the best way to skim the fat from the surface of the liquid is to dip a kitchen towel in water, wring it out, and place 2 or 3 ice cubes in it. Dip the section of the towel with the ice cubes into the surface of the liquid, and all the floating particles of fat will freeze to the cubes.

Braised Lamb Shanks

8 servings

8 lamb shanks	2 cloves garlic
2 cups carrots, cut into small cubes	1 bay leaf
1 cup celery, cut into small cubes	12 black peppercorns, slightly bruised
1 cup chopped onion	4 tbsp. shortening
3 cups green peas	2 cups water
2 to 3 tbsp. Chef's Salt (see page 60)	

1. Crush the garlic to a pulp with 1 tsp. of the Chef's Salt. Mix the rest of the Chef's Salt with the garlic pulp and rub into the surface of the lamb shanks.

2. In a heavy skillet, heat the shortening to the smoking point. Add the lamb shanks four at a time and, turning them, brown the surface. Remove and brown the remainder.

3. Place the shanks in a roasting pan. Rinse the frying pan with 2 cups water, scraping off all bits adhering to the pan. Then pour the liquid over the shanks. Cover the roasting pan and bake in a preheated 350-degree oven for 30 minutes.

4. Add the onion, and another cup of water if necessary. Bake for 30 more minutes.

5. Add all the remaining vegetables except the green peas. Lower temperature to 325 degrees. Roast for 30 more minutes. Add the green peas, remove the lid, add water if necessary, and keep braising for another 30 minutes. Baste frequently. Serve.

CHEF'S SECRET: The procedure as given will give a beautiful color to the lamb shanks, and the vegetables won't be overcooked because they are added later. Because the lid is removed for the last 30 minutes, the liquid from the roasting pan will reduce to an excellent *au jus*.

If you like, you can pour 1 cup or more red wine over the shanks for the last 30 minutes. This is especially desirable if you plan to serve wine with them.

POULTRY

CHICKEN

Roast Chicken
Breaded Chicken
Stuffed Roast Chicken
Chicken Paprikash
Chicken in Champagne Sauce
Chicken à la King

Chicken Fricassee
Chicken Cordon Bleu
Broiled Chicken
Stuffed Legs and Wings
Sweet and Sour Chicken
Chicken with Tarragon

DUCK

Roast Duckling

Duck in Avocado

TURKEY

Roast Turkey
Turkey Breast Steaks

Turkey Chowder
Turkey Hash

OTHER FOWL

Roast Goose
Roast Pheasant
Pigeon Pie
Roast Quail
Roast Partridge in Grape Leaves

Roast Mallard Duck
Rock Cornish Hens
Capon Breast and "Quail Eggs" in a
    Nest of Green Noodles

*E*ven if the eater's first choice is always meat, the shopper's first choice is always poultry—probably not just for price alone, but for the simple reason that the shopper most likely is the one who does the cooking, and the variety of ways poultry can be cooked is almost unlimited. So is the variety of tastes, textures, and shapes. Just think of a crisp, succulent roast duckling or a majestic turkey on the Christmas or Thanksgiving table, the cold fried chicken in the picnic basket, or all the other poultry possibilities.

The first and most important rule in poultry cooking is to be sure that the birds are fresh. It is no big problem to recognize freshness as long as the poultry is refrigerated, but how do you check freshness if it is frozen? First of all, go to a reputable store and, if possible, peek at the thermometer which is located somewhere in the frozen food cabinet. The closer to zero the temperature is, the better the quality of the frozen fowl. Then check the label and watch for the pointers which can betray long-stored, dehydrated merchandise: the package material is damaged at the corners; the skin is discolored somewhat, lighter around the neck and the tail end of the bird and on the outside of the drumstick; in other places a dryness of the skin is also evidence of long-stored poultry. Of course, after defrosting at home, further signs will be noticeable: a rancid odor and a texture of the skin resembling a dry sponge or a piece of cork.

Do not forget, proper freezing does not harm poultry at all, and it is much easier to maintain perfect quality in the frozen stage than in any other way. The damage is done by improper freezing and improper storage.

The temptation to buy chicken on sale and freeze it at home is often great. How to do it? Split the chicken in half or cut it into serving-size pieces. Pack each half or piece separately in plastic wrapping, and try to press out as much air from each package as possible. Then wrap the packages in aluminum foil. Lay them all flat—next to each other, never on top of each other—in the bottom of your frozen-food cabinet, and place other packages of frozen food on top of them. Remember, cold air always travels downward, and therefore foods freeze much faster if they have an already frozen layer of products on top of them. Poultry stored in this way will keep up to eight weeks, but do not try to store it for any longer.

Poultry

CHICKEN

Roast Chicken

4 servings

2 2½- to 3-lb. roasting chickens
2 tbsp. Chef's Salt (see page 60)
2 stalks celery
few slices carrot
1 cup chopped onion, including the
skin

small clove garlic
4 to 6 tbsp. shortening
2 cups water

1. Wash the chickens, being sure to take out every little bag hiding in the front or back cavity. Wipe dry and rub inside and outside with Chef's Salt. Let stand at room temperature for 30 minutes to 1 hour.

2. Place all the vegetables, including the garlic clove, in a roasting pan. Add the water. Place the chickens, breast up, on top of the vegetables.

3. Heat the shortening to the smoking point and pour the hot fat over the breasts.

4. From here on, you can choose between two methods: (a) put the chicken in a preheated 425- to 450-degree oven and keep basting it with its own cooking liquid, every 10 minutes, for 1 to 1½ hours; or (b) put the chicken in a 350-degree oven, close the door, and roast for 1 to 1½ hours, basting only once after 1 hour of cooking.

5. Check the internal temperature in the thickest part of the breast and on the inside of the thigh. It must be 185 degrees both places. Or, if you do not have a thermometer, pierce with a long sharp needle. No pinkish liquid should come out; the juices oozing out should be clear.

CHEF'S SECRET: The first method is the method that chefs use in famous, high-class restaurants in Europe. It requires constant attention, but, of course, results in a much tastier chicken which is crisp on the outside and moist and tender on the inside. The second method is easier and gives the housewife time for other things, but the chicken prepared by this method never compares in taste to that prepared by the first method.

The basting of the skin with the hot shortening gives the chicken a beautiful color.

Breaded Chicken

8 servings

2 2¼- to 2½-lb. fryers, cut into serving pieces	4 whole eggs
2 cups milk	½ cup milk
2 cups flour	½ cup water
3 tbsp. Chef's Salt (see page 60)	4 to 6 cups bread crumbs
	shortening for frying

1. When cutting the chicken into serving pieces, separate the thighs from the drumsticks, cut each breast in half, leaving a part of the breast meat on each wing, and, if you wish, cut two separate back pieces.

2. Take out all the small bones like the rib cage, backbone, collarbone, etc., leaving only the main bones in the pieces.

3. Mix the flour with the Chef's Salt. Beat the eggs with the ½ cup milk and the water, then strain through a sieve.

4. Dip each chicken piece in the 2 cups milk, let the milk drip off, then dip it in the flour-spice mixture. Be sure to completely cover with the flour mixture. Shake off excess flour and then dip in the egg wash. Turn the piece to be sure no dry spots remain, then place the piece on the top of the piled up bread crumbs. Sprinkle more bread crumbs over the chicken until completely covered, then gently but firmly press down so that the crumbs really adhere to the chicken. Shake off excess crumbs and lay the chicken parts on a paper-covered tray, skin side up. Continue until all chicken is breaded.

5. In a large frying pan which has a lid, heat half of the shortening to approximately 360 degrees and carefully, one by one, put in the chicken pieces, skin side up. Add the chicken slowly so that the fat remains hot. Cover the pan, adjust the heat to medium, and cook for approximately 10 to 12 minutes.

6. Remove cover, turn pieces, and fry, uncovered, for another 10 minutes or so. Remove the pieces to a warm place on absorbent paper and keep warm until served.

CHEF'S SECRET: By straining the egg-milk-water mixture, called egg wash, you avoid having big parts of the egg white adhere to some pieces so that there is not enough of the egg wash for other pieces. Also, the straining makes the coating even.

If you want to avoid lumps of flour and bread crumbs on your fingers, designate one hand as "wet" and the other as "dry." With the wet hand, handle the uncoated chicken, dip it into and remove it from the milk, and place it on the flour. Sprinkle flour over it with the dry hand, and coat it and lift it out with the dry hand. Place it in the egg wash with the dry hand, lift it out with the wet hand, and then finish with the dry hand. It sounds complicated, but if you learn the trick you can prepare large amounts of chicken without ever getting lumps on your fingers.

It is important to cover the pan while the bottom of the chicken is frying, as this keeps it tender. Frying the pieces without a cover after turning makes the skin crisp.

Stuffed Roast Chicken

6 to 8 servings

1 large (5- to 6-lb.) roasting hen	1 cup chicken stock
8 oz. chicken livers	1 cup milk or cream
1 1-lb. loaf of Italian or French bread,	½ tsp. freshly ground black pepper
1 day old	1 to 1½ tsp. Chef's Salt (see page 60)
½ cup finely minced onions	1 small carrot, sliced
1 tbsp. fat	1 medium onion, sliced
2 tbsp. chopped parsley	½ cup shortening
4 whole eggs	

1. Cut or break the bread into pieces about the size of a walnut. Pour 2 to 3 cups lukewarm water over the pieces of bread and let stand for a few minutes. Press out and discard the liquid.

2. Sauté the minced onions in the 1 tbsp. fat.

3. Run the chicken livers through a food mill, meat grinder, or blender. Add to the bread together with the eggs, sautéed onions, freshly ground black pepper, parsley, milk, and chicken stock. Work the mixture with both hands until evenly blended.

4. Fill the cavity of the roasting hen with some of the dressing.

5. Loosen the skin from the flesh through the neck opening and, with your index finger, loosen the skin along the breast to the thighs, loosening over the thighs as well.

6. Place a couple of tablespoons of the dressing between the skin and flesh and gently massage it down between the skin and flesh of the thigh. Keep repeating on both sides of the roasting hen until all, or almost all, of the dressing has been used and is under the skin.

7. Secure the neck opening by sewing with a few stitches; secure the back opening with a poultry skewer; then tie the two legs together to the tail.

8. Rub the surface of the skin with Chef's Salt.

9. Place all the vegetables in the bottom of a roasting pan. Add enough water to cover the bottom of the pan and place the roasting hen, breast up, on top of the vegetables.

10. Heat the shortening to the smoking point and pour, smoking hot, over the breast of the roasting hen.

11. Pierce the skin throughout the whole stuffed surface, at about ½-inch intervals, using the same needle used for sewing.

12. Cover the pan and roast in a preheated 350-degree oven for 2 to 2½ hours. Reduce the heat to 300 degrees, add some more liquid to the roasting pan, and roast for an additional 30 minutes without the cover.

13. Let stand for at least 30 minutes before cutting and serving.

CHEF'S SECRET: If you feel your finger won't be long enough to get to the thigh from the neck opening, brush the handle of a cooking spoon with some oil and, after loosening the skin from the flesh on the breast, insert the cooking spoon handle and carefully loosen the skin to and over the thigh.

Piercing the skin will prevent it from bursting at a weak spot.

If you wish, roast the chicken without stuffing; bake the stuffing in an oven-proof casserole or glass container and serve it separately.

Chicken Paprikash

4 servings

1 2½- to 3-lb. frying chicken	3 tbsp. tomato purée
5 tbsp. lard or shortening of your choice	1 clove garlic
	1 tsp. salt
black pepper and salt, to taste	2 cups chicken stock or water
5 tbsp. sweet Hungarian paprika	1 medium-sized bell pepper
1 cup finely chopped onion	1 cup sour cream

1. Cut out the backbone of the chicken and split into three pieces crosswise. Cut the neck in two pieces, cut off the drumsticks, and split the thighs lengthwise in half along the bone. Cut off two joints of each wing; cut the breast crosswise in half, leaving the first wing joint on. Cut the gizzard into four pieces and the heart in half.

2. Sprinkle all the pieces of chicken with salt, black pepper, and 1 tbsp. paprika.

3. Melt 4 tbsp. of the fat in a large heavy sauté pan. When hot, put in the chicken pieces and very quickly sauté over medium heat until the chicken meat turns white and is firm to the touch. Remove all chicken except the back, gizzard, heart, and neck. Keep warm.

4. Increase the heat and add the chopped onion, 2 tbsp. paprika, tomato purée, and the garlic which has been mashed with the 1 tsp. salt. Stir these ingredients until the fat sizzles. Add 1 cup stock, cover the pan, and cook until onions become pulpy.

5. Return the sautéed chicken and its juice to the pan. Add another teaspoon salt, the bell pepper cut into finger-length slices, and the remaining stock. Cook, covered, for an additional 25 to 30 minutes, over medium heat, or until the chicken is tender.

6. In a small saucepan, heat the remaining tablespoon of fat and add 2 tbsp. paprika. Stir until heated through, being careful to prevent burning. Pour this over the cooked chicken.

7. Remove 3 large spoonfuls of cooking liquid from the pan. In a small bowl, stir this liquid into the sour cream. Pour the sour cream mixture over the chicken and remove from heat. Serve while hot.

CHEF'S SECRET: If you follow the directions for the onions, you will have the perfect consistency and taste. Depending on the onion you use, the time it takes to turn into a pulp will vary. You must watch carefully.

Only the best imported Hungarian or Spanish paprika will give the very special taste that Chicken Paprikash is famous for. If you can't get it in your regular grocery, look for it in a specialty store.

Chicken in Champagne Sauce

8 servings

2 2¼- to 2½-lb. fryers, cut into serving pieces
4 tbsp. butter
2 tbsp. other shortening
2 tbsp. finely minced shallot or 1½ tbsp. finely minced scallions (white part only)
2 tbsp. Chef's Salt (see page 60)
1 tsp. mace
½ tsp. nutmeg

3 tbsp. concentrated orange juice
1 10½-oz. can chicken broth
5 oz. fresh mushrooms (large, if possible)
2 cups champagne, or 1 cup white wine and 1 cup club soda
1 tsp. sugar
3 tbsp. cornstarch
⅓ cup water

1. Dissolve the cornstarch in the water.

2. In a large skillet or frying pan, melt the butter with the other shortening. Sprinkle the Chef's Salt on the chicken pieces and, when the shortening is smoking hot, quickly brown the skin side of each piece of chicken.

3. Remove chicken to a casserole and cover. To the frying pan, add the orange concentrate, the shallots, spices, and canned chicken broth.

4. Stirring constantly, bring this mixture to a slow boil. Remove it from the heat, cool for 4 to 5 minutes, then pour it over the browned chicken pieces. Cover the casserole and place it in a preheated 350-degree oven.

5. Cook for approximately 1 hour with the lid on, then test for doneness. Remove some of the sauce and stir into it the sugar and the cornstarch mixture. Bring to a boil, stirring constantly, and cook until thickened. Pour back into the casserole.

6. Quickly wash the mushrooms, cutting off the stems to use for some other purpose.

7. Gently mix the mushroom caps among the chicken pieces. Pour in the 2 cups champagne. Let the casserole stay in the shut-off oven or in a warm place for 1 hour. Then remove the pieces of chicken to a serving platter. Serve the sauce separately in a sauce boat.

CHEF'S SECRET: The characteristic taste of the champagne sauce comes from the orange concentrate, the mace, and the champagne. The wine and club soda mixture is a substitute for the champagne; of course, no substitute is perfect, but it works.

If you were to pour the boiling sauce over the browned chicken pieces, the muscles would tighten up and get tough. That is why we recommend that you let the sauce cool for a few minutes.

If you prefer, you may omit the mushrooms and add orange rind prepared as follows: Cut enough very thin strips of orange rind, the yellow part only, to have about 3 to 4 tbsp. Boil the orange rind first in 2 cups water, discard water, then boil again in 2 more cups water. Rinse in cold water and soak it in the champagne or wine–club soda mixture for about 10 minutes before mixing into the sauce.

Chicken à la King

8 to 10 servings

1 5-lb. roasting chicken
2 ribs celery, coarsely chopped
2 medium-sized carrots, coarsely
    chopped
1 medium-sized onion, cut in 4 pieces
1 clove garlic, crushed
3 tbsp. Chef's Salt (see page 60)
1 bay leaf
2 whole cloves
10 whole peppercorns, crushed
1 cup milk
1 cup light cream

½ cup flour
1 tbsp. cornstarch
2 tbsp. butter
2 tbsp. chicken fat (skimmed from top
    of stock)
3 small green peppers
3 whole pimientos, canned
20 medium-sized mushroom caps,
    washed
2 ribs celery, peeled
chopped parsley

1. In a large stock pot, place the chicken, coarsely chopped celery, carrots, onion, garlic, Chef's Salt, herbs, and spices. Add enough water to cover. Bring to a boil, then reduce to a simmer for approximately 2½ hours, leaving the lid ajar.

2. Remove the chicken and place it on a platter to cool at room temperature. Strain the stock. Reserve stock and vegetables separately.

3. Prepare the cream sauce base by mixing the milk and cream with the flour and cornstarch. Be sure it is well blended. Melt the butter and fat in a small saucepan and heat it until it bubbles. Pour the milk-flour-starch mixture into the hot fat. Stir over medium heat until thickened. With a wire whip, whip in enough strained stock to make a sauce of medium consistency which coats the back of the spoon.

4. Remove all meat and skin from the bones of the chicken. Discard the bones; save the skin. Save one side of the breast to garnish the dish. Cut the rest of the meat into ¾-inch cubes.

5. In a blender jar, place 2 cups sauce, some of the vegetables from the stock, and about a third of the skin. Blend at high speed until completely puréed. Add more stock if necessary. Stir this mixture into the rest of the sauce.

6. Cut the peppers and pimientos into ¾-inch pieces. Blanch the peppers in boiling water for 5 minutes. Drain. Add peppers, pimientos, and mushrooms to the sauce. Simmer for 5 minutes. Add the cut-up chicken and continue heating just long enough for the chicken to be hot.

7. Serve the Chicken à la King in a large casserole. Garnish with the remaining chicken breast cut into strips on the bias (Chinese cut). Cut the celery the same way as the breast and blanch it in boiling water until tender, using as little water as possible in order to retain its bright green color. Attractively arrange the celery with the chicken breast on the top of the dish.

CHEF'S SECRET: It is better to let the roasting chicken stay at room temperature for 2 to 3 hours before starting the cooking than to start from the refrigerated stage. Don't try to bring the liquid to a boil too quickly; start slowly. Once it reaches the boiling point, don't let it boil more than 1 or 2 minutes before reducing the heat. This method will make the meat juicy and more tender.

Green peppers sometimes tend to give a bitter taste when cooked. Blanch them in boiling water for 1 or 2 minutes, then rinse with cold water.

Chicken Fricassee

4 servings

1 3-lb. chicken	1 sprig parsley
12 small boiling onions, peeled	1 pinch thyme
salt	½ bay leaf
pepper	12 medium-sized mushrooms, washed
4 tbsp. lard or chicken fat	juice of ½ lemon
4 tbsp. butter	2 egg yolks
3 tbsp. flour	½ cup heavy cream
3 cups chicken stock	4 tbsp. butter

1. Split the chicken down the back into two halves. Cut the breast from the thigh and drumstick, then cut the drumstick from the thigh. Cut off the wing tips and discard. Sprinkle pieces with salt and pepper.

2. In a large heavy-bottomed saucepan, lightly brown the pieces of chicken in hot fat and butter. Remove to platter.

3. Lightly brown the onions in the same pan, then return the browned chicken to it.

4. Sprinkle the flour over the chicken and onions. Toss pieces until flour is absorbed.

5. Add the stock and herbs. Bring to a boil, cover, and cook gently for 35 minutes or until chicken is tender.

6. Add mushrooms and lemon juice. Cover and cook for 5 more minutes.

7. Remove chicken, onions, and mushrooms from the sauce and place on a serving platter or in a casserole. Pick out bay leaf and parsley and discard.

8. Mix the egg yolks with the cream in a small bowl. Slowly ladle a small amount of the hot sauce into the yolks and cream. Stir. Pour this into the rest of the sauce and heat to the boiling point, over medium heat, stirring constantly with a wire whip. This mixture should not be allowed to boil. Remove from heat and whip in the butter. Pour sauce over chicken.

CHEF'S SECRET: One of the oldest chicken dishes ever recorded is Fricassee. We can find it in almost every European cookbook from the sixteenth and seventeenth centuries.

For this dish the onions should be lightly browned. Heat the fat before adding the onions; when adding them, distribute them evenly over the bottom of the frying pan. Keep an eye on them until the edges start to brown, then immediately return the chicken pieces to the pan. The caramelized onions give the Fricassee its characteristic taste.

When you separate the yolks from the whites for mixing with the cream, be sure that as little as possible of the egg white remains on the yolk, because the white will harden and leave lumps in the sauce.

Chicken Cordon Bleu

8 servings

8 large, boneless chicken breast halves,
   approximately 8 oz. each
8 1½- by 3½-inch oblong pieces of
   cooked, ready-to-eat ham
8 1½- by 3½-inch oblong pieces of
   Swiss, Muenster, or Gruyère cheese
salt
black pepper

flour for dusting the pieces
3 eggs
¼ cup milk
¼ cup water
3 to 4 cups bread crumbs
1 egg white
butter and shortening

1. Remove the skin from the pieces of chicken. Lay the chicken pieces, with the side from which the skin was removed down, on a cutting board and gently flatten with a mallet.

2. Sprinkle each with salt and pepper and brush the surface with the egg white, which has been slightly beaten with a fork and strained through a sieve.

3. On the left side of each large breast, place a slice of cheese and a slice of ham, one on top of the other. Fold the right side over the ham and cheese and press the edges together. Shape each portion into a nice oval. Freeze the pieces for 1½ to 2 hours.

4. Beat the 3 eggs with the milk and water, then run through a sieve.

5. One by one, remove the pieces from the freezer. Dust with flour, then dip in egg wash, being sure to completely coat the surfaces. Then, place each in the bread crumbs, covering and gently pressing the crumbs into the surface. Refrigerate.

6. Melt enough butter and another type of shortening of your choice to have about ½ inch in the bottom of the pan. When the fat gets hot, carefully add two or four of the pieces at a time, depending on the size of the skillet.

7. Cook until nicely browned, approximately 5 to 7 minutes; then place each portion on absorbent paper and keep in a warm place until ready to serve.

CHEF'S SECRET: If you can't get the large halved chicken breasts, buy double or whole breasts and use half for the bottom and the other half for the top.

The pounding serves two purposes: the first is to make the breast larger, and the second, which is even more important, is to make the thickness even so the cooking time will be uniform.

If you want to test the shortening for the proper degree of heat, drop one or two of the larger bread crumbs into the fat. If the bread crumb immediately comes to the surface in the midst of a little white foam, the shortening is ready.

Broiled Chicken

2 servings

1 2-lb. broiling chicken
salt
freshly ground black pepper

2 tbsp. oil
2 tbsp. melted butter

1. Split the broiler along the backbone. Flatten it with your hand. Season with salt and pepper; brush with a mixture of oil and butter.

2. Preheat broiler.

3. Place chicken on broiling pan, breast side up, and place the pan 4 inches from the heat.

4. Broil for 30 to 40 minutes, turning and basting every 10 minutes. Broil breast side up the last 10 minutes. Adjust the pan by lowering it from the heat if the skin is getting too brown.

CHEF's SECRET: If you like the skin of the broiled chicken crisp, then wipe it before broiling with a dry kitchen towel and don't put any salt on the skin.

If you like a nice brown glaze on the broiled chicken, sprinkle some granulated sugar through a sieve over the surface of the chicken just before the last minute or two of broiling. It won't be sweet, but will have a "professional-looking" shine.

Stuffed Legs and Wings

12 pieces

8 chicken wings	salt
4 chicken livers	pepper
4 chicken legs, about 8 oz. each	4 eggs, beaten
4 breakfast link sausages	3 cups Italian bread crumbs
flour	lard or oil for deep-frying

1. Using a sharp knife, loosen the skin and flesh around the base of the second wing joint, toward the tip. When it loosens, grip the bones in your right hand and the meat in your left, then gently pull out the two bones.

2. Cut the chicken livers into small pieces.

3. Stuff some of the pieces into the pocket of each wing.

4. Starting at the tip end of the thigh, remove the bone from the leg without cutting into the meat. Cut into the joint where the thigh and drumstick meet. Cut the tendons, cutting toward the bone gently but firmly from the outside of the flesh until you have cut them all around just under the top end of the drumstick bone. Scratch back the meat from the bone using a paring knife, and with one fast movement you can then remove the drumstick so that the chicken leg is turned inside out.

5. Place a sausage in the place where the bone was and turn the flesh back into the original position.

6. Place the fat in a heavy frying pan and heat it slowly on medium heat. Preheat oven to 350 degrees.

7. Season the flour with salt and pepper. Dredge the stuffed wings and legs in the flour; dip them in the beaten eggs; then roll in the bread crumbs.

8. Deep-fry the legs in hot fat until golden brown. Place on a sheet pan and finish cooking for 15 to 20 minutes in the oven. Deep-fry the wings while the legs are baking.

CHEF's SECRET: In order to easily place the breakfast sausages in the chicken legs, first freeze the sausages for a while.

For easy boning, see the drawings on page 102.

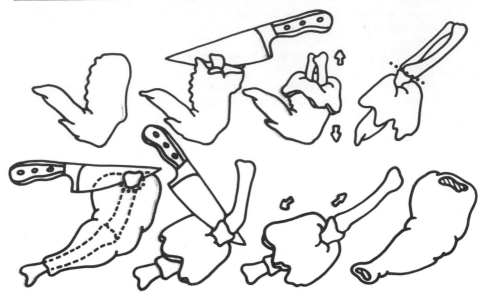

Sweet and Sour Chicken

8 servings

2 2¼-lb. chickens
1 cup tomato purée or 4 tbsp. tomato
    paste diluted with enough water to
    make 1 cup liquid
1 No. 2 can pineapple chunks
2 cups bell pepper, cut into ½-inch
    squares
2 cups onion, sliced ⅓ inch thick, then
    cut crosswise
10 to 12 cherry tomatoes (optional)
1 tbsp. flour

4 tbsp. cornstarch
1½ tsp. salt
light sprinkling of ginger powder
light sprinkling of white ground pepper
1 tsp. granulated sugar
1 to 1½ cups oil
2 tbsp. sugar
1 cup white vinegar
2 tbsp. or more soy sauce, depending
    on taste

1. Bone and cut the chicken into bite-sized pieces. Remove the skin if
desired. Sprinkle chicken pieces with soy sauce and about 1 tbsp. of the
vinegar, turning the pieces until all are moist.

2. Mix the cornstarch, flour, salt, ginger, and white pepper.

3. Sprinkle about one-third or one-fourth of the chicken pieces at a time
with the cornstarch-flour-spice mixture and then fry in very hot oil. Transfer
the pieces to a casserole. After all chicken is fried, discard the oil.

4. Quickly blanch the green peppers, then the onions in boiling water for
10 seconds, and immediately cool in ice water.

5. In a saucepan, combine the liquid from the pineapple, vinegar, and
tomato purée and bring to a boil. When boiling, add the onions, pineapple,
and green pepper. Pour the whole mixture over the chicken pieces and fold
over 2 to 3 times. Add sugar.

6. Correct seasoning; if you feel the sauce is not thick enough, mix some
cornstarch with cold water and add to the dish, drop by drop, until thickened.

Add more soy sauce or more sugar or cut down on the vinegar, depending on taste. If you like, garnish with cherry tomatoes.

CHEF'S SECRET: This is a very simple dish, but extremely good. Many butcher shops sell chicken that is boneless and in bite-sized pieces; take advantage of this or substitute a pound of lean pork cubes or small pieces of veal for the chicken. Chinese homemakers often make this dish from a mixture of chicken and pork.

The soy sauce and vinegar sprinkled on the chicken gives the "oriental" taste to the chicken, as does the ginger.

You can prepare all the ingredients in the morning, but don't mix them together. Keep the blanched vegetables, sauce, and chicken separate; then heat them all in a casserole in the oven for 45 to 60 minutes at 350 to 375 degrees or heat on top of the range, stirring constantly.

Chicken with Tarragon

8 servings

1 large roasting hen or capon	1 bay leaf
1 tbsp. dried or 2 tbsp. fresh chopped tarragon	1 tsp. slightly bruised peppercorns
	1 cup vinegar
1 tbsp. Chef's Salt (see page 60)	enough water to completely cover the hen
1 carrot, sliced	
2 celery stalks, sliced	1 envelope unflavored gelatin for each 3 cups cooking liquid
1 onion, cut into 4 pieces	
1 clove garlic	4 to 6 sprigs fresh tarragon

1. In a pot large enough to hold the hen or capon, place all ingredients except the gelatin and the fresh tarragon sprigs. Slowly and carefully, bring to a very gentle boil. Immediately reduce heat and simmer until a thermometer inserted into the thickest part of the breast registers 180 degrees. Remove from heat.

2. Pour off the liquid, straining it first through a sieve and then through a wet kitchen towel. Measure the quantity of liquid. Mix the dry gelatin with 2 to 3 tbsp. water for each package gelatin used. Add to the strained cooking liquid.

3. Let the chicken cool enough to be able to handle, then rinse under cold water, inside and out, and wipe dry. Lay breast up in a container large enough to hold it.

4. Bring the strained cooking liquid with the gelatin just to the boiling point, but don't boil. Remove it from the heat and cool it by pouring it into a shallow container with a large surface.

5. Place the fresh tarragon on the breast of the hen and secure it with a few toothpicks, then slowly ladle the liquid over the hen.

6. Refrigerate overnight. Remove the toothpicks and serve cold.

CHEF'S SECRET: This is a simple but very elegant dish. The chicken must remain very white.

If you like the gelatin mixture tart, add some vinegar or tarragon vinegar according to your taste. If you like a golden aspic, add a few drops of yellow food coloring to the chicken liquid when you add the gelatin.

If you want to decorate the hen with cut-outs of the aspic (as this type of gelled liquid is called), pour some in a very straight-sided shallow container and let it gel in the refrigerator; then cut the desired shapes with a knife or a small cookie or aspic cutter.

If your aim is ease of serving rather than elegance, remove all flesh after the bird is cooked and cooled enough to handle. Lay the flesh in a dish and ladle on the liquid. Float the tarragon sprigs on top.

DUCK

Roast Duckling

2 to 4 servings

1 4½- to 5-lb. duckling
Chef's Salt (see page 60)
1 carrot, washed, scraped, and coarsely
  chopped
2 stalks celery, coarsely chopped
1 medium-sized onion, coarsely
  chopped

1 or 2 cloves garlic, thinly sliced
3 to 4 tbsp. lard, duck fat, or chicken
  fat
3 to 4 black peppercorns
1 small piece of bay leaf
sprinkling of marjoram

1. Preheat the oven to 300 to 325 degrees.

2. Use a roasting pan with a tight-fitting cover. Put the lard, duck fat, or chicken fat into the roasting pan. Reach into the vent end of the duckling and remove the neck and giblets, which will be inside the body cavity. Rub the inside and outside of the duckling with Chef's Salt.

3. Place the duckling, breast down, directly on top of the lump of fat in the roasting pan. Place the cut vegetables and garlic inside, on, and around the duckling. Add about 1 to 2 inches of water to the pan. Add the peppercorns, bay leaf, and marjoram. Cover and place in the preheated oven.

4. After 2 hours, take the roasting pan out of the oven and very carefully remove the duckling to a platter. Let it cool completely. If it is not completely cooled, the dish will not turn out properly.

5. To finish, split the duckling lengthwise by standing it on the neck end and, with a sharp knife, cutting from the tip of the tail directly down the center. To quarter, each half may again be cut (see drawing).

6. Place the cold, split duckling pieces, cut side down and skin side up, on a slightly greased cookie sheet. Return to a 425- to 450-degree oven for 18 to 22 minutes. Before serving, remove the first two joints of the wing, leaving only the third.

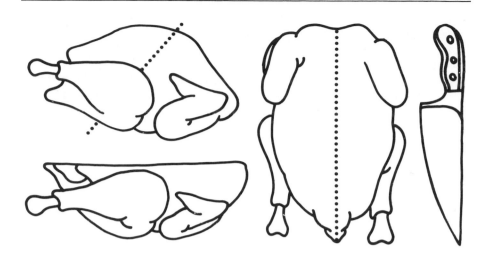

CHEF'S SECRET: The success of a roast duckling starts with the buying. For best results, buy the best. A 4½- to 5-lb. duckling is the most satisfactory and economical size. It is perfectly safe and even advisable to buy frozen duckling. Look for the mark of government inspection on the package. Store in a freezer or the freezing compartment of the refrigerator until ready to use. Before using, let the duckling defrost overnight in the bottom of the refrigerator. After it has been defrosted completely and the flesh feels soft, preparation may begin.

After the duckling has been removed from the roasting pan to cool, it can be safely kept at room temperature all day. Or, if the weather is very hot and humid, store the duckling in the refrigerator after it has cooled to room temperature. It is important to bring it back to room temperature about an hour before finishing. Do not reheat right from the refrigerator.

Perhaps you wonder why fat is added to the duck, which is a naturally fat bird. As the water starts to heat in the roasting pan, the fat becomes liquid and forms an even surface over the top of the water. The surface of fat has a boiling point of 360 degrees, while the water boils at 212 degrees. Without the fat, the water would create a vapor surrounding the duck in the covered roasting pan. This would give the bird a steam-cooked, undesirable taste, and would prevent the fat under the duck skin from oozing out as it does in dry air.

Duck in Avocado

6 servings

3 ripe, but firm, avocados
1 qt. water
juice of 1 lemon
the breast and thigh meat from a whole
    roasted duckling
6 medium-sized oranges, peeled and
    segmented
lettuce leaves

¼ cup chopped pecans or toasted
    sliced almonds
6 tbsp. mayonnaise (see page 214)
2 tbsp. frozen undiluted orange juice,
    defrosted
parsley sprigs
orange wedges (optional)

1. Peel the avocados, cut them in half, and immediately dip them in the water with the lemon juice added to keep them from discoloring.

2. Be sure the duck meat is skinless and boneless. Cut it into bite-sized pieces.

3. Mix the duck meat with the orange segments. Divide into six portions. Fill the avocado halves, which have been placed on a platter lined with crisp lettuce leaves, with the portions of meat and oranges.

4. Mix the concentrated juice with the mayonnaise and spoon this over each stuffed avocado. Top each with the nuts. Decorate with parsley sprigs and orange wedges.

CHEF'S SECRET: Always peel the avocado first and then cut it in half. This is important, because if avocados are ripe enough to be eaten, the halves would be mashed during the peeling process.

If you leave the pits in after halving the avocados and dipping them in the lemon water, you can wrap the avocados in plastic wrap and keep them all day in the refrigerator. They won't discolor.

You can give this dish an oriental flavor by mixing 1 tbsp. soy sauce into the 6 tbsp. mayonnaise, replacing the orange with canned tangerine segments, and grinding some roasted sesame seeds over the dish. (The sesame seeds are available in very handy little plastic throw-away grinders in grocery stores carrying oriental foods.)

When using the canned tangerine segments, you can greatly improve the taste by pouring off the canned syrup, rinsing the segments quickly in cold water, then transferring them to a plastic container. Squeeze the juice of 1 lemon over them and, if you like, add 1 or 2 tbsp. brandy and enough water to cover. Chill in the refrigerator overnight.

TURKEY

Roast Turkey

8 servings

For the turkey:
1 10- to 12-lb. turkey, ready to roast
4 tbsp. Chef's Salt (see page 60), mixed if desired with 1 tsp. thyme or poultry seasoning
1 cup each coarsely chopped carrots, celery, onions, and turnips
1 cup cold shortening (butter or lard)

1 clove garlic, sliced
1 tsp. slightly bruised peppercorns
1 large brown paper bag, without any printing on it, large enough to hold the turkey
For the gravy:
giblets

thyme	2 cups cream or half-and-half
oregano	2 tbsp. flour (or more if you prefer a
1 tbsp. fat	thicker gravy)
2 cups water	Chef's Salt (see page 60)

1. Remove the giblets from the turkey, making sure that none is left in the neck cavity.

2. Rub the turkey inside and outside with Chef's Salt and place about one handful of the mixed chopped vegetables in the cavity.

3. Place the remaining vegetables, garlic, and peppercorns in the bottom of a large roasting pan. Add enough water to have about 1 to 1½ inches in the bottom of the pan.

4. Cover the turkey breast and legs evenly with the shortening, then place the turkey in the brown paper bag and set on top of the vegetables in the pan.

5. Roast in a preheated 325-degree oven for 3 to 3½ hours or until a meat thermometer inserted into the thickest part of the thigh registers 185 degrees.

6. For the last ½ hour of roasting, open the paper bag and tear off as much of the paper as possible. Increase the heat to 425 to 450 degrees and baste the breast every 8 to 10 minutes.

7. While the turkey is roasting, wash and clean the giblets. Cut the heart, gizzard, liver, and as much of the meat from the neck as possible into pieces about the size of a cranberry. Sprinkle with a pinch of Chef's Salt, thyme, or oregano. Fry over high heat in the 1 tbsp. fat until brown, then pour 2 cups water in the pan, cover, and simmer slowly until needed for the gravy.

8. When the turkey is done, remove from the oven, transfer to a serving platter, and keep warm for at least 1 hour before serving.

9. Strain the cooking liquid. Discard the turnip and the spices, then press the remaining vegetables through a sieve. Add the pulp to the cooking liquid.

10. Add the cooked giblets to the cooking liquid and bring the mixture to a boil. When boiling, stir into it the cream or half-and-half mixed with the flour.

CHEF'S SECRET: A few years ago it was my job to test different turkey roasting methods. We tried every method we found or could conceive, but again and again, for some reason, the turkey roasted in the brown paper bag came out the best.

Turkey Breast Steaks

4 servings

4 8- to 12- oz. turkey breast steaks or a boneless turkey breast, 4 to 4½ inches thick, cut into 4 steaks (see drawing, page 108)	salt and pepper according to taste

1. Gently pound the turkey steaks with a mallet. Sprinkle with salt and pepper and pan-fry over medium heat until brown.

2. If you prefer, brush with shortening and broil 8 inches from the source of heat, turning frequently to avoid burning.

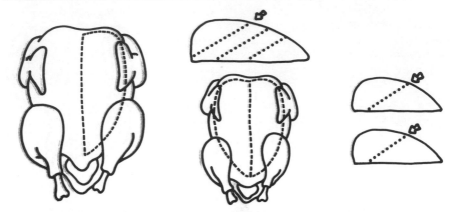

CHEF'S SECRET: If you pan-fry the steaks, immediately after placing them in the pan, start to shake the pan back and forth so they won't stick.

If you wish, you can flour the steaks before frying and add 2 to 3 tbsp. of water or stock to the frying pan when they are done to make a little thin gravy.

Don't try to fry the steaks in butter, but put a small piece of butter on each and let it melt before serving. It will greatly improve the taste.

Turkey breast steaks are relatively new and people who have never tried them are reluctant to do so, but once they do they keep eating them.

Turkey Chowder

8 servings

4 lb. turkey wings
4 tbsp. shortening
1 No. 2 can creamed corn
1 No. 2 can whole-kernel corn
1 cup celery, diced to the size of a kernel of corn
½ cup bell pepper, diced to the size of a kernel of corn
1 cup onion, diced to the size of a kernel of corn

1 bunch green parsley
1 bay leaf
1 piece celery
2 tbsp. salt
½ tsp. freshly ground black pepper
2 to 3 egg yolks
1 cup cream or half-and-half
2 qt. water

1. Tie the parsley, the bay leaf, and the celery together.

2. Wash the wings, cover with water, and bring to a boil. Let boil for 3 to 4 minutes, then pour off the water.

3. In a large soup pot, melt the shortening and add the fresh vegetables and half of the salt. Cook over high heat, stirring, until the vegetables start to brown. Reduce the heat; add the turkey wings, the rest of the salt, the black pepper, and the parsley bouquet. Cover the wings with the 2 qt. water, put on the lid, and simmer for 2 to 2½ hours.

4. Remove the meat and let it cool. Remove the parsley bouquet and discard. Remove the flesh from the bones; discard the bones.

5. Return the meat to the chowder and add both cans of corn. Simmer for 15 additional minutes.

6. Mix 2 to 3 egg yolks with the cream or half-and-half and place in the bottom of a large soup tureen. Stirring constantly, add a few tablespoonfuls of the hot chowder to the egg yolk–cream mixture; add more hot liquid, then pour in all the chowder and serve.

CHEF'S SECRET: Do not be misled by the name "chowder," because this is a main-course dish. The few minutes' preboiling of the turkey wings will improve the taste of the chowder and will remove a considerable amount of the turkey fat under the skin.

This soup would be thick enough to eat without adding the egg yolk–cream mixture, because of the creamed corn and the thoroughly-cooked vegetables, but of course it would not taste the same.

If fresh corn or frozen corn is available, by all means use it instead of the canned kernels, but do not substitute for the canned creamed corn.

Turkey Hash

4 to 6 servings

3 cups cooked turkey breast, coarsely chopped
1 cup light cream
2 tbsp. butter
2 tbsp. flour
2 cups milk
½ cup heavy cream
salt
white pepper
1 egg yolk, beaten
2 tbsp. whipped cream

1. Place the chopped turkey in a saucepan with the light cream and cook slowly on low heat until the cream is reduced to about half the original quantity.

2. In another small saucepan, melt the butter, add the flour, and cook until it turns a golden color. Stir in the milk with a wire whip. Cook this sauce on low heat until it has reduced to about 1 cup. Stir frequently to prevent sticking. After it has reduced, stir in the heavy cream.

3. Add 1 cup of this sauce to the turkey. Season with salt and pepper.

4. To the remaining sauce, add the egg yolk and fold in the whipped cream.

5. Pile the hash on a serving dish or in a heat-proof casserole and spread the egg yolk sauce over the top. Place under a low broiler flame until tiny brown dots speckle the sauce. Serve immediately.

CHEF'S SECRET: Dip two fingers in some shortening and coat the pan before pouring in the light cream and chopped turkey. Do this off the fire and place the frying pan on the range after the ingredients are in it. Don't stir the ingredients in the pan; shake the pan instead.

When the light cream comes to a boil, be very careful; start to stir and keep stirring, then remove it from the range and keep warm until you make the other sauce.

This dish may be served in patty shells, pastry shells, or on lightly buttered toast instead of in the casserole.

OTHER FOWL

Roast Goose

8 servings

1 8- to 10-lb. goose
1 onion
1 tart apple
3 tbsp. Chef's Salt (see page 60)
1 large clove garlic
½ tsp. caraway seed (optional)
1 tsp. marjoram (optional)

4 tbsp. shortening
enough water to have 2 inches in the
    bottom of roasting pan
Kitchen Bouquet
1 to 2 tbsp. cornstarch
⅓ cup water

1. Preheat the oven to 350 degrees.

2. Remove giblets from the goose. Near the opening of the cavity you will find 2 large lumps of fat under the skin. Remove these, cut them into small pieces, and, in a small heavy pot, over medium heat, render out the goose fat.

3. Mash the garlic with 1 tbsp. of the Chef's Salt and, if used, the marjoram and caraway seed. Rub the inside and outside of the goose with this mixture.

4. Cut the apple and onion into quarters and place them in the cavity of the goose. Mix the remaining Chef's Salt into the water in the roasting pan; then place the goose in the pan.

5. Strain the rendered goose fat and then heat it to the smoking point. Pour half of it over the breast of the goose, then turn the goose breast side down and pour the other half of the hot fat over it.

6. Cover the roasting pan, place it in the oven, and roast for 2 to 2½ hours or until a thermometer inserted into the thickest part of the thigh and into the breast registers 180 degrees.

7. Remove the goose and let it stay breast down in the covered roasting pan for about 30 minutes. Then remove it to a tray and let it stay at room temperature for at least 3 hours.

8. Pour the juice from the roasting pan into a fairly tall, narrow container to allow the fat to come to the top. Skim off as much as possible. Refrigerate the roasting liquid until you can remove all the fat.

9. Taste the juice; if salty, dilute it with a little water. Add a few drops of Kitchen Bouquet and heat the juice to the boiling point.

10. Mix the cornstarch with the ⅓ cup water and stir 1 to 2 tbsp. of this mixture into the juice, depending on how thick or thin you prefer the juice.

11. One hour before serving, preheat the oven to 475 to 500 degrees.

12. Heat 4 to 5 tbsp. of the goose fat to the smoking point. Place the goose on a low-edged pan, breast up, and pour the hot fat over the goose. Place in the oven and roast for 30 minutes. Shut off the oven and leave the goose in

for an additional 10 minutes. Then remove, place on a serving platter, and let stand in a warm place at least 20 minutes.

CHEF'S SECRET: The hot fat will make the goose skin very crisp. The salt that is added to the water in the roasting pan will prevent the juices from the goose flesh from oozing out, so that the goose remains juicy and tender.

Roast Pheasant

8 servings

2 large pheasants	2 or 3 stalks celery, coarsely chopped
2 tsp. salt	2 bay leaves
½ tsp. black pepper	bacon
¼ tsp. crushed juniper berries	2 to 3 cups water
½ tsp. paprika	4 to 6 tbsp. melted shortening, prefer-
3 or 4 carrots, coarsely chopped	ably lard or bacon drippings
1 large onion, coarsely chopped	

1. Preheat the oven to 325 to 350 degrees.
2. Rub the completely defrosted pheasants with a mixture of the salt, black pepper, crushed juniper berries, and paprika.
3. Place the coarsely chopped vegetables and the bay leaves in the bottom of a deep roasting pan which is large enough to hold the pheasants. Lay the pheasants on the vegetables and brush the skin with the melted shortening.
4. Add the water to the roasting pan, cover, and place in the oven. Roast for approximately 2 hours.
5. Remove from the oven and let stand for 10 to 15 minutes. Then remove the birds from the roasting pan, turn them breast up on a tray, and let them stay at room temperature for at least 4 or 5 hours. Or, after cooling, cover them with plastic or foil and leave them in the refrigerator overnight.
6. Before serving, split each pheasant into quarters, cover with bacon, and roast at 450 to 475 degrees for 20 to 25 minutes. Serve at once with Port Wine or Madeira Sauce (see *Chef's Secret*, page 206).

CHEF'S SECRET: If the birds are frozen, defrost by leaving in the refrigerator overnight. If you are in a hurry, defrost under running tap water.

If you have a "great hunter" in the family, he will bring the birds home skinned—and probably tougher. In this case it is advisable to use an extra cup of water and to roast the birds a little more than 2 hours. You will also need more bacon to cover the pheasants in this case.

If the bird brought home by the hunter should turn out to be tough and inedible, don't give up; cut it into small pieces, grind, then run through a blender and make a good pâté from it.

Juniper berries are often unavailable in food markets, but ask in ethnic pharmacies. You can buy as many as a pound at one time and keep them for years; they are not like other spices that rapidly lose their pungency. Be sure to crack them gently with a mallet in the corner of a kitchen towel before using. If for some reason you can't get any juniper berries, use an ounce of gin for each bird.

Regular sliced bacon will do for covering, but if you are lucky enough to have a friendly butcher nearby, buy a 1-lb. slab of bacon and ask the butcher to slice it into rectangular pieces from the top toward the rind by laying it flat on the electric meat slicer. Place a double sheet of wax paper which is a little larger than the rectangles of bacon between each and freeze what you don't use. This way, the bacon will always be available for other occasions.

Pigeon Pie

8 servings

4 squabs
enough pastry for 1 9-inch double-crust pie
2 tbsp. finely minced shallot or scallion (white part only)
1 tsp. salt
¼ tsp. white pepper
1 tsp. sweet basil
4 tbsp. butter

2 tbsp. oil
4 tbsp. flour
approximately 2 cups heavy or light cream
1 whole egg, well beaten
1 cup chicken stock or 1 cup water mixed with ½ chicken bouillon cube

1. In a heavy pan, sauté the shallot or scallion in the butter and oil. Cut the squabs into four pieces each and add to the pan along with the salt, pepper, and sweet basil. Reduce the heat to very low, cover, and cook for about 30 minutes, stirring once in a while.

2. Remove the pieces of squab. Let cool, then bone. Discard bones and skin; return the meat to the pan.

3. Increase the heat to medium. Sprinkle half of the flour over the top, stirring to blend, then add the chicken stock or the water with the bouillon. Keep stirring. Add half the cream and reduce the heat to low.

4. Mix the egg with the rest of the cream and the remaining flour. Pour this through a fine sieve into the pan, stirring constantly. Remove from the heat.

5. Bake the bottom crust in a 9-inch glass pie dish for 10 minutes at 350 degrees. Spoon in all the meat, leaving quite a bit of the sauce in the pan. Cover with the second crust and bake at 350 degrees for 20 to 25 minutes. If you wish, brush the top crust with a little melted butter or egg wash, or, if you like a very shiny pie crust, with an egg yolk combined with ½ tsp. sugar and 1 tsp. water.

6. Dilute the remaining sauce with enough water to make it the consistency of a medium white sauce. Simmer for 10 minutes and serve in a sauce boat with the pie.

CHEF'S SECRET: Prebaking the bottom crust helps to prevent a soggy bottom, especially if you brush the pie pan with shortening before putting in the pie dough and then brush the dough itself with the shortening before baking. This is not usually necessary for other pies, but it enhances this dish.

If you wish, you can proceed as follows: preheat the oven to 425 degrees; bake the top crust on a cookie sheet; bake the bottom crust completely; cool, then spoon the mixture into the bottom crust, set the prebaked top in place, cut into eight wedges, and serve immediately.

If you wish, add 3 to 4 oz. sliced, lightly sautéed mushrooms to the mixture.

Roast Quail

8 servings

8 quails
salt
pepper
1 lb. ground ham or 1 12-oz. can
   chopped ham

8 bay leaves
8 slices ranch-style bacon (thickly sliced)
1 10½-oz. can chicken broth, or ½ can chicken broth and 1 cup white wine

1. Preheat oven to 450 to 475 degrees.
2. Split each quail on the back. Sprinkle with salt and pepper.
3. If you are using canned chopped ham, chop it finely. Divide the ground ham or the canned chopped ham into eight equal portions. In the cavity of each quail, place 1 bay leaf and a portion of the meat.
4. Wrap a slice of the ranch-style bacon around each bird and tie with a string which is much longer than needed, so that it is not necessary to tie a knot.
5. Roast the birds breast down for 5 minutes in the preheated oven. Turn the birds and baste each with 2 tbsp. of the canned chicken broth or the chicken broth–white wine mixture and roast for 10 minutes breast up.
6. Shut off the oven; leave the birds in the oven for another 8 to 12 minutes. Serve with Port Wine or Madeira Sauce (see *Chef's Secret*, page 206).

CHEF'S SECRET: Some homemakers have an aversion to canned meats which is absolutely unfounded. The canned chopped ham, or any canned meat that is packed under government inspection by a reputable company, will contain nothing but a very satisfactory quality of chopped ham. Its texture and taste will pleasantly counterbalance the taste of the quail without overpowering it.

A very festive way to serve the quail is as follows: Prepare 1 package green noodles according to package directions. Brush 1 lb. long macaroni with 2 to 3 tbsp. oil; toast it under the broiler on a cookie sheet, then cook according to package directions. When preparing the macaroni, keep turning them under the broiler, being careful not to let them burn. To serve, mix the green noodles and the prepared macaroni, butter the mixture, and make a nest for the birds on a serving platter.

Roast Partridge in Grape Leaves

8 servings

8 partridges
salt
pepper
juniper berries
bay leaves
2 or 3 apples
½ cup lard or bacon drippings
½ cup butter
18 slices country bacon, thickly sliced

1 jar grape leaves
1 12-oz. can chopped ham
1 medium head firm white cabbage
2 tbsp. chopped onion
½ tsp. caraway seed
1 tbsp. sugar
½ tsp. salt
⅓ cup white wine
⅔ cup water

1. Rub the partridges inside and outside with salt and pepper.

2. In the cavity of each, place 2 or 3 whole juniper berries, a piece of bay leaf, and a wedge of apple.

3. In a large skillet, heat the lard or bacon drippings and the butter to the smoking point. Pan-fry the birds on each side, turning frequently, until the skin gets brown. Remove the birds, discard the fat, and let the birds cool.

4. Wrap around each bird 2 slices of country bacon and enough grape leaves from a jar to cover the whole bird. With strong white kitchen thread, secure the grape leaves all around the bird.

5. Slice the cabbage into finger-thick slices. Finely chop the canned ham and the remaining two slices of country bacon.

6. Sauté the chopped bacon with the chopped onion, over medium heat, until the onion turns glossy.

7. Place the sautéed bacon-onion mixture in the bottom of a casserole. Add the cabbage, chopped ham, caraway seed, sugar, salt, and white wine mixed with the water. Place the grape leaf–wrapped birds over this mixture, cover, and cook over medium heat for 45 minutes, then reduce the heat to low and cook for an additional hour. Serve.

CHEF'S SECRET: The grape leaves in the jar are available among the Near Eastern or Greek food items in stores. If they are not available in the jar, you can use fresh grape leaves if you can get them, but first blanch them in water with 2 to 3 tbsp. vinegar added. The outside leaves of the cabbage may also be substituted for grape leaves.

You can prepare this dish ahead of time by proceeding as directed until all ingredients are in the casserole. Then bake in the oven for about 2 hours at 325 degrees.

Roast Mallard Duck

8 servings

2 mallard ducks	buttermilk to cover or a mixture of but-
salt	termilk and sour cream
pepper	shortening (preferably lard or bacon
crushed juniper berries	drippings)

1. If the skin comes off easily from the foot of a mallard duck, and if the beak is soft and light in color around the nostrils, the bird is young and can be roasted as you would roast a pheasant, except that the juice should not be used. If the bird is old, remove the skin completely.

2. Cut the duck into four pieces; sprinkle with salt, pepper, and crushed juniper berries.

3. Pan-fry the pieces of duck in the shortening for 10 to 15 minutes, then discard the shortening.

4. Place the pieces in an ovenproof dish. Fill the dish with enough buttermilk or buttermilk–sour cream mixture to completely cover the pieces of duck. Place in a preheated 325-degree oven for 3 to 4 hours. Serve.

CHEF'S SECRET: Roast mallard duck and other wild ducks sometimes have a peculiar odor and flavor. You can minimize this by boiling 3 qt. water with

3 cups vinegar and 2 tbsp. salt and, when boiling, pouring it over the raw, quartered wild ducks and letting it stay until lukewarm. Discard water, rinse the ducks with warm water, then proceed with the cooking.

Even a very tough old duck, if prepared according to the recipe, will be palatable and tender.

Rock Cornish Hens

4 servings

4 Rock Cornish game hens, defrosted	sweet paprika
2 cups poultry dressing, any kind you like (optional)	poultry seasoning
	soft butter
salt	4 or 8 rings raw onion
pepper	4 sprigs fresh sweet basil or tarragon

1. Wipe each bird inside and outside with a damp cloth. Sprinkle with salt. Stuff with dressing if you wish.

2. Place breast side up on a large square sheet of foil measuring 16 by 16 inches. Sprinkle the skin with salt, pepper, paprika, and poultry seasoning.

3. Preheat oven to 350 degrees.

4. Place one or two rings of raw onion and a sprig of herb on each bird.

5. Wrap the birds in aluminum foil and roast in a roasting pan or other shallow pan for 45 minutes to 1 hour.

6. Remove the birds from the oven. Open the foil carefully to avoid a sudden burst of steam.

7. Increase the heat to 425 degrees. Brush the birds with butter.

8. Put the birds back in the oven for 5 to 10 minutes with the foil turned back so they can brown. Serve with the juices from the foil.

CHEF'S SECRET: If you stuff the Rock Cornish game hens, the cooking time will be at least 1 hour to 1 hour and 15 minutes instead of the 45- to 60-minute cooking time. The aluminum foil should be opened up 10 minutes earlier for stuffed birds because much more moisture will develop from the stuffing.

If you want the birds to have a very delicate flavor, carefully pour over each breast, just before serving, 1 tbsp. of a fruit-flavored dry brandy (definitely not a sweet fruit-flavored cordial) such as pear, plum, or kirsch.

Capon Breast and "Quail Eggs" in a Nest of Green Noodles

4 servings

For the capon breast:	2 to 3 cups water
1 7½-lb. capon	Chef's Salt (see page 60)
1 medium-sized carrot	
1 medium-sized onion with skin left on	*For the "quail eggs":*
2 stalks celery	8 oz. raw capon meat
6 or 8 truffle slices	3 oz. ham
3 tbsp. lard	2 egg whites
1 tbsp. salt	1½ cups heavy cream

⅛ tsp. nutmeg
½ tsp. salt
3 yolks of hard-boiled egg
yellow food coloring
2 qt. water
1 tbsp. salt

For the sauce:
pan juice from cooked capon
1 cube beef bouillon or 1 tsp. beef extract
1 tbsp. cornstarch

3 tbsp. water
½ cup champagne or white wine
few drops Kitchen Bouquet

For the green noodle nest:
1 1-lb. package green noodles
salt
3 tbsp. butter
3 tbsp. fat skimmed from the cooked
  capon
2 tbsp. freshly chopped green parsley

1. To prepare the capon, first remove the wings by gently lifting the capon by a wing and, using a sharp knife, cutting at the natural joint. Next remove the thighs and legs, cutting at the natural joint but leaving some of the skin from the thigh attached. Now remove the breast meat, starting on the back near the wing cut and cutting toward the carcass. You will have to trim the meat from the wishbone, cut it loose from the top of the keel bone, then gently pull the entire breast loose from the keel bone.

2. Remove the meat from the thighs of the capon.

3. Turn the boned capon breast skin side up. Gently loosen the skin from the meat on each side of the breast and slide 3 or 4 slices of truffle into each opening, forming a row on either side of the breast.

4. Turn the breast back over and sprinkle the flesh with Chef's Salt. Lay the boned thigh meat on the breast and sprinkle additional Chef's Salt on the meat. Fold the sides of the breast around the thigh meat and shape into a neat roll.

5. Cut the vegetables coarsely and place in the bottom of a roasting pan. Lay the capon breast on top of the vegetables, with folded edges on the bottom.

6. Heat the lard in a small saucepan until it starts to smoke. Pour over the breast of the capon. Sprinkle about 1 tbsp. salt around the capon and on the vegetables, and add water until it is about an inch deep in the bottom of the pan. Cover roasting pan with a tight-fitting lid or with aluminum foil.

7. From the carcass of the capon, legs, wings, and so forth, cut 8 oz. flesh into tiny cubes or strips. Discard tendons, cartilage, and connective tissues. Grind the small pieces in a meat grinder 2 or 3 times, removing the blade each time and cleaning off the connective tissues. Then, in an electric blender, purée the meat with the egg whites, 1 cup of the cream, nutmeg, and salt. To do this you will have to work with small amounts, adding first a few pieces of the meat mixture, then a little egg white, then cream, more meat, and so on. This mixture must be completely smooth.

8. Remove ½ cup of the above mixture, and refrigerate the rest.

9. Purée the ham, hard-boiled egg yolks, and remaining cream. Add the ½ cup of capon purée to this mixture. Color this ham-capon purée so that it resembles the color of egg yolks.

10. Oil the bottom of a pan or a piece of aluminum foil and pour the ham-capon mixture onto it. Place in the freezer until firm.

11. Once the mixture is firm, cut it into small pieces and form small balls, about ½ inch in diameter. Return to freezer for about 15 minutes.

12. Bring the water and salt to a boil in a large pan.

13. To form the "eggs," put about 1 to 1½ tbsp. of the puréed capon into the palm of your hand, place an egg-yolk ball in the middle of the mixture, spoon an additional 1 to 1½ tbsp. of capon purée over the ball, and, with the help of a tablespoon, form into the shape of an egg. Make sure the ball remains in the center and that it is completely covered with the capon purée. Drop into the boiling water. Continue making eggs until you have used all the mixture and all the balls. Simmer the eggs in the boiling water for 5 to 7 minutes or until firm. Remove and immediately place in cold water.

14. Cook the green noodles in salted water according to package directions. Drain, rinse in cold running water, then place in a bowl of cold water.

15. Preheat oven to 350 degrees.

16. About 2 hours before serving time, place the roasting pan with the capon breast in the oven and bake for 1 hour. Remove cover, increase temperature to 450 degrees, and return to oven for 15 minutes or until browned on top.

17. Remove capon breast from oven and reduce oven temperature to 300 degrees. Strain the juice from the roasting pan into a saucepan. Put the saucepan over medium heat and simmer until reduced by half.

18. Add the bouillon or beef extract to the juice and stir until dissolved. Mix the 3 tbsp. water with the cornstarch. Stir the cornstarch-water mixture into the juice, bring to a boil, then reduce the heat again to a simmer. Add the wine and the Kitchen Bouquet; remove from heat but keep warm.

19. Drain the green noodles, place in a skillet, and add the butter and capon fat. Sauté for about 10 minutes, then add the parsley and continue heating for about 5 minutes.

20. Place the green noodles in a 10-inch pie dish or a shallow ovenproof dish, forming a nest. Place the cooked capon breast in the center of the nest. Arrange the quail eggs around the capon breast, on the noodles. Spoon a small amount of sauce over the top of the capon and eggs. Return to the oven for 15 minutes.

21. Remove from oven, spoon a little additional sauce over the top, and serve immediately.

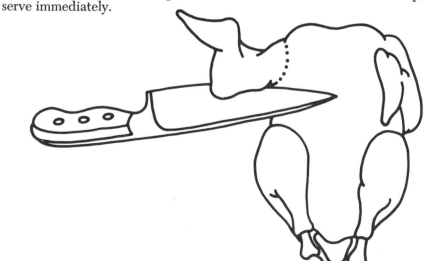

CHEF'S SECRET: When you lift the capon by holding one wing, you can feel where the joint goes from the wing into the bones of the carcass. If you cut toward the moving part then it will be very easy, even the first time, to cut off the wing with one motion. (See drawing, page 117.)

Here is the greatest secret: Don't keep your knives among other kitchen tools in a drawer, as they will never be sharp if you do. Keep the knives separate and, if possible, always in a plastic slip case.

In the instructions we mention that between grindings you should disassemble the grinder and remove the connective tissue from the blade. If you don't do this, the holes of the grinder will become blocked and the blade will be dislocated and pushed away.

FISH &

SHELLFISH

FISH

Four Times Sole
  Poached Sole
  Sautéed Sole
  Baked Fillets of Sole
  Sautéed English Style
Baked Gamefish
Fried Fish
Whole Salmon

Poached Salmon in Champagne
  Sauce
Trout in Nightgown
Bass with Fennel
Flounder Fillets
Poached Turbot
Fish Pudding
Tuna-Beans

SHELLFISH

Shrimp de Jonghe
Shrimp with Garlic and Parsley
Shrimp Creole
Shrimp Tree

Shrimp in Beer Dough
Shrimp in Dill Sauce
Lobster Parisienne
Lobster Thermidor

*O*nce a lady asked me on my television program, "How should a fresh fish smell?" When I said it shouldn't, she could not understand. She believed, the poor soul, that fresh fish smells fishy!

Most older cook books advise housewives to check the eyes of the fish. "If the eyes are clear, the fish is fresh; when they are broken, and covered with a haze, they are old." The advice is not bad but not too practical. Fish fillets, steaks, and slices have no eyes, not even skin and scales. So the modern housewife really should be told that the smell—better to say the lack of it—is her only guide. And, of course, the reputation of the dealer.

Frozen fish are a big question mark in the minds of many housewives. They should not worry. Today the most modern, expertly run food-processing plants freeze all kinds of fish with the utmost care. Commercially frozen fish are prepared and chilled under proper conditions, with the best possible controls. Unfortunately, the same cannot be said about fish caught by sportsmen and frozen at home. Do not forget that "freezer" is a misnomer; the housewife has no real freezer in her home. What she mistakenly calls a freezer is nothing but a frozen-food-holding cabinet. It is designed, made, and sold as a home storage unit for merchandise that has been purchased properly frozen.

This, of course, does not mean that the housewife cannot attempt, even fairly successfully, to freeze fish at home. The rules are simple. If you are interested, see the Chef's Secret under gamefish.

Fish & Shellfish

FISH

Four Times Sole

8 servings

Poached Sole

8 3½ - to 4-oz. fillets of sole	1 bay leaf
2 qt. water	2 to 3 sprigs parsley
1 tbsp. salt	1 stalk celery
1 cup vinegar	1 sliced carrot
10 to 12 black peppercorns	1 piece lemon rind, 2 by 1 inches

1. Combine all the ingredients except the fish fillets and bring to a boil. Boil for 15 minutes over medium heat.

2. Place the fillets in a shallow pan and ladle the hot liquid slowly over the fillets.

3. Over low heat, bring fillets and liquid to a gentle boil. Remove from the fire after 2 minutes and cover. Let stand for 3 to 4 minutes, depending on the thickness of the fillets. Serve immediately.

Sautéed Sole

8 3½ - to 4-oz. fillets of sole	1 cup all-purpose flour
4 tbsp. oil	salt and pepper to taste
4 tbsp. butter	

1. In a heavy sauté pan, slowly heat the oil and the butter. Mix the seasonings with the flour and sprinkle the fillets liberally with the mixture, turning fillets over so that both sides are sprinkled. Gently press the flour mixture into the fillets, then lift by one end and shake off excess.

2. When the shortening is hot, place the fillets in the pan, side by side. Turn over immediately.

3. Gently shaking the pan, cook the fillets over medium heat for 3 to 4 minutes. Remove to a serving platter or to individual plates. Serve immediately.

Baked Fillets of Sole

8 3½- to 4-oz. fillets of sole   1 cup white wine
salt and pepper to taste   1 cup water or 1 cup fish stock or Court
2 to 3 tbsp. butter   Bouillon (see page 131)

1. Preheat the oven to 350 degrees. Carefully brush an ovenproof dish with the butter.

2. Salt and pepper the fillets and fold them in half across the width. Place them, slightly overlapping, in the dish.

3. Mix the white wine with the water, stock, or Court Bouillon. Bring the mixture to a rolling boil and spoon the hot liquid over the fish.

4. Cover the ovenproof dish with its own cover or with aluminum foil. Bake for 15 to 25 minutes, depending on the thickness of the fillets.

Sautéed English Style

8 3½- to 4-oz. fillets of real Dover sole   1 cup bread crumbs
8 to 10 tbsp. butter   salt and pepper to taste
4 tbsp. oil

1. Heat the oil and 4 tbsp. of the butter together in a heavy sauté pan or frying pan. Melt the remaining butter separately, with the oil.

2. Mix the salt and pepper with the bread crumbs. Dip one side of each fillet in the melted butter and then press it, buttered side down, into the bread-crumb mixture.

3. Place the fillets with the uncoated sides down into the hot shortening in the pan. Tilt the pan and spoon the shortening over the bread-crumb-covered side, using a long wooden-handled spoon.

4. Remove the fillets to a hot serving platter and serve.

CHEF'S SECRET: If you use frozen fillets, defrost them by submerging them in room-temperature water after removing them from their cardboard box. If they are wrapped in cellophane or plastic, start defrosting them while they are still wrapped and remove the fillets later.

According to U.S. government regulations, Dover sole must be flown into the country frozen; this is "real" Dover sole. However, all kinds of sole are sold under the name Dover. All soles and flounders belong to the same family, but the texture, flavor, and water content of Dover sole are entirely different from the others.

If you use real Dover sole, the fish handler will probably fillet the fish for you.

In many fish stores and supermarkets, it is possible to buy individual frozen sole fillets or, even better, fresh rex sole, lemon sole, or grey sole.

All uncooked sole fillets are very easy to handle, but only true Dover sole remains firm after cooking. Therefore, be very careful in handling the cooked fillets. With a fairly large spatula eased under the fillet so that nothing hangs over on the sides, you can carefully lift the fish from the pan or cooking dish.

The English style of sautéing requires some skill. Try it first with only one or two fillets. In this case, of course, don't heat all the shortening at once. Learn to tilt the pan so that you can spoon the hot shortening easily, without touching the fillets.

Baked Gamefish

3 servings for each pound whole fish

(Amount of ingredients depends on the
   size of fish)
gamefish
salt
pepper
garlic salt
oil

butter
1 fresh or dried herb, such as parsley,
   fennel, or dill
lemon juice
sliced lemon
fresh green parsley for decoration

1. Preheat oven to 350 degrees. Lay fish in a flat, shallow dish, lined with aluminum foil and slightly coated with oil.

2. Sprinkle the inside of the fish with lemon juice, then with salt, pepper, and a very small amount of garlic salt. Rub salt and pepper into the top skin of the fish and coat the fish lightly with oil.

3. Bake until the fish is flaky and firm to the touch. The amount of time varies, depending on the size of the fish.

4. Pour off the oil and coat the fish with soft, room-temperature butter. Sprinkle with the herb of your choice and return to the oven for 3 to 5 minutes.

5. Remove the fish from the oven and place on a serving dish. Decorate with lemon slices and fresh green parsley.

CHEF's SECRET: Gamefish refers to all fish that a sportsman is permitted to catch, as opposed to fish purchased from a market. Husbands are proud fishermen and will be appreciative if the gamefish they catch and bring home is served.

You may freeze a gamefish if you don't want to cook it immediately, but don't keep it frozen longer than a month. The proper way to freeze the fish is:
1. Be sure the fish is completely cleaned and gutted.
2. Scrape off all scales and discard.
3. If you want to keep the head on, be sure to take out the gills, because they are very bitter and will spoil the whole fish.
4. Rinse the inside and dry the fish on an absorbent paper towel. If the fish weighs 2 lb. or more, place a double sheet of aluminum foil or plastic wrap in its cavity. This will be a great help in defrosting the fish.
5. Wrap the fish first in plastic wrap, then in aluminum foil. After it is frozen, pack it in freezer paper or in a box for protection during storage.

If you plan to bake the frozen fish without thawing it first, you should pre-pare it before you freeze it. After washing and wiping the cavity, spread the room-temperature butter on the skin; sprinkle the inside with lemon juice, salt, pepper, and garlic salt. Rub some oil into the skin and, in this case, pack it in double aluminum foil instead of plastic wrap.

To bake, start the frozen fish at 300 degrees instead of 350 degrees. Leave it completely wrapped in the foil. Open the foil when a toothpick easily pierces the fish at its thickest part and finish the baking at 350 degrees according to the recipe.

To defrost an unprepared fish before baking, the best way is to submerge it in cold water in a sink and keep it there until it reaches the temperature of the water and is flexible.

Some gamefish are very dry. Before baking these fish, cut gashes in the fish about 1½ to 2 inches apart and insert ½ slice bacon in each gash. (See drawing.)

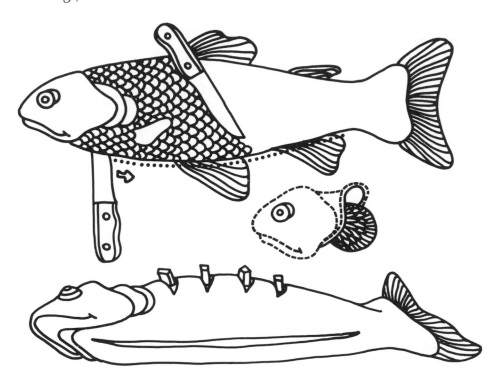

Fried Fish

8 servings

8 4- to 6-oz. fish fillets	2 cups plus 2 to 3 tbsp. milk
salt and pepper to taste	1 cup flour

2 large eggs or 3 medium eggs
4 cups fresh, dry, good-quality bread
  crumbs

oil, butter, or lard—combination of
two

1. Thoroughly mix salt and pepper into the flour. Put 2 cups of the milk into a pie pan or flat soup plate. Beat the eggs with the remainder of the milk and put in a separate plate or pie pan. Have the flour and bread crumbs ready on separate sheets of wax paper.

2. One at a time, dip the fish fillets first into the milk, being sure to coat completely. Shake off excess milk. Lay the milk-dipped fillet on the flour and toss flour over it, covering completely. Gently press the floured fillet with a spatula so that the flour adheres to the milk. Then shake off the excess flour.

3. Dip the flour-coated fillet into the egg wash. Let the excess egg drip off, then bury completely in the bread crumbs and press gently but firmly so that the breading adheres to the egg.

4. Lay the prepared fillets on a tray. When they are all breaded, fry them over medium heat in a heavy frying pan filled ¾ to 1 inch deep with the shortening of your choice. Turn only once, carefully, with a spatula and keep them warm on absorbent paper until serving.

CHEF'S SECRET: You can bread hundreds of pieces of fish or meat without having lumps on your fingers and without messing up the flour or bread crumbs if you follow this easy rule: With one of your hands, handle only the raw fillet, the milk-dipped fillet, and the egg-dipped fillet. With your other hand, handle the flour-dipped fillet and the crumb-dipped fillet. In this way, your wet hand never touches the dry ingredients, so the crumbs cannot stick to your fingers.

Whole Salmon

15 to 20 servings

1 whole salmon, 5 to 6 lb., ready for
  stuffing
salt and pepper to taste
3 envelopes unflavored gelatin
1 3-oz. package cream cheese
1 large carrot

red food coloring
1 tbsp. sugar
juice of 1 lemon
2 cups water
small, pitted black olives
oil

1. Preheat oven to 375 degrees. Line a large baking pan with a double thickness of aluminum foil. Wash the salmon with a cloth dipped in cold water mixed with the juice of half a lemon. Sprinkle salt and pepper generously in the inside cavity and sprinkle half an envelope of dry gelatin evenly on the inside surface.

2. Fold a piece of aluminum foil into three layers. Make sure the folded piece is as long as the salmon plus 3 inches on both ends, and as wide as the salmon at its thickest part. Pour some oil on this aluminum strip. Oil the double aluminum sheet in the pan. Place oiled aluminum strip on the foil in the pan and lay the whole salmon on the strip.

3. Rub the skin with salt and pepper (about 2 tbsp. for a salmon this size). Cover the tail of the salmon with several layers of foil, well oiled both inside and outside.

4. Place the fish in the oven and bake for 1 to 1½ hours, depending on thickness, or until it is firm to the touch and flakes easily. Baste it with oil 2 or 3 times during the baking. Remove from the oven and let cool until it is easy to handle.

5. In the meantime, slice the carrot crosswise into ⅛-inch slices and blanch the slices for 8 to 10 minutes by dropping them into boiling water. Rinse until cool and then keep in cold water.

6. Dissolve the remaining 2½ envelopes of gelatin in ½ cup cold water. Mix the sugar, the 2 cups of water, the juice of half a lemon, and ½ tsp. salt. Bring the mixture to a boil. When it reaches the boiling point, stir in the dissolved gelatin. Remove from the heat as soon as the gelatin mixture starts to boil again. Cool slightly.

7. In an electric mixer, start to mix the cream cheese and add, drop by drop, 4 tbsp. of the lukewarm gelatin. Add 2 to 3 drops of red food coloring to the rest of the gelatin.

8. Using a kitchen scissors, carefully cut off the skin of the salmon, leaving a 1-inch border on both sides. With your finger, starting by the head and working toward the tail, very carefully remove the dark grey substance running along the middle of the salmon where the back fillet and belly fillet meet. (See drawing.)

9. Set the pink gelatin into an ice water bath and, with a soft brush, brush it onto the surface of the salmon flesh. The first coat will soak in quickly, but the second coat will cover the flesh and remaining skin and give the fish a shiny appearance.

10. Scrape the cream cheese–gelatin mixture into a decorating bag with a plain ¼-inch tube. Run a line at the border of the flesh and the skin all around the gelatin-coated surface. If you have left the head on, draw a circle around the eye and fill it in with half of a black olive. Run a line around the mouth and the edge of the gill. Decorate the tail with straight lines.

11. With a small scalloped cookie cutter, cut enough slices of the carrot to decorate one long cream cheese line with the carrot flowers.

12. Split the pitted black olives in half. Dip the olives in the pink gelatin and press one half onto the middle of each carrot flower. Chill the fish thoroughly in the refrigerator. Serve it with mayonnaise (see page 214).

CHEF'S SECRET: If you order the salmon boned and ready for stuffing, your fish dealer will remove all the bones from it so it will be very easy to cut when serving.

The multi-folded aluminum foil strip with the 3-inch extended ends makes it easy to lift the baked fish out of the foil-lined pan and to place it on the serving platter.

If you don't have a serving tray or platter large enough for the fish, draw the outline of the fish, leaving about 1 inch all around, on a piece of corrugated cardboard. Cut it out with a sharp knife and cover it neatly with aluminum foil. After you place the fish on the foil platter, you can fold back the foil and stick long-stemmed fresh green parsley, watercress, or curly endive under the fish so it covers the edges.

Cream cheese mixed with gelatin is the easiest decorating material for any housewife; it will stay nice and firm overnight, without discoloration, so that you can completely finish the decorating a day in advance when preparing for a party.

Blanching the carrots will preserve their color. They won't dehydrate, and coating them with a little gelatin will give them the appearance of black-eyed Susans. This decoration is very effective and colorful, and no skill is needed to do it.

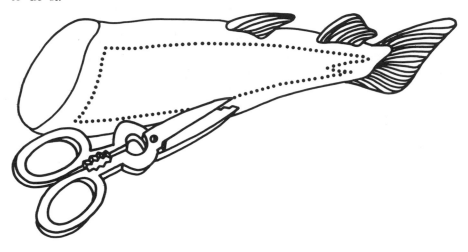

Poached Salmon in Champagne Sauce

8 servings

8 salmon steaks, 5 oz. each
4 tbsp. butter
1 cup half-and-half
1 tbsp. flour
1 tbsp. cornstarch
salt and white pepper to taste
⅛ tsp. mace

1 tsp. granulated sugar
1 cup dry champagne or, if not available, dry white wine
8 slices black truffle or 4 black olives (optional)
1 egg yolk

1. In a shallow dish, poach the salmon steaks in simmering, lightly salted water for 6 to 8 minutes, depending on their thickness. Remove them carefully with a wide spatula to a warm serving platter.

2. Melt the butter in a saucepan. In a bowl, mix the flour, cornstarch, sugar, mace, salt, and pepper. Slowly stir in the half-and-half, mixing until the mixture is completely free of lumps.

3. Pour this mixture into the warm butter and stir until it starts to bubble. Immediately remove from the fire and stir in the champagne or wine, reserving 3 tbsp. of the champagne.

4. When the champagne is completely mixed into the sauce, put the sauce back on low heat and stir until it boils again. Remove and set it in a warm place, and let it stand until serving time.

5. Just before serving, mix the reserved champagne with the egg yolk. Spoon a little of the hot sauce into the yolk-champagne mixture. Stir it and then pour slowly into the sauce. Spoon the sauce over the salmon. Decorate with truffles or halved olives; serve immediately.

CHEF'S SECRET: The mace enhances the champagne flavor but too much of it would spoil the sauce, so be very careful when using it.

The egg yolk will give the desirable faint yellow hue to the sauce. If for any reason you want to omit it, replace it by adding 1 tsp. more cornstarch and one drop of yellow food coloring to the sauce. Of course, the starch is added with the other dry ingredients.

If you must use an ordinary white wine instead of champagne, add a few drops of lemon juice or orange juice and 2 to 3 tbsp. ginger ale or club soda to it before stirring the wine into the sauce.

Trout in Nightgown

8 servings

8 fresh or frozen rainbow trout, 3 to 4 oz. each, or same size fillets cut from larger trout	1 tbsp. chopped fresh parsley ½ cup cream and ½ cup milk, or 1 cup half-and-half
1½ cups fresh button mushrooms	salt and pepper to taste
2 tbsp. butter	4 tbsp. oil
2 tbsp. flour	8 thin crêpes (see page 262)

1. Preheat oven to 350 degrees. Sprinkle trout lightly with salt and pepper.

2. Rinse mushrooms quickly and shake or swing dry in a towel. Chop them very fine.

3. Melt the butter in a saucepan. Add the finely chopped mushrooms and stir, over high heat, for a minute or so.

4. Blend the flour into the half-and-half or cream-milk mixture and add this to the mushroom mixture. Add parsley and a little salt and cook, stirring constantly, until it becomes a thick, greyish-brown substance.

5. Press the mixture through a fine sieve or run it through the blender.

6. Cut the 8 crêpes so that each resembles a long nightgown (see drawing). Divide the mushroom purée into eight portions and spread one-eighth on one side of each nightgown. Set aside.

7. In a large pan, bake the fish (skin side up, if fillets) in the oil for approximately 15 minutes. Then cover each fish with a nightgown so that the side with the mushroom paste is on the fish. Bake the fish for another 8 to 12 minutes, depending on the size.

8. Remove to a serving platter. Decorate with lemon wedges and parsley. Serve with Sauce Louis (see page 215), or with mushroom sauce (see page 208) or homemade mayonnaise (see page 214).

CHEF'S SECRET: Clean the fish thoroughly and pat it dry with paper towels. This will make the trout's skin very tasty.

It is difficult to determine when the cream-flour mixture should be poured into the mushrooms. When a dark liquid starts to ooze from the pieces of mushroom, it is time to pour in the mixture.

If you have any extra mushrooms, and if you have a few more crêpes, you may thin this mushroom purée with a few tablespoons of sour cream, spread it on the crêpes, roll them jelly-roll fashion, and bake them with the fish.

Sometimes the crêpes start to curl up and dry out on the cut edges during baking. To prevent this, you can brush the nightgowns with a soft food brush dipped in a little milk or water.

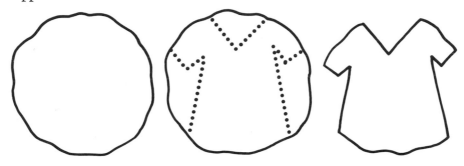

Bass with Fennel

6 servings

1 2½-lb. sea bass, cleaned, head and tail removed	2 cups dry white wine
salt	4 tbsp. butter
black pepper	4 tsp. fennel seeds, ground
	chopped parsley

1. Preheat oven to 375 degrees.
2. Score both sides of the fish with a sharp knife.
3. Sprinkle inside and outside with salt and pepper.
4. Place in a casserole dish that is large enough to hold the fish comfortably.
5. Add the wine; dot with 2 tbsp. of the butter and sprinkle the fennel seeds over the top.
6. Cover with a lid or foil; bake for about 20 minutes or until the fish is tender.
7. Remove the fish to a large serving platter.
8. With a wooden spoon, swirl the remaining 2 tbsp. of butter into the pan juices until melted. Pour over the fish. Sprinkle with chopped parsley and serve immediately.

CHEF'S SECRET: To score the fish with a sharp knife can be disastrous, as you can slash it instead of scoring if you are not careful. To avoid this, take a very sharp pointed knife and wrap its blade with a strong paper strip such as a folded double page of a newspaper, so that only a half-inch of the blade's tip is exposed. Secure the paper cover on the knife with masking tape or transparent tape, and score the fish holding the knife by the covered blade. Don't hesitate to plunge the knife, since it can't go deeper than a half-inch. If you do much scoring of fish, beef, ham, pork, and so forth, it is worthwhile to prepare an old knife for scoring by permanently taping it with electrician's tape. Be sure to keep it clean.

To remove the fish easily to a large serving platter, triple fold heavy-duty aluminum foil with both ends 3 inches longer than the fish itself. First lay the foil, lightly oiled, into the casserole, then lay the fish on it. It will be easy to lift the foil and discard it after the fish is securely on the platter.

To swirl the butter into the pan juices, strain the juices from the casserole into a saucepan. Bring the juice to a boil. Make sure your swirling butter is hard and cold. Break it into 6 or 8 pieces, and as soon as they are in the pan, lift the pan off the flame and swirl the butter into the hot juice with a wooden spoon. If you wish, you may sprinkle a few drops of lemon juice into the sauce. Definitely serve lemon in some form with this fish.

Flounder Fillets

8 servings

8 flounder fillets, 4 to 6 oz. each	3 tbsp. milk
salt and pepper to taste	bread crumbs
1½ lemons	shortening for frying
flour	parsley for decoration
3 medium eggs	

1. Salt and pepper the fillets and squeeze some lemon juice from the ½ lemon over them. Then bury them one by one in the flour. Press hard with both palms so that they are completely coated with the flour; be sure that no part of the fish remains uncoated.

2. Beat the eggs and milk together. Remove the fish from the flour and dip them into the egg wash. Let the excess egg wash drip off, then bury, again one by one, in a large pile of dry bread crumbs. Press with both hands so that the bread crumbs adhere to the egg wash.

3. Carefully lay the fillets on a tray and cover with wax paper. After about 10 minutes, gently turn each one over.

4. Heat shortening in a large frying pan, using enough so that you have a depth of about three-fourths of an inch. It is preferable to use a mixture of two fats, such as oil and lard, oil and butter, or butter and lard. Fry the fish until it is golden brown. Remove to absorbent paper toweling. Serve it with the remaining lemon, sliced or cut in wedges, and parsley.

CHEF'S SECRET: The lemon juice sprinkled on the flounder gives a very good flavor to the fish and keeps it firm. It is very important to "bury" the fillets in the flour and the crumbs, because if any part of the fish is exposed to the shortening during frying, the shortening will seep in between the coating and the fish, causing the coating to fall off.

Beat the eggs and milk with a fork. Then let the mixture run through a fine sieve. This will break up the egg white so that no large amount will stick to the fillet.

Poached Turbot

2 to 4 servings

2 1-lb. fillets of turbot, skin removed
2 tbsp. butter

For Court Bouillon:
1 cup dry white wine
1 qt. water or 2 cups water and 2 cups
   clam juice
2 carrots, diced

2 medium onions, diced
2 shallots, minced
3 small sprigs parsley
1 tsp. salt
½ tsp. thyme
½ bay leaf
6 peppercorns, crushed

1. Place all ingredients except the butter and the turbot in a large saucepan. Bring to a boil, reduce heat, and simmer for 1 hour.

2. Strain this Court Bouillon through a fine sieve.

3. Butter a deep ovenproof casserole and place the turbot fillets in it, with the side from which the skin was removed up. Cover with the Court Bouillon, with at least one inch of the liquid above the surface of the fillets. Cover the casserole with a lid or with aluminum foil.

4. Place the casserole over low heat. Maintain the liquid at a simmer for 20 minutes. The flesh should flake when separated with a fork.

5. Carefully lift the fish from the Court Bouillon and let it drain on a platter.

CHEF'S SECRET: Unfortunately, the law does not always protect the consumer as it should. Besides the fact that real turbot is a very expensive fish, other countries pack much lower-quality species and call them turbot. When you buy turbot, be sure that the fish you buy is extremely firm, snow white, and has no "watery" appearance. NO BARGAINS EXIST IN TURBOT. The price per pound is comparable to that of lobster. Turbot, just like real Dover sole, firms up when cooked, so you won't have any difficulty in lifting the pieces from the Court Bouillon.

Leftover poached turbot makes the world's finest fish salad when mixed with chopped celery and mayonnaise. Keep this in mind while shopping.

Fish Pudding

4 to 6 servings

1 lb. halibut, sole, haddock, or cod
   fillets
3 egg whites

1 cup heavy cream
1 tsp. salt
¼ tsp. white pepper

1 pinch cayenne
¼ tsp. nutmeg
¼ tsp. celery salt

few drops onion juice
butter

1. Preheat oven to 350 degrees.
2. Put fish through food chopper, using finest blade.
3. Put ground fish in a bowl and set it in a pan of ice water.
4. Slowly stir in the egg whites; beat with a wire whip to keep mixture smooth.
5. Stir in cream very slowly.
6. Add salt, pepper, cayenne, nutmeg, celery salt, and onion juice.
7. Let stand at room temperature for 1 hour.
8. Pour the mixture into a well-buttered 1-qt. mold. Set the mold in another baking dish which has 1 inch of hot water in the bottom. Cover the mold with foil.
9. Bake about 45 to 60 minutes or until firm. Serve warm or chilled. If you like, pour off the juice which will form around the mold.

CHEF'S SECRET: If you do not have a food chopper, use a blender. Cut the fish in finger-sized pieces and blend at low speed.

If you use an electric blender, place the container in the freezer for about 2 hours before using it instead of putting it in a pan of ice water.

Be sure that the cream you use is heavy whipping cream and that it is very fresh. Lighter cream will not do.

Tuna-Beans

10 servings

1 lb. dried white (haricot) beans
salt
water
½ cup olive oil
1 clove garlic, crushed
5 to 6 large ripe tomatoes, peeled and
chopped

12 oz. canned white-meat tuna fish in
oil, broken into large pieces
1½ tsp. sweet basil
freshly ground black pepper

1. Soak the beans in cold water for at least 8 hours.
2. Drain the beans and cook in salted water until tender, about 1½ to 2 hours. Keep them covered with water throughout the cooking time. Drain.
3. Heat the oil in a large saucepan. Sauté the garlic until browned.
4. Discard the garlic pieces and add the tomatoes. Sprinkle lightly with salt; cook for 10 minutes over high heat.
5. Stir in the beans and tuna fish.
6. Sprinkle with sweet basil and plenty of pepper. Cook for 10 minutes longer over low heat. Serve very hot.

CHEF'S SECRET: In better grocery stores, you can get canned white beans. If you don't want to cook your own, you can use two cans of beans, drained and rinsed under hot and then cold water.

To peel the tomatoes, place 1 qt. water in a small pot and bring it to a boil. Drop in not more than two tomatoes at a time and leave them for 30 seconds. Immediately remove and place the tomatoes in ice water to chill. If the tomatoes are unripe, this may require 35 to 40 seconds instead of 30 seconds.

Italian imported canned plum or pear tomatoes can be substituted for the fresh tomatoes.

If you don't trust yourself with the garlic, use garlic salt or liquid garlic instead. But if you want the real thing, use a whole clove and crush it gently with the side of a coffee cup, first rubbing the clove in the corner of a kitchen towel.

SHELLFISH

Shrimp de Jonghe

6 servings

2 lb. shrimp, cooked, peeled, and de- veined
butter to line the casserole
¾ cup dry white wine
½ tsp. black pepper
¼ cup butter

1 cup fresh bread crumbs
2 garlic cloves, chopped very fine and put through a garlic press
2 tsp. sweet basil
½ tsp. salt
1 tbsp. chopped parsley

1. Preheat oven to 350 degrees.
2. Select the proper-sized casserole; the shrimp should cover the bottom while slightly overlapping each other.
3. Coat the bottom and sides of the casserole with butter.
4. Place the shrimp in the casserole as described in step 2.
5. Add the wine and sprinkle with pepper.
6. Mix all the remaining ingredients with the ¼ cup of butter in a small bowl until well blended.
7. Dot the entire surface of the shrimp with the butter mixture. Be sure the dots are the same size and that all the shrimp are covered.
8. Bake for 20 to 25 minutes, or until the butter is melted and bubbly and the surface browned. Serve immediately.

CHEF'S SECRET: To coat the casserole evenly, chill the dish in the refrigerator, then brush it with melted butter.

Be sure that the wine you use is definitely "dry." If you don't know about wine, ask your wine dealer instead of ruining the dish.

If possible, avoid using commercial bread crumbs for this dish. Make your own from leftover French or Italian bread by crushing it with a rolling pin.

The best part of the Shrimp de Jonghe is the juices which will develop during baking. Be sure that you have plenty of fresh bread on the table and encourage the guests to dip the bread in the juices and eat it.

Shrimp with Garlic and Parsley

8 servings

32 to 40 medium or 24 to 32 large raw shrimp, peeled and deveined
3 large cloves garlic, peeled, sliced, and slightly crushed
4 tbsp. butter

4 tbsp. oil
salt and freshly ground pepper to taste
2 tbsp. dry cocktail sherry or any other dry white wine
½ cup freshly chopped parsley

1. Place the garlic in a small, cold saucepan. Put the pan over medium heat and add the butter and oil. Heat until the edges of the garlic start to turn light brown. Strain the shortening through a sieve into a frying pan.

2. Add the shrimp to the frying pan at once and add half of the parsley. Keep turning the shrimp with a spatula until they become firm and turn pink. Remove them to a serving platter.

3. Add the wine to the juices in the pan. Add the remainder of the parsley, season with salt and pepper, and bring to a boil. Pour this mixture over the shrimp immediately. Serve on toast, over rice, or on mashed potatoes.

CHEF'S SECRET: Handling the garlic according to directions will give you all the flavor you need without any garlic particles.

Cooking some of the parsley with the shrimp, then adding more at the last minute, gives two distinctively different flavors.

Cooking the liquid out of the shrimp and mixing it with the wine and shortening makes a tasty sauce which will be absorbed by the toast, rice, or potatoes.

Shrimp Creole

6 servings

⅓ cup oil
½ cup diced onion
¼ cup diced green pepper
¼ cup thinly sliced celery
¼ cup flour
1 cup hot water
1 8-oz. can tomato sauce
½ cup tomato catsup
1 tsp. salt

1 tsp. sugar
¼ tsp. garlic salt
2 bay leaves
1 pinch thyme
1 dash Tabasco sauce
1 lb. shrimp, peeled, deveined, and thawed
2 tsp. lemon juice

1. In a heavy cast-iron skillet, heat the oil to the smoking point.

2. Sauté the onion, celery, and green pepper until tender.

3. Stir in the flour, then the hot water.

4. Add all the remaining ingredients except the shrimp and lemon juice. Cook over low heat for 15 or 20 minutes.

5. Add the shrimp; cook for an additional 4 minutes.

6. Remove from heat; discard bay leaves.

7. Add the lemon juice. Stir. Serve over cooked rice.

CHEF'S SECRET: The proper way to sauté the onion, celery, and green pepper is as follows: First put the onion in the heated oil, stir it, and cover it. Don't lift cover for about 4 minutes. Then lift the cover, add the celery and green pepper, and stir vigorously. Cover again and set the heat at medium.

The best way to stir in the flour is to use a small strainer to shake the flour evenly over the surface of the sautéed vegetables. Then stir and, while stirring, add the hot water.

Shrimp Tree

servings depend on size of tree

styrofoam cone	shrimp
parsley	cherry tomatoes

1. Buy a styrofoam cone in a dime store, department store, florist's shop, or florist supply store. Secure the styrofoam cone in any container you choose.

2. With a sharp tool such as an ice pick, make holes in the cone and insert in each hole a very small bunch of parsley sprigs tied together firmly with a green florist wire.

3. Sprinkle the whole tree liberally with ice-cold water and cover it with a water-dipped kitchen towel. The tree will stay surprisingly fresh this way in the refrigerator for as long as three or four days.

4. Using toothpicks, place on it peeled, boiled shrimp, cherry tomatoes, or any other bite-sized tidbits which will look appetizing.

CHEF'S SECRET: To make the little bunches of parsley, cut the stems of the sprigs at an angle so that after you wrap them with florist wire they will form a point and stick into the foam without breaking.

Keep the parsley fresh by soaking the bunches in ice water as you are making them; then place them on the tree.

Shrimp in Beer Dough

8 servings

24 large raw shrimp, split in half lengthwise	½ tsp. baking powder
2 whole eggs	¾ tsp. salt
1 cup flour	1 to 1½ cups beer
	shortening for frying

1. If possible, leave a part of the tail on both halves when splitting the shrimp in half.

2. Combine the dry ingredients in a mixing bowl.

3. Separate the eggs. Add the yolks to 1 cup of beer and stir the egg yolk–beer mixture into the dry ingredients.

4. With an electric beater, beat the egg whites until they form soft peaks. Do not over-beat. Gently fold the whites into the beer dough. If it is too stiff, add a little beer; if too loose, sprinkle a little flour over the top and gently fold it into the dough with a spatula.

5. Heat enough shortening to cover a depth of 1½ to 2 inches in a frying pan until it starts to smoke. Holding the shrimp by the tail, dip them one by one into the beer dough and fry until golden. Place on absorbent paper. Serve hot.

CHEF'S SECRET: Be sure that eggs, flour, and beer are at room temperature, and make the mixture about 30 minutes before you plan to use it.

The consistency of the perfect beer dough is similar to American pancake batter. It is very hard to give exact measurements for this dough recipe because of the differences in flour, size of eggs, and so forth. Try one or two shrimp before you cook the others. Then you will be able to adjust the dough if necessary. If a shrimp loses its coating when placed in the hot shortening, you need more flour. If it sinks to the bottom of the frying pan, you need more beer.

This beer batter may also be used for strips of summer sausage or salami, Swiss cheese, thin strips of fish fillet, and other foods.

Shrimp in Dill Sauce

8 servings

2 cups small shrimp (about 1½ lb.)
4 tbsp. butter
2 tbsp. oil
1 cup milk
4 tbsp. flour
1 cup freshly chopped dill

½ to 1 cup chicken broth or water (depending on how thick a sauce is desired)
salt and pepper to taste
2 to 3 tbsp. vinegar or lemon juice
1 cup commercial sour cream

1. Cook shrimp, rinse under cold tap water, and keep at room temperature.
2. Melt the shortening in a saucepan. Combine the flour with the milk, add a little salt and pepper, and stir the flour-milk mixture into the shortening together with 1 tbsp. freshly chopped dill.
3. Keep stirring until the mixture starts to cook. Remove it from the fire and dilute it with chicken broth or water. Correct seasoning by adding more salt or pepper if needed.
4. Just before serving, bring the sauce to a boil again. Add the shrimp and the sour cream, then add most of the dill and the vinegar or lemon juice. Serve with boiled rice or mashed potatoes. Sprinkle top with the reserved dill.

CHEF'S SECRET: The boiled shrimp will not dry out or get rubbery if kept at room temperature in tepid water.

Adding lemon juice or vinegar to the sauce will strengthen the dill taste.

Depending on the sour cream you use, you may have to add a very little sugar to improve the taste.

Lobster Parisienne

8 to 10 servings

1 live lobster, 3 to 4 lb.
boiling, salted water, with a handful of seaweed thrown in if possible

1 large head iceberg lettuce
2 cucumbers, 6 to 7 inches long, 1½ to 2 inches in diameter

8 small or medium grade AA eggs, hard-boiled, or 8 firm, ripe tomatoes, 1½ inches in diameter
1 stalk celery, chopped fine
1 cup homemade or good-quality mayonnaise (see page 214)
salt and white pepper to taste

few drops Worcestershire sauce
2 envelopes unflavored gelatin
1 cup water
few drops red food coloring
truffle slices
parsley

1. Plunge the lobster into the boiling, salted water and cook it until the shell turns completely red. Immediately place the pot in the sink and start running cold water into the pot to cool it. As soon as you can handle the pot, pour off the water, then refill the pot with cold water and add 3 to 4 trays of ice cubes. Leave the lobster in the ice water until completely chilled. You can do this the day before and then refrigerate the lobster overnight after it has chilled in the ice water.

2. Once the lobster is completely chilled, lay it on its back. Holding the tail firmly in one hand, cut out the belly membrane, starting under the middle of the tail fins and cutting toward the body, inside of the armor along the scalloped edge. Repeat on the other side. Lift the membrane from the tail in one piece.

3. Insert a finger under the tail end and loosen the meat where the tail is secured to the armor. The flesh of the tail will start to curl up as you press your finger in deeper and deeper. Hold the flesh with your thumb; when your finger reaches the point where the body armor and the tail armor meet, press your thumb and finger firmly, and gently remove the tail meat in one piece. Set it aside.

4. Reach into the body cavity and remove the lobster's stomach and the coral or emerald. Discard the stomach; save the coral or emerald for decorating canapés (see page 8).

5. Hold one of the larger claws firmly with one hand. Using a lobster scissors, cut into the soft membrane that separates the large claw from the last joint of the leg. Using only the tip of the scissors, gently cut into the large claw, about half an inch from one edge. Remove the scissors, insert it again so that it is pointing to the opposite edge, and cut again. Repeat this, alternating sides and forming 2 half circles which will meet, so that you can lift out the bottom of the claw armor and then remove the claw meat. You will have to make a cut at the joint of the claws in order to remove the meat. Repeat this procedure with the second claw.

6. Cut the head of lettuce in half, using a stainless steel knife. Place one half, cut side down, on a large oval platter. Cut some of the remaining half head of lettuce into shreds and cover the bottom of the platter. Mount the lobster shell so that both its claws are encircling the lettuce and its body and tail gently slope to the opposite end of the serving platter. Secure the lobster to the lettuce with toothpicks, bamboo skewers, or thin florist wire. Refrigerate.

7. Cut each cucumber in half crosswise. Cut off ends. Form two crowns from each half as follows: With a small knife, cut halfway into the cucumber with a diagonal cut, turn a little and make another cut in the opposite direction, forming two sides of a triangle. Continue around the center of the halved cucumber, reversing the diagonal cuts but always forming a "v" shape. Once you have cut completely around the cucumber, the two sections

should pull apart and the top of each will form a crown (see drawing, page 139).

8. Using a melon-ball cutter, remove from the crown end the soft pulp of each cup.

9. Peel the hard-boiled eggs. Cut a slice from the top and bottom of each egg. With a melon-ball cutter, remove some of the egg white and yolk, forming egg cups. Be careful not to break through the sides. You can substitute tomatoes for the cucumbers or eggs if desired. Be sure, if you use tomatoes, that they are firm and won't collapse after you remove the inside.

10. With a very sharp knife, cut 8 thin slices from the tail meat. Cut from the red surface of the claw meat 8 tiny diamonds. Set aside.

11. Chop and mix the remaining lobster meat, the insides of the hard-boiled eggs, and the celery; add the salt, white pepper, and Worcestershire sauce. Gently fold in the mayonnaise.

12. Divide this mixture between the cucumber crowns, eggs, or tomatoes. Chill.

13. Dissolve the gelatin in ⅓ cup of the water. Bring the remaining ⅔ cup of water to a boil, and stir the dissolved gelatin into the boiling water. Remove from the fire. Pour ½ cup into another small container and add to it a few drops of red food coloring.

14. Place the container of tinted gelatin in an ice water bath until it reaches a consistency similar to egg white. Remove it immediately from the cold water bath and brush a coating over the lobster shell.

15. Add a few drops of lemon juice or vinegar and a sprinkling of sugar or salt to the ½ cup of clear gelatin. Stir it gently until it starts to get syrupy. Refrigerate it for a few minutes or put it in an ice water bath. Using a soft, small pastry brush, coat each of the lobster medallions cut from the tail meat with a very thin coat of the gelatin and arrange the medallions along the back of the lobster tail. Decorate each medallion with a slice of truffle or the diamonds cut from the lobster claws. Lightly brush over the top of the decoration with gelatin.

16. Arrange the salad cups along the side of the platter, in front of the lobster. Decorate with parsley. Serve with additional mayonnaise or Sauce Louis (see page 215).

CHEF'S SECRET: Many housewives hate to kill a lobster and hate even more to plunge it into the boiling water or to heat it slowly to death. A very fast, secure, and humane way is to press the lobster to the table with one hand, grab the middle fan between the thumb and index finger, and turn it quickly and firmly in a clockwise direction, making a full circle. If you don't want to do this, buy the lobster alive and then ask the fishmonger to do it for you. Of course, if you let him do it, cook the lobster as soon as you get home.

A properly cooked lobster will stay overnight in a cool part of the refrigerator without any spoilage.

To be sure that the tail doesn't curl up after boiling, you can tie the body and tail to a piece of wood or press it gently between two cookie sheets before refrigeration.

If you want your Lobster Parisienne to look very professional, cut the two long antennae to the same length and insert a florist wire in each. (The antenna is hollow, so the wire will go in easily.) Then tie the two wires together and bend the antennae into a nice arch. This must be done right after chilling the cooked lobster. An hour later, the antennae will be too brittle.

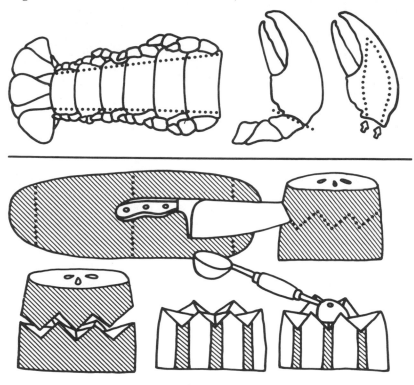

Lobster Thermidor

4 servings

2 live lobsters, 1½ to 2 lb. each
4 tbsp. butter
2 tsp. flour
¾ cup heavy cream
1 cup canned chicken broth
salt
Spanish paprika

1 or 2 drops Tabasco or sprinkling of cayenne (optional)
2 tbsp. medium sherry
4 slices of day-old white bread, crusts removed, torn into pea-sized pieces and dried

1. Boil and cool the lobster according to the directions given in the recipe for Lobster Parisienne (page 136). Split the lobster lengthwise, remove the meat from the tail and claws, and discard stomach and membrane. Wash the shells and place them, cut side down, on a cookie sheet. Refrigerate.

2. Cut all the lobster meat from the tail, body, and claws into cubes. Melt 1 tbsp. butter in a heavy saucepan. Stir the flour into the cream, being sure that there are no lumps. Add the chicken broth to the cream-flour mixture.

3. When the butter is hot and bubbly, gently pour in the cream-flour-broth mixture, stirring constantly. Add salt, paprika, and Tabasco or cayenne. Bring the mixture to a boil.

4. Add lobster meat. Using a ladle to stir, gently ladle the sauce and the

lobster meat together over medium heat until the mixture starts bubbling again. Then remove from the heat and add the sherry.

5. Melt the remaining 3 tbsp. of butter in a frying pan. Add the bread. Heat, tossing the bread in the butter until the butter is absorbed. Remove from the fire.

6. Divide the lobster mixture among the half shells. Sprinkle with the butter-toasted bread and brown it under the broiler for 2 to 3 minutes, or until the crumbs start to brown. Serve immediately.

CHEF'S SECRET: You can boil the lobster and make the sauce a day ahead. If you wish, remove and cube the lobster meat, press it gently into a plastic container, and pour the sherry over it. Keep it like this overnight in the refrigerator.

Regular bread crumbs would never do for this dish. You have to have day-old bread. Hold the bread in one hand and tear off pea-sized pieces with the other, being careful not to press the bread so that it becomes solid.

For this dish, if possible, use unsalted butter. It will make a big difference.

If you happen to ruin the lobster shells while cleaning, don't worry. Proceed as above, but empty the Lobster Thermidor into an ovenproof casserole. Sprinkle the crumbs over the top and bake in a 450-degree oven for 8 to 10 minutes. Place the casserole in the middle of a silver tray and surround the edges with broken pieces of lobster shell. Sprinkle with parsley.

EGGS, CHEESE, RICE, & PASTA

EGGS

Scotch Eggs

Eggs Benedict

Eggs Frou-Frou

Farmer's Omelet

CHEESE

Cheese Service

Breaded Swiss Cheese

Welsh Rarebit

Cheese Balls

   Blue Cheese

   Cheddar Cheese

   Swiss Cheese

RICE

Italian Risotto

Rice Salad

Mushroom Rice

Rice à la Grecque

Rice Croquettes

PASTA

Spaghetti Bolognese

Fettuccini à la Romano

Noodle Kugel

Lasagna

Galuska (Spaetzle)

*F*or a Hungarian married to a Japanese and living in the United States, rice cooking can be frustrating. For decades I learned to admire the skill of women who could cook rice so that every grain stayed separate. Then I started to learn to admire women who could cook rice that stuck together enough to be picked up with chopsticks. I learned rules according to which it was forbidden, or at least unadvisable, to wash rice for longer than two to three seconds in a sieve under running water. And other rules according to which you had to wash rice for minutes, then let it soak in water for at least one-half hour before cooking. Finally, I realized that all these rules are right and valid, depending on what dish, from what country, is being prepared and what type of rice is being used. (The best advice I can give on this is to read the instructions on the box, because the packer knows best the product which is packaged.)

If you want the rice just as a plain accompaniment to Eastern Mediterranean dishes, the best way is to pre-fry the rice, stirring it constantly, in oil and butter mixed with another shortening. For dishes of Middle Europe, pre-fry with lard, and then add the required liquid and cook the rice over low, constant heat or bake it in the oven. For other dishes, first boil the rice in water and then add the required shortening, mostly butter. For Far Eastern or Oriental dishes, simply boil the Japanese rice according to the package instructions.

The same applies to cooking pasta, but the main rule here is not to overcook. Nothing is as bad as soggy noodles, spaetzles, or macaroni. The cooking time depends very much on the product; the quality of the product depends on the amount of egg used in proportion to the flour. The best way to keep cooked pasta is in ice-cold water to cover. Of course, before reheating, it should be shaken until dry.

Eggs, Cheese, Rice, & Pasta

EGGS

Scotch Eggs

8 servings

8 pullet or small eggs, hard-boiled and peeled
1½ lb. ground meat (mixture of pork and beef, veal and beef, veal and pork, or 8 oz. each type of meat)
1 tsp. salt

¼ tsp. or more freshly ground black pepper, depending on taste
2 raw eggs
1 cup cold water
flour and bread crumbs
shortening

1. Combine the ground meat, salt, pepper, 1 raw egg, and the cold water and mix by hand until the mixture is a smooth, even consistency. Divide the mixture into eight portions.

2. Wet one palm and place a portion of the meat mixture into it. With the other hand, flatten the mixture until it is large enough to completely encase a hard-boiled egg.

3. Place a hard-boiled egg on the flattened portion of meat and, with both hands, form an egg-shaped meat ball, being sure the surface is smooth and even and that the hard-boiled egg is completely covered. Repeat until all eight eggs are covered. Refrigerate for 1 hour.

4. Prepare an egg wash by beating the second raw egg with 2 to 3 tbsp. water. Be sure no big lumps of egg white remain.

5. Roll each chilled egg in flour, dip in the egg wash, and then roll in bread crumbs. Refrigerate for 4 hours.

6. Deep-fry the eggs in hot shortening for 5 minutes. Transfer them to an absorbent surface and keep them warm in a preheated 200-degree oven for about 30 minutes before serving.

CHEF'S SECRET: This is a very popular "bar" dish in England. It is very good made with canned pork products, such as canned chopped ham or minced ham, instead of the ground pork.

Refrigerating the eggs for an hour before breading allows them to become firm, so that they may be easily handled during the breading. Letting them stay in the refrigerator for 4 hours between the breading and the frying serves the same purpose. Of course, it is possible to prepare the eggs a day ahead, up to the deep-frying. Just keep them refrigerated until you are ready to fry them.

After 5 minutes' deep-frying, the meat mixture covering the eggs will be cooked but the hard-boiled egg inside will still be cold. This is why it is necessary to place them in the oven. If you want to serve them cold, let them cool after deep-frying for at least 1 hour. Split them in half or quarters and serve with or without mayonnaise.

Eggs Benedict

2 servings

¾ cup butter
3 egg yolks
2 tbsp. cold water
¼ tsp. salt
1 tsp. lemon juice
1 qt. water
¼ cup white vinegar

4 fresh eggs, at room temperature
4 slices Canadian bacon, medium thickness
2 English muffins, split in half
4 thin slices black truffle or 4 black olive halves

1. Prepare a Hollandaise Sauce as follows: Place the bottom of a double boiler over low heat and add enough water to have the upper part submerged in it. Bring the water to the simmering point.

2. Melt the butter in a small saucepan. Do not let it bubble or boil.

3. Place the egg yolks and 2 tbsp. cold water in the top of the double boiler. Set the top part into the bottom part. Beat the yolks with a wire whip until they become frothy and slightly thickened. Do not overcook.

4. Remove the pan from the water and place it on a wet towel.

5. Slowly incorporate the melted butter into the egg yolks, beating in a circular motion.

6. Add salt and lemon juice. Stir. Let the sauce stand in a warm place until ready to assemble.

7. Place the 1 qt. water and the vinegar in a saucepan and bring to a simmering point over low heat.

8. Break each egg into a cup. Slip the egg from the cup onto the surface of the water. Wait until it sets before you add another.

9. Poach each egg until the white is solidly white and no longer transparent; the yolk must remain runny. It will take about 2½ to 3 minutes. Keep the water simmering.

10. Remove each egg with a slotted spoon. Drain on paper toweling. Keep warm in a 150-degree oven until ready to serve.

11. Quickly heat the bacon on both sides in a hot skillet.

12. Toast the inside of each muffin under a broiler or in a toaster.

13. To assemble, place toasted English muffin halves, cut side up, on a large serving platter. Place a slice of bacon on each. Top with a well-drained egg. Spoon 1 to 1½ tbsp. Hollandaise Sauce over each egg. Garnish with a slice of truffle or olive. Serve immediately.

CHEF'S SECRET: Do not try this recipe for the first time when you have guests. Try it at least once when you are not in a hurry. You will find, after one or two tries, that it is easier to do than it sounds. The main thing to watch is that the water in the bottom of the double boiler never stops simmering, but never starts to boil.

Instead of making the Hollandaise Sauce, try the following at least once: In a small saucepan, for each person, melt together 2 tbsp. commercial cheese spread, 1 tbsp. heavy cream or half-and-half, and a dash of Tabasco or a small sprinkling of cayenne. Spread the sauce over the eggs and place them under the broiler for 1 minute. Or, for each person, mix 2 tbsp. commercial sour cream with 1 tsp. tomato paste, a small pinch of sugar, and a few drops Worcestershire sauce. Spoon the mixture over the eggs, sprinkle them with grated Parmesan cheese, and place them under the broiler for 1 minute. From here on, you can dream up your own variations.

Eggs Benedict have nothing to do with the Benedictine Order. This dish was originated by a Boston restaurant man named Benedict. His chef allegedly left him and went to New York to work in one of the great plush downtown luncheon places around the turn of the century, and this is where the dish became famous.

Eggs Frou-Frou

6 servings

6 poached eggs	3 hard-boiled egg yolks, pressed through a sieve
¾ cup frozen peas	
¾ cup frozen asparagus tips	1½ cups homemade mayonnaise (see page 214), cold
¾ cup frozen whole string beans, diced	salt
1 tbsp. unflavored gelatin	pepper
2 cups canned chicken broth, free from fat, at room temperature	ice cubes
yellow food coloring	parsley sprigs

1. Cook the three green vegetables, separately, according to package directions. Drain and refrigerate.

2. Make an aspic by mixing the gelatin with the chicken broth. Bring the mixture to a boil, stir, then remove from the heat. Color a pale yellow with the food coloring.

3. Place the ice cubes in a bowl and add cold water. Place the pan of aspic

in the ice water and stir until it begins to gel, but remains a liquid. Remove from the water.

4. Place the cold eggs on a cake rack and set the rack in a shallow pan.

5. Measure out ½ cup aspic and stir it into 1 cup of the cold mayonnaise. Add the sieved egg yolks. Salt and pepper to taste.

6. Spoon this mixture over the eggs until they are completely coated. Keep the coating even and do not let little holes or bubbles form. Coat the eggs 2 or 3 times, refrigerating after each coat. Collect the drips from the pan and reheat over low heat, then cool by stirring over the ice water, to use again.

7. Place a slice of truffle or black olive on each egg.

8. Glaze each egg with the aspic until a thin, shiny coat adheres to it. Refrigerate.

9. Add the remaining mayonnaise, including the unused portion used to coat the eggs, to the cold vegetables. Stir in ¼ cup of the aspic. Place in a decorative mold and refrigerate.

10. Pour the remaining aspic in a small flat pan and place in the refrigerator to gel.

11. When the vegetables have gelled, unmold onto a serving platter. Dice the aspic into small cubes, using a sharp knife. Surround the vegetable mold with the cubed aspic. Place the eggs on the diced aspic. Decorate with parsley sprigs.

CHEF'S SECRET: This is a beautiful dish and is definitely worth the little work involved.

You may add 1 tsp. sugar and a little salt to the liquid in which you cook the aspic. It will make the aspic's flavor much more pungent.

The French word "aspic" scares many housewives. They think it is something very complicated, although it is nothing but a gelatin dish without sugar or fruit flavor.

If you like, remove 3 to 4 tbsp. of the broth and substitute a small amount of white wine or lemon juice for added flavor.

It is best to stir the gelling aspic with your finger. When you feel the temperature become cooler than your body temperature, or when your fingers feel sticky if you press them together and then pull them apart, the aspic is ready to work with. It is advisable to have some hot water on hand in case you overchill the aspic in the ice water bath. You can immediately place the pan into the hot water, remelt, then repeat.

To poach the eggs, see the directions given in Eggs Benedict, page 144. After poaching, for a "professional" look, trim the edges of the white.

Farmer's Omelet

4 servings

6 large or 8 medium eggs
1 cup milk
½ tsp. salt
¼ tsp. freshly ground black pepper
4 to 6 tbsp. shortening (preferably bacon drippings, lard, or butter)

1 cup diced boiled potatoes (or any leftover potatoes except mashed)
½ cup diced ham
½ cup minced onion
4 strips bacon, cut in half
parsley sprigs

1. Place the bacon in a cold frying pan and fry over medium heat, turning frequently. Remove to absorbent paper.

2. Add the onions to the bacon fat and fry until they turn slightly brown. Then add the potatoes and ham. Keep turning with a spatula, browning lightly, then remove to a warm container.

3. In a bowl, beat the eggs, milk, salt and pepper.

4. Heat the shortening in a frying pan. Depending on the size of the pan, pour in all or half of the egg mixture. As soon as it starts to set, spread the ham, potatoes, and onion (or half of the mixture) on top of the eggs.

5. Loosen the edges of the eggs with a spatula and carefully fold the omelet in half. Slide onto a serving platter and cover each portion with two slices of bacon. Decorate with parsley sprigs and serve.

CHEF'S SECRET: This dish is known all over Europe; it is a kind of European "chop suey." Instead of ham, any leftover roast or steak would do. If you do not have potatoes or do not care to use them, green peas, green beans, or any similar vegetable may be substituted.

CHEESE

Cheese Service

Cheese is the most abused of all food items, especially among the so-called "gourmet foods." On many occasions, even at the "gourmet dinners" of eating societies where they strive for propriety and perfection, a mortal sin is committed: The cheese is served right from the refrigerator. This makes even the world's best cheese inedible.

In the winter time, cheese should be kept at room temperature all day long on the day it will be served. In the summer, or during warm weather, keep it at room temperature for at least 2 hours before serving. Very "runny" cheeses, of which Camembert and Brie are the two most popular, can be left in their wrappings and should not be cut far in advance. However, cheeses such as Edam, Port Salut, Swiss, and Cheddar can be precut, covered with a wet cheesecloth or absorbent paper towel, and then covered with plastic.

Not only by tradition, but for chemical reasons, cheese never should be served on any type of metal platter. Wood, marble, glass, plastic, fresh straw, or grape leaves are all proper, and all emphasize the importance and elegance of the cheeses.

Travelers know that in elegant French, Swiss, or other restaurants, or in the homes of aristocrats and true gourmets, where the service is the most beautiful silver, the cheese course is served on an old wooden plank or a piece of marble which has been in the family or in the restaurant for a decade or a century, even though the quality of the cheese is the very highest.

This custom has other than traditional reasons, as was demonstrated not too many years ago. One of the giant American corporations purchased a small independent cheese company, built a magnificent new manufacturing facility, and for more than a year could not produce one piece of edible cheese. This manufacturer consulted a European cheese manufacturer from the old traditional school, who had recently changed his famous old factory to a new, automated manufacturing plant with great success. When he arrived and looked at the factory, he immediately asked what had happened to the old building. When he was told that the old building was still standing, although it was locked up and for sale, he felt very relieved. He told the manufacturers that they should remove as many of the old wooden surfaces from the former factory work tables, wall coverings, and storage shelves as possible, rush them to the new factory, and incorporate the wood all over. This suggestion worked a miracle, and the aroma and taste of the cheese, which was seemingly lost forever, is now the same as it was before the crisis. The fungi living on the wood through the years established a "working relationship" with the molds of the cheese, and the biochemical mixture gave the cheese its characteristic, inimitable flavor.

If you are interested in cheese, you can make a good test at home. Buy a piece of true Roquefort, Danish blue, Italian Gorgonzola, and if available a piece of English Stilton. You will note that all four have a seemingly identical greenish-blue mold (which nowadays is mechanically injected to expedite ripening). However, they are only similar, not identical, because they come from different natural caves where centuries of cheese manufacturing have established a very special strain of fungus or mold, which gives to each a characteristic, inimitable identity.

If you leave the four pieces of cheese together for a few days at room temperature, under a glass dome, you will notice that all four will lose their characteristics. The molds will all turn yellow or brown and all the cheeses will acquire the same sharp, acid, unpleasant taste. This happens because the molds kill each other. On the other hand, if you keep the four pieces separately, each on a different plate under a small glass dish, each one will remain fresh, pleasant-tasting, and edible after the same length of time.

In France and elsewhere on the Continent, cheese is served with white, soft-centered, crusty bread or with a juicy dark rye bread. In England, it is served with special cheese biscuits. Both ways traditionally are correct and both can be very pleasant. However, one unforgivable thing is frequently done: stale, rancid, imported cheese biscuits are used just for tradition's sake.

If neither crusty French or Italian bread nor fresh, crisp cheese biscuits are available, freshly made, lightly buttered toast is the best substitute.

Fruits are the natural accompaniment for cheese. Apples and grapes are especially appropriate, but fresh figs, avocados, peaches, and other fruits are also delightful.

Breaded Swiss Cheese

8 servings

8 slices rindless Swiss cheese, 2 oz. each	flour
3 eggs	bread crumbs
3 tbsp. water	6 to 8 tbsp. oil
1 pinch salt	6 to 8 tbsp. butter
	fresh watercress or parsley

1. Prepare an egg wash by beating the eggs with the water and salt.
2. Coat the slices of cheese by first dipping in the flour, then in the egg wash, and finally in the bread crumbs.
3. Heat the oil and butter in a frying pan. Over fairly high heat, fry the breaded cheese about 2 minutes on each side or until the pieces turn golden brown.
4. Garnish with watercress or parsley and serve.

CHEF'S SECRET: This is one of the finest European luncheon dishes, but you must use a good-quality imported Swiss cheese such as Gruyère. Other cheeses would turn gummy.

Do not try to lift the pieces of cheese from the frying pan with a fork; use a slotted metal spatula.

This is one of the few breaded dishes that cannot be breaded ahead of time. It must be breaded just before frying.

Welsh Rarebit

4 servings

2 tbsp. butter	1 tsp. Worcestershire sauce
1 lb. sharp Cheddar cheese, shredded	½ cup beer
½ tsp. powdered mustard	2 eggs, slightly beaten
1 dash cayenne	8 slices crisp toast
½ tsp. salt	parsley sprigs

1. Melt the butter over direct heat in the top part of a double boiler.
2. Add the cheese and heat, stirring occasionally, until the cheese is completely melted.
3. Place the pan over the boiling water in the bottom of the double boiler and add the seasoning.
4. Combine the beer with the eggs and pour the mixture into the melted cheese. Cook until thickened, stirring frequently.
5. Serve over toast points, garnished with parsley.

CHEF'S SECRET: If you read this recipe carefully, you will see that the top of the double boiler is used first over direct heat; then, after the cheese is completely melted, it is put above the boiling water in the bottom part.

This is done because of the amount of time it would take to melt the cheese over the boiling water. An even better method is to make the Rarebit right in a fondue dish, if you have one.

If for any reason you cannot use the beer, substitute club soda for it. The carbonation is necessary if the dish is to be of the proper consistency. Of course, for a festive occasion, you can replace the beer with champagne.

Cheese Balls

3 balls

Blue Cheese

8 oz. crumbled blue cheese, Roquefort, or Gorgonzola
2 3-oz. packages cream cheese, at room temperature
4 oz. butter, at room temperature
1 tbsp. brandy
few drops Worcestershire sauce
½ cup finely chopped pecans

Cheddar Cheese

8 oz. grated sharp Cheddar cheese
2 3-oz. packages cream cheese, at room temperature
4 oz. butter, at room temperature
1 tbsp. prepared mustard
1 tsp. paprika
few dashes Worcestershire sauce
2 tbsp. paprika

Swiss Cheese

8 oz. finely grated Swiss cheese
2 3-oz. packages cream cheese, at room temperature
4 oz. butter, at room temperature
2 tbsp. cognac or brandy
light sprinkling of salt
white pepper
2 to 3 tbsp. sesame seeds

1. For each cheese ball, mix all ingredients except the last one listed in each case.

2. With wet hands, form the mixtures into balls. Then roll each ball in the last ingredient listed (i.e., roll the Blue Cheese Ball in chopped pecans, the Cheddar Cheese Ball in paprika, and the Swiss Cheese Ball in sesame seeds).

CHEF'S SECRET: These cheese balls are very handy and can be made a long time in advance. They can be stored in the refrigerator for up to 1 week or in the freezer for up to 1 month.

You can make all the balls in the same mixing bowl if you start with the mildest—the Swiss cheese—then do the blue cheese and, finally, the Cheddar.

It is important that you wet your hands with enough cold water to make your palms cool before you start to form the balls. If you have difficulty rolling the balls in their coatings, refrigerate the balls for several hours, then roll them between your palms, this time wet with hot water, so that the surface of the balls starts to melt. You can then roll them in the coatings and they will be sure to stick.

If you like the balls fluffy and airy, it is possible to beat the mixture in an electric mixer, using a paddle instead of a wire whip. Start by beating the softened butter; then add the cream cheese, bit by bit. Add the liquid if any is used, then fold the cheese into the mixture, beating at a lower speed.

RICE

Italian Risotto

8 servings

2 cups rice	black pepper and salt, to taste
1 package frozen green peas	1 cup grated Romano, Parmesan, or
8 oz. chicken livers	similar sharp cheese
4 tbsp. oil	2 tbsp. butter
1 small clove garlic	

1. Cook the rice in lightly salted water, according to package directions. Do not overcook. Quickly rinse the rice in a colander under running cold water. Shake as dry as possible.

2. While the rice cooks, heat the 4 tbsp. oil with the garlic, slightly crushed, until the edges of the garlic start to brown. Remove and discard the garlic clove.

3. Pat the chicken livers dry with a paper towel. Grind fresh pepper over each chicken liver but do not salt them.

4. Fry the livers in a covered frying pan over medium heat, being sure they do not touch each other and turning once in a while. To test for doneness, pierce the thickest part with a sharp object; if no more red liquid comes out, they are done. Remove them from the fire and keep covered in a warm place.

5. Cook the green peas according to the package directions.

6. To serve, slice as many nice, even slices as possible from the larger parts of the chicken livers. Salt the remaining pieces and mince them so they are about the size of the peas. Gently mix together the rice, the green peas, and the minced chicken livers.

7. Press the mixture into a bowl which has been brushed with the 2 tbsp. butter. Unmold the rice on a serving platter. Press the slices of chicken liver around the edge of the rice and sprinkle all the cheese on the top.

CHEF'S SECRET: In Italy, this dish is not a side dish but a main dish. Besides the green peas, Italian cooks sometimes use young snap beans. Also, prosciutto ham slices are sometimes alternated with the chicken liver slices.

It is important that you do not salt the chicken livers before cooking them, as salting will make them tough. If the frying is done over high heat, the edges will be tough and brittle. If done over low heat, they will become soft and unpleasant. This is why it is so important to maintain a medium heat.

Patting the livers dry also helps to insure the proper texture.

Covering the pan saves your hands because chicken livers tend to spatter while frying.

Rice Salad

8 servings

4 cups cooked cold rice	1½ to 2 tbsp. sugar
1 cup cooked green peas	½ cup oil
2 eggs, beaten	⅓ cup vinegar
1 tbsp. shortening	enough water to increase the amount
½ cup finely chopped sweet gherkins	of vinegar to ½ cup
½ cup finely chopped dill pickles	leftover cold meat cut into matchstick-
½ tsp. salt	size strips or small cubes (optional)
¼ tsp. white pepper	

1. Over very slow heat, in 1 tbsp. barely melted shortening, cook the 2 beaten eggs into a small omelet. Cook on one side just until the eggs are set, then gently loosen the edges with a spatula and carefully turn the omelet over and cook until firm. Remove from the heat and set aside to cool.

2. Mix the rice with the green peas and pickles.

3. Cut the omelet into a perfect square, then chop up the trimmings and mix them with the rice mixture.

4. Cut the square omelet into thin matchstick-size julienne strips. Cut the leftover meat, if any, the same size.

5. Mix the salt, pepper, sugar, oil, and vinegar-water mixture together into a vinaigrette. Pour the vinaigrette over the rice mixture.

6. Decorate the top with the julienne strips of egg and, if used, leftover meat. Serve chilled.

CHEF'S SECRET: The best way to make the flat omelet or egg pancake is to first beat the 2 eggs vigorously with a fork and then run the mixture through a fine sieve so that no lumps of the white remain. The heat under the pan and the shortening in the pan must be just warm, not hot.

Many people commit a great error when making vinaigrette by dissolving the salt, sugar, and spices in the vinegar and then adding the oil. It is much better to mix the spices in the oil, preferably with a wire whip in a stainless steel, glass, or plastic bowl (an aluminum bowl will darken the dressing because the wire whip will take off some of the aluminum oxide). If you do not believe that it matters whether the spices are mixed first with the oil or with the vinegar, make a simple test: Make the vinaigrette twice, using the same bowl and wire whip. Make the vinaigrette first by mixing the spices into the oil, and then make it again by mixing the spices into the vinegar. You will taste the difference. The reason this difference exists is that the oil has no physical or chemical properties to pick up and hold moisture for any length of time, but it does have the physical properties to pick up solids and other oils. Thus, if you first mix the spices with the oil, the oil will remain tasty even if it should separate from the vinegar for any reason.

Mushroom Rice

8 servings

2 cups rice	4 tbsp. freshly chopped parsley
water	2 tbsp. butter
½ tsp. salt	black pepper to taste
3 tbsp. oil	butter for brushing the bowl
5 oz. fresh, sliced mushrooms	

1. Heat the oil in a saucepan. Add the rice and stir until the rice turns yellow. Add the salt and slightly less water than required according to package directions, cover, and bring to a boil. Reduce the heat and simmer until the water is absorbed and the rice is tender.

2. Quickly sauté the mushrooms and the parsley in the butter.

3. Add the mushroom-parsley mixture to the cooked rice and add black pepper to taste. Gently toss together.

4. Press the rice mixture into a lightly buttered bowl, then invert onto a serving platter and serve immediately.

CHEF'S SECRET: If you like the Mushroom Rice with a stronger mushroom flavor, mince 3 or 4 mushrooms finely, sauté them with the rice in the oil, and then cook them with the rice. Or, after sautéing and before cooking, sprinkle the rice with ¼ tsp. mushroom powder.

If you do not have time to watch the rice while it simmers, preheat the oven to 300 degrees and, when the rice comes to a boil, cover the saucepan and place it in the oven.

The easiest way to press the Mushroom Rice into the bowl is to pile in the rice (do not fill the bowl to the rim), then place over it a sheet of plastic wrap or wax paper and press down with a plate which is just a little smaller than the bowl itself. This will prevent unevenness and will make the removal of the molded rice easier.

To unmold, fold a kitchen towel into thirds, using a towel large enough when folded to come up on both sides of the bowl. Remove the plastic covering from the bowl and place the rice-filled bowl in the middle of the towel. Put the serving platter upside down over the rice bowl and with both hands, tightly holding the bowl to the serving platter with the towel, invert it quickly onto the serving platter (see drawing, page 153).

Rice à la Grecque

8 servings

2 cups rice	1 small can tiny white onions
1 medium-sized onion, finely minced	1 clove garlic, slightly crushed
3 tbsp. butter	2 tbsp. chopped pimiento or fresh red
water	bell pepper, if available
½ tsp. salt	Greek or black olives
8 oz. Italian sausage meat	parsley sprigs
1 package frozen peas	butter for brushing the bowl

1. Sauté the minced onions and the garlic in the butter until the onions turn glossy. Discard the garlic.

2. Add the rice to the pan with the onions and stir until the rice turns slightly yellow. Add the salt and slightly less water than required according to package directions and bring to a boil. Simmer until the water is absorbed and the rice is tender.

3. Form the sausage meat into balls the size of a cherry, then fry in a separate frying pan until browned.

4. Cook the peas according to package directions.

5. Rinse the white onions under cold running water.

6. Add the sausage meat, peas, and white onions to the cooked rice-onion mixture. Gently toss together and heat through.

7. Add the chopped pimiento or bell pepper to the rice mixture.

8. Lightly butter a bowl and press the rice mixture into it. Turn out onto a serving platter. Garnish with the olives and parsley sprigs and serve immediately.

CHEF'S SECRET: This recipe, to the best of my knowledge, is one of the original recipes of Escoffier. Of course, it is adapted from a restaurant form to a household recipe, and there have been other minor changes. It is the finest accompaniment for roast capon, roast chicken, or roast turkey. It is also excellent with squab or veal.

To keep this dish as colorful as possible, try to undercook the peas. Leave the pan uncovered during the cooking so they will remain vivid green.

If you cannot get Italian sausage meat, buy regular sausage meat and, for each 8 oz. meat, dilute ½ tsp. oregano and ¼ tsp. ground coriander in 2 tbsp. water. Mix the water-spice mixture into the sausage meat and form the balls. If only link sausage is available, sprinkle it before frying with the amount of spices indicated above.

Rice Croquettes

8 servings

2 cups rice	4 egg yolks
4 cups water	1 whole egg
½ tsp. salt	flour
2 cups milk	bread crumbs
6 tbsp. sugar	shortening
1 tsp. vanilla	

1. In a medium-sized saucepan, bring the rice, water, and salt to a boil. Let boil for 3 to 5 minutes. Pour off the water, then add the milk, sugar, and vanilla. Continue cooking until the milk is absorbed and the rice is tender.

2. Beat the egg yolks until lemon-colored and fluffy, then add the beaten egg yolks to the rice, stirring constantly. Cook over medium heat until the mixture is thickened.

3. Remove the rice from the heat and spread it out evenly in a shallow pan. Let it cool completely.

4. Divide the rice mixture into equal portions. With wet palms, form each portion into a cone shape.

5. Prepare an egg wash by beating the whole egg with 2 tbsp. water.

6. Roll the shaped croquettes in the flour; dip in the egg wash, then into the bread crumbs.

7. Fry each croquette in hot shortening until golden brown. Serve immediately.

CHEF'S SECRET: This basic recipe can be changed into many different interesting flavors or even a completely different dish. For instance, you may omit the sugar and the vanilla and add 6 tbsp. finely grated, pressed-out raw carrots, a little additional salt, and a little black pepper. After frying, stick a small sprig of parsley in the thickest end of each cone, and serve the croquettes with any saucy meat dish as a very interesting garnish.

For a very unusual dessert dish, omit the sugar and add 4 to 6 tbsp. grated chocolate or a small amount of chocolate chips (first chopped with a knife) and serve the chocolate rice croquettes with a vanilla sauce. Another interesting European dessert may be made by placing a pitted prune sprinkled with a little cinnamon in the middle of each croquette as you are forming them. Then roll them into a ball, bread, and fry.

You can fry the Rice Croquettes in the morning or the afternoon, place them on an absorbent paper without letting them touch each other, and, before serving, reheat in a preheated 350- to 375-degree oven for approximately 15 minutes.

PASTA

Spaghetti Bolognese

8 servings

8 to 12 oz. ham, coarsely chopped
2 cups coarsely chopped onion
½ cup thinly sliced carrots
1 cup thinly sliced green stalk of celeriac or, if not available, 2 cups thinly sliced pascal celery
8 oz. butter
1 cup olive or corn oil
1 lb. ground beef
1 lb. ground pork shoulder
1 cup or more Italian white wine or tart domestic white wine
1 10½-oz. can beef consommé

1 10½-oz. can chicken consommé
2½ cups water
1 lb. chicken livers
1 pinch ground nutmeg
1 pinch ground coriander
¼ tsp. or more ground black pepper
salt, depending on the saltiness of the ham
4 tbsp. cornstarch
2 cups heavy cream
spaghetti, cooked according to package directions
grated Parmesan or Romano cheese

1. After measuring the ham, onion, celeriac, and carrots, chop each ingredient finely, then mix them together in a bowl and set aside.

2. Melt 1 tbsp. of the butter and 1 tbsp. of the oil in a heavy skillet or saucepan over medium heat. Add the finely chopped ham-vegetable mixture and cook, stirring once in a while, until the mixture starts to turn brown.

3. Remove the mixture from the heat and pour it into a large saucepan. Keep warm.

4. In the same skillet, heat 2 tbsp. of the shortening (butter and oil). Alternately add small amounts (about the size of a walnut) of the pork and beef, starting with the pork. After each addition, try to press the meat apart so that no large lumps remain. Continue until all the meat has been added and no pieces are bigger than the size of a green pea.

5. Increase the heat to high. Add the wine and bring the mixture to a boil,

stirring with a spatula or cooking spoon. Boil until almost all the wine and the liquid which oozes from the meat have evaporated.

6. Now, transfer the browned pork and beef mixture to the large pan. Add the consommé and 2 cups of water and bring to a vigorous boil. Reduce the heat to very low, cover, and simmer for 30 to 35 minutes, stirring once in a while.

7. Add the spices.

8. In the same frying pan used before, over high heat, melt the remaining mixture of oil and butter and fry the chicken livers for 3 to 4 minutes. Remove them from the heat and, as soon as they are cool enough to be handled, chop them into small cubes.

9. Dissolve the cornstarch in the remaining ½ cup water and add to the sauce along with the chopped chicken livers. Cover and leave over very low heat for about 10 minutes.

10. Stir the cream into the sauce and continue heating until the cream has warmed. Taste and add more salt if needed. Serve over spaghetti. Top with grated cheese.

CHEF'S SECRET: For a perfect dish, it is better to undercook than to over-cook the spaghetti. Do not use spaghettini; however, this sauce can be served over macaroni or mostaccioli.

If possible, try to buy prosciutto or a prosciutto-type, salty, dry ham such as Southern country ham or Westphalian ham. If you must use regular ham, try to get a lean piece.

There is a great difference in the taste and aroma of the green stalks of the celeriac or celery root, which are dark green, thin, and very fragrant and pungent, and the crisp, whitish or yellowish-green, much less pungent pascal celery. If you use the pascal celery, use the greener outside stalks.

Using the same skillet is a great advantage, but make sure nothing sticks to the pan because it will burn during the next step. If you have to clean the pan between steps, do not wash it; just wipe it with paper towels.

This sauce freezes well, especially if the cream is not added. When you want to use the frozen sauce, heat it in a water bath if possible. This will take longer, but will keep it from burning. Once it is heated, stir in the cream and continue heating just until it is warm enough to serve.

The best sauce can be ruined if the wrong cheese is used on it. Definitely try to use freshly grated Parmesan or Romano.

Fettuccini à la Romano

8 servings

1 lb. imported fettuccini; if not available, 1 lb. fettuccini-type noodles (the long variety, if possible)
2 tbsp. oil
1 small clove garlic, slightly crushed
8 oz. butter

6 oz. grated Swiss cheese (preferably Gruyère)
6 oz. grated Romano or Parmesan cheese
1 cup heavy cream
peppercorns

1. Cook the fettuccini until just barely tender, according to the package directions. Try not to break the long noodles.

2. In a large, heavy skillet, over medium heat, warm the oil with the garlic. As soon as the garlic edges turn yellow, remove and discard it.

3. Add half of the butter to the oil and let it melt. Add half of each type of cheese, stir, then add the noodles. Gently, but firmly, keep turning the noodles, cooking over medium heat.

4. Make a well in the middle of the pan and pour the cream into it. Fold the noodles and cheese into the cream.

5. Quickly place the mixture on a hot serving platter. Place the unmelted butter and the rest of the two cheeses on the top. Rush to the table, give a good grinding of fresh black pepper, fold it once more, and serve.

CHEF'S SECRET: Do not be afraid to use the garlic. It will not give a garlic taste to the noodles.

Not all the cheeses of Rome are available here and, after many tries, I have found that the most satisfactory and most "Roman" result comes from the mixture of Gruyère and a good Parmesan. If possible, make the dish at the dining table or close to the dining table so the guests can see. If a person is clever at using two forks and at lifting long noodles in the air and dropping them down, he can easily win the reputation of a master chef without knowing anything about cooking.

Noodle Kugel

8 servings

4 tbsp. melted butter	1¼ cups sugar
1 lb. broad noodles, boiled and drained	¼ tsp. salt
4 eggs, separated	1 cup raisins
1 tsp. ground cinnamon	½ cup chopped nuts
¼ tsp. ground nutmeg	jelly or jam (optional)

1. Preheat the oven to 350 degrees.

2. Add the melted butter to the noodles.

3. Beat the egg yolks with the sugar; blend in the spices and the salt. Add to the noodles.

4. Beat the egg whites until stiff, but not dry. Fold the egg whites into the noodles. Pour one-third of the mixture into a 2-qt. baking dish. Sprinkle one-half of the raisins and nuts in. Add another third of the noodle mixture, the remaining nuts and raisins, and then the rest of the noodle mixture.

5. Bake in the preheated oven for 45 minutes or until set. Serve hot. If you like, offer warmed and diluted jelly or jam.

CHEF'S SECRET: The success of the Noodle Kugel depends greatly on a very "light hand" and on the speed with which you can complete the steps. The best way to mix the egg yolk–sugar mixture into the noodles is to pour the mixture directly from the mixing bowl over the noodles, which must be dripped perfectly dry, and then to gently fold them together with a rubber spatula. The same method should be used for the addition of the egg whites.

If you want to unmold the Noodle Kugel before serving, brush the inside of the baking dish with butter or oil and sprinkle it generously with bread crumbs mixed with a little bit of sugar before pouring the Kugel in.

If the raisins are not especially fresh, soak them a short time in lukewarm water, but do not plump them; plumping will make them lose their taste and texture.

Lasagna

8 servings

1 1-lb. package lasagna noodles	2 8-oz. cans tomato sauce, Italian-style
1 recipe Sauce Bolognese (see page 156)	if possible
	1 tsp. oregano
8 oz. ricotta cheese	½ tsp. fennel seed
2 cups grated Parmesan cheese	4 tbsp. oil

1. In a large pot, bring to a boil enough water to completely cover the lasagna noodles. Pour the oil on the boiling water and add the lasagna noodles, one by one, being careful not to break the curly edges. Cook according to the package directions. After cooking, rinse the noodles quickly with cold water and lay them out on a dry surface, preferably on a towel.

2. Combine the tomato sauce with the herbs.

3. Grease an ovenproof dish, which is not too deep, and cover the bottom and sides of it with lasagna noodles. Be sure the edges overlap.

4. Pour a part of the Sauce Bolognese over the noodles. Cover with a second sheet of lasagna noodles, then some of the tomato sauce mixture, then small dots of the ricotta cheese, distributing evenly. Lightly sprinkle some of the grated Parmesan over the ricotta cheese, spoon on more of the Sauce Bolognese and then continue with another layer of the noodles, tomato sauce, ricotta cheese, Parmesan cheese and Sauce Bolognese. Use all the lasagna noodles, Sauce Bolognese, ricotta cheese and 1 cup of the Parmesan cheese. Over the top layer of noodles, just add tomato sauce and then sprinkle with the remaining Parmesan cheese.

5. Bake in a preheated 350-degree oven for about 1 hour. Shut off the heat and let the Lasagna stay in the oven for another 30 minutes.

CHEF'S SECRET: The oil on the top of the water will prevent the lasagna noodles from sticking together.

If you cook the lasagna noodles according to the package directions, you will notice that they are not completely cooked. This is as it should be, since they will be baked for an hour and should not turn into mush.

Leaving the Lasagna in the oven for ½ hour after baking will settle the layers. It will not only be tasty, but will be much easier to cut and serve.

You can freeze the leftover Lasagna packaged in aluminum foil. Reheat it from the frozen state, spooning some tomato juice or, if you have any on hand, some tomato sauce over the top.

Galuska (Spaetzle)

8 servings

3 cups flour   1 tsp. salt
4 eggs   4 to 6 tbsp. butter
1 cup milk

1. Fill a large pot about two-thirds full with water. Add approximately 1 tsp. salt for each quart of water used. Cover and bring the water to a boil, then set the heat so the water remains at a gentle boil.

2. With a fork, beat the eggs with the milk.

3. In a large mixing bowl, combine the flour and salt with the beaten egg mixture. Stir with a wooden spoon, until the batter is smooth and all the flour is incorporated.

4. With a tablespoon, spoon the dough into the boiling water, taking an amount about the size of an almond each time. Continue until all the dough is used.

5. Cover the pot three-quarters of the way, leaving an opening so that the steam and foam which develop as the Galuska cook can escape. Stir once in a while. Cook until all the Galuska are on top of the water. Test one of the larger Galuska by cutting through it to be sure that no raw center remains.

6. Pour into a colander and immediately rinse very quickly and briefly with cold water. Shake as dry as possible.

7. Place the Galuska in a frying pan and distribute the butter over the top. Let it melt, then gently turn the Galuska with a spatula and keep them warm until served.

CHEF'S SECRET: Do not overwork the dough, as this will result in hard, chewy Galuska.

To cut down on the work, pour one-third of the dough onto a dinner plate. Hold the plate close to the edge of the pot with the simmering water and quickly spoon the almond-sized portions into the water by first dipping the spoon into the water and then taking the dough from the edge of the plate. If you use this method, no dough will stick to the spoon and all the Galuska will be approximately the same size.

VEGETABLES

LEGUMES

Purée of Yellow Split Peas   Barley Pilaf
Lentils

ROOTS

Carrots with Dill in Cream Sauce   Pan-Roasted Potatoes
Turnips or Rutabagas

LEAVES

Creamed Spinach   Sweet-Sour Red Cabbage
Sorrel   Brussels Sprouts
Sweet-Sour German Cabbage   Kohlrabi

OTHERS

Zucchini   Green Peas
Acorn Squash   Braised Celery Hearts
Ratatouille   Braised Endive
Artichokes   Asparagus
Eggplant   Spring Vegetable Mixture
Beans Polonaise

*S*ome years ago I luckily acquired a tremendous menu collection, mostly from the second half of the nineteenth century up to the end of the 1920's. Many times, going through some of the more interesting pieces or reading one after the other at random, I noticed that in European households and in restaurants, inns, and clubs the main emphasis at the noon meal was on the vegetable; meat or poultry was served with it just as a small embellishment. Of course, this type of vegetable was the cooked-to-death, thickened-with-roux variety prepared for filling the stomach. The idea of having meat for the main part of the menu, with vegetables playing second fiddle, is Anglo-Saxon and, mainly for economical reasons, American. The Eastern European and Middle European staple is the starch; the Western European is the vegetable; and the American is a balance of all three with the emphasis on meat. Of course, tastes and trends are also changing on our continent. Boston beans are baked overnight, and Southern turnip greens with hamhock and black-eyed peas are placed on the stove at five o'clock in the morning to be ready for five o'clock in the afternoon.

In my opinion, most vegetables taste much better if they are cooked only for a very short period with as little water as possible, or in many instances without water, just in their own liquid extracted by slow heating. In the last ten to fifteen years, the Far Eastern vegetable cooking method has been increasing in popularity. The vegetables are cooked just enough so as not to be raw anymore and heated through. This way they remain crunchy and vivid in color, retain their identity, and are much more satisfying.

$\mathcal{V}egetables$

LEGUMES

Purée of Yellow Split Peas

8 servings

1 lb. split peas
2 tbsp. butter
2 tbsp. bacon drippings or other shortening

1 cup thinly sliced onion
2 cups shortening for frying
black pepper and salt to taste

1. Cook the split peas according to the package directions.
2. Add the butter and bacon drippings to the cooked split peas and run them through a food mill or a blender. (If you use a blender, some additional liquid such as canned chicken broth, soup stock, or water will be needed. Do not used canned consommé.) Add salt and pepper to taste. Keep warm.
3. Preheat the shortening to the smoking point. Separate the slices of onions into rings and add them to the hot shortening in small amounts. Precook the onions until they are limp and the edges start to turn yellow. Remove them with a slotted spoon and place them on absorbent paper. Cover with another absorbent paper and pat them dry. This can be done ahead of time.
4. Before serving, reheat the shortening. Add the onions and fry them over high heat until they get brown and crisp. Remove with a slotted spoon to absorbent paper; after 2 to 3 minutes, sprinkle them over the top of the Purée of Yellow Split Peas. Serve.

CHEF'S SECRET: It used to be an overnight task to cook split peas, but this is no longer the case. Manufacturers are precooking or tenderizing the peas so that they are easy to cook.

The secret of crisp onions is to cut the slices very thin and to cook them twice. This way they will not be greasy and will almost caramelize. If the onions are very moist when sliced, pat them dry on absorbent paper or on a kitchen towel before separating the rings.

Lentils

8 servings

4 cups dry lentils
1 piece smoked pork jaw, approximately 8 to 12 oz., or the same amount of smoked picnic ham or bacon
1 cup finely chopped onion
1 cup coarsely chopped carrot
4 tbsp. bacon drippings, lard, or other shortening

¼ tsp. finely minced garlic
1 tbsp. salt
1 bay leaf
¼ tsp. white pepper
1 tbsp. sugar
4 tbsp. vinegar
sour cream and/or additional vinegar (optional)

1. Soak the lentils overnight in 12 cups water.
2. Mash the garlic with the salt. In a large pot, melt the shortening. Add the onion, carrot, bay leaf, garlic-salt pulp, sugar, and pepper. Cover and cook over medium heat for 10 minutes.
3. Pour off the remaining soaking water, if any, from the lentils. Quickly wash the lentils.
4. After 10 minutes' cooking, add half the lentils, in small amounts, to the onion-carrot-spice mixture, stirring constantly. Add the jaw, or bacon or ham, then add the rest of the lentils.
5. Add enough water to barely cover the lentils. Bring the mixture to the simmering point, then adjust the heat to low and cook the lentils until tender.
6. Once the lentils are done, shut off the heat. Stir in the vinegar and let the lentils stand, covered, for 15 to 20 minutes. To serve, offer sour cream in a sauce boat, or additional vinegar, or both.

CHEF'S SECRET: To test the lentils for doneness, use the same procedure that is used to test beans. Remove a spoonful of the lentils from the pan. Gently blow on the lentils. If the skin breaks and starts to peel back, the lentils are done.

Press the lentils through a food mill if you desire a purée of lentils.

Barley Pilaf

8 servings

1 lb. barley
1 clove garlic, split in half crosswise
4 tbsp. oil
2 tbsp. butter
4 tbsp. finely minced onion
½ cup dried Zante currants or, if not

available, ½ cup dark raisins, chopped
2 to 3 tbsp. pine nuts or pistachio nuts (optional)
salt and black pepper to taste
½ cup toasted slivered almonds

1. Cook the barley according to package directions. These vary from manufacturer to manufacturer, so be careful to read the label.
2. When the barley is done, heat the oil in a large frying pan. Add the garlic, cut surface down. When the edges start to turn yellow, remove garlic and discard.

3. Add the finely minced onion to the frying pan and cook until limp, stirring constantly.

4. Add about one-third of the barley to the onion; keep stirring. Add the raisins or currants and the pine nuts or pistachio nuts, if used. Toss together, then add the rest of the barley. Stir gently with a fork. Season with salt and pepper to taste.

5. To serve, place the barley-raisin-onion mixture into a cone-shaped or round mold and press in with a wet, folded cloth. Unmold onto a serving platter. Melt the butter and pour over the top of the mold, then sprinkle with the toasted slivered almonds, or toast the slivered almonds in the butter and pour the mixture over the top of the mold.

CHEF'S SECRET: I learned this recipe in Morocco, where they also always sprinkle some cilantro over the top. Cilantro is available in Latin American stores. It has a very characteristic, pleasant, perfumed fragrance.

In all better places, the barley mold is always cone-shaped. If you do not have a cone-shaped dish at home, you can purchase a cone-shaped soup strainer or so-called "China cap." Or make a cone from a flexible cardboard and cover the inside and outside with aluminum foil.

If barley is not available, this typical pilaf can be made from kasha, rice, or egg barley (a type of noodle), and of course you can substitute ingredients for the raisins and pine nuts or select additional ingredients.

If you cannot get the small currants and you use the large dark raisins, do not try to chop them with a knife. It will be a messy and never-ending job. Snip each raisin in two or three pieces with a kitchen scissors and the job will go very quickly.

ROOTS

Carrots with Dill in Cream Sauce

8 servings

4 cups thinly sliced, fresh, young
  carrots
1 cup water
2 tbsp. butter
1 tsp. salt

½ tsp. sugar
⅛ tsp. white pepper
2 tbsp. all-purpose flour
1 cup heavy cream
3 tbsp. freshly chopped dill weed

1. Place the carrots, water, butter, salt, sugar, and white pepper in a heavy pan. Bring the liquid to a rapid boil and cook until the carrots are tender.

2. Stir the flour into the heavy cream.

3. When the carrots are tender, pour the liquid off into another saucepan. Bring this liquid to a boil; then, stirring constantly, add the flour-cream mixture.

4. Simmer the sauce slowly for 10 to 15 minutes.

5. After the sauce has cooked, add the freshly chopped dill and the carrot slices. Hold in a warm place for at least 15 minutes before serving.

CHEF'S SECRET: The amount of moisture in carrots varies, depending on where they are purchased and on their freshness. It is easy to adjust the liquid in the recipe after cooking. If there is too much, simply discard some; if not enough, add a small amount of water. To test the water content of carrots, bend one before cutting or slicing. If the carrot is easy to bend and slow to go back to its original shape, the moisture level is very low; if it snaps with a noise when bent or cut, and splits in a lengthwise direction, it is oversaturated with water.

The amount of sugar may not be enough for certain carrots. If so, simply add a little more.

Fresh dill weed, or the tender young dill leaves, is sold in bunches in season and can be frozen for a year-round supply. Holding the dill by the stem ends, dip a bunch in boiling water for 2 or 3 seconds. Immediately place in ice water to chill. Shake out some of the water but leave the bunch moist. Roll very tightly in aluminum foil and freeze. Once frozen, pack the aluminum-wrapped rolls in a plastic bag and store in the coldest part of your freezer. The dill will stay fresh for as long as a year. To use the frozen dill, remove it from the freezer just before it is needed. With a sharp knife, slicing crosswise, cut as much as needed. Repack and freeze the rest immediately.

Turnips or Rutabagas

8 servings

2 lb. yellow turnips or rutabagas, peeled and cut into 1-inch cubes
enough water to cover
8 tbsp. butter, or 4 tbsp. butter and 4 tbsp. other shortening

2 to 4 tbsp. soup stock, canned chicken broth, or slightly salted hot water
salt and fresh pepper to taste

1. Measure the water to be sure there is just enough to cover the turnips. Bring the water to a boil. When boiling, add the turnip cubes, one by one, slowly enough to keep the water boiling constantly.

2. Cook the turnip cubes until tender, or until they can be easily pierced with a toothpick. Pour off the cooking liquid and quickly rinse the turnips in cold water. Shake dry.

3. Melt the shortening in a heavy pan.

4. Mash the turnips; add salt, freshly ground pepper, and the stock, broth, or water. Add the melted shortening. Serve at once.

CHEF'S SECRET: With this cooking method, the turnips will keep their typical flavor, which is somewhat bitter but very pleasant.

Pan-Roasted Potatoes

8 servings

2 lb. potatoes
3 tbsp. lard

3 tbsp. butter
2 tsp. salt

1 tbsp. paprika	2 tbsp. finely chopped parsley
½ tsp. black pepper	1 tbsp. caraway seed

1. Wash and peel the potatoes, then wash them again. Cut them into uneven cubes, approximately 1 inch each.

2. Place them in a large pot with enough cold water to cover plus one inch. Add the caraway seeds and 1 tsp. of the salt.

3. Bring the potatoes and liquid to a boil over medium heat. As soon as the water starts to boil, remove the pan from the fire and let stand for 5 minutes.

4. Pour off the water, place the potatoes in a bowl, and let them stand at room temperature until cooled.

5. Combine the remaining salt, black pepper, and paprika.

6. Place the butter and lard in a large, heavy frying pan. Add the cold potatoes and sprinkle the top with the salt mixture.

7. Place the cold frying pan containing the cold shortening and potatoes over medium heat and heat it slowly, turning the potatoes gently with a spatula once in a while. Fry until the potatoes heat through and start to turn a light golden brown color.

8. Remove to a serving dish. Sprinkle the potatoes with the chopped parsley and serve.

CHEF'S SECRET: If you precook the potatoes according to the directions, removing the pot from the fire as soon as the water starts to boil, letting it stand for 5 minutes, then draining the water, the 1-inch cubes will be just barely cooked and will not have raw centers. If you should immediately start to fry them without cooling to room temperature, they would become overcooked and would break. If you let them cool and slowly reheat them, they will be piping hot but not overcooked.

The paprika will give the potatoes a beautiful golden color with only a fraction of the amount of shortening which would otherwise be needed to achieve this color. Potatoes prepared in this way will not be greasy and will retain the real potato taste.

LEAVES

Creamed Spinach

8 servings

2 lb. fresh or 2 12-oz. packages frozen spinach leaves	1 cup chicken stock or water
2 slices white bread, crusts removed	1 small clove garlic
1 cup milk	1 tsp. salt
salt	freshly ground black pepper to taste
2 tbsp. flour	1 egg

1. Soak the slices of bread in the milk.

2. Place the fresh, washed spinach leaves in a large amount of lightly salted boiling water. Cook for 5 minutes. Drain and cool by rinsing with cold water. Shake dry. If frozen spinach is used, prepare it according to package directions.

3. Chop the spinach very fine, by hand, using a large French knife on a wooden board.

4. Mash the white bread soaked in the milk. Add the egg.

5. Mash the garlic with the 1 tsp. salt. Stir the flour and the garlic-salt mixture into the chicken broth or water.

6. Rinse a large saucepan with cold water. Do not dry. Heat the cooked spinach over medium heat until it starts to bubble and the bubbles break with a sound as they rise. Add the chicken broth or water mixture, stirring vigorously with a wooden spoon or wire whip. Adjust the heat to low and cook the mixture, covered, for 10 minutes, stirring once in a while.

7. Before serving, stir in the pulp made from the milk and bread. Correct the seasonings, if necessary, with salt and black pepper. Serve.

CHEF'S SECRET: If you grind the spinach through a meat grinder or a food mill, all of the liquid will come out and only the fibers will remain. When the leaves are chopped by hand, the knife cuts through only the cells directly under the edge of the knife, without pressing the others to remove all the juice.

The milk-soaked bread thickens the spinach and adds a mild filler which heightens the spinach flavor. If you used enough flour to thicken the spinach without the bread, the flavor would be floury.

Sorrel

8 servings

1 lb. fresh sorrel
2 tbsp. shortening (preferably half butter)
1½ tbsp. flour
1 tsp. sugar
salt and pepper to taste
2 cups canned chicken broth, or a mixture of 1 cup milk and 1 cup chicken broth, or 1 cup milk and 1 cup water with 1 chicken bouillon cube dissolved in the water
1 cup sour cream
⅓ cup buttermilk or milk

1. Cook the sorrel in boiling salted water for 5 minutes. Drain and rinse with cold water to cool the sorrel. Shake dry.

2. Chop the sorrel with a large knife on a wooden chopping board.

3. Melt the shortening in a heavy saucepan. Add the flour and stir over medium heat until the mixture turns into a uniform light beige and starts to bubble.

4. Remove from the fire. Stir in the 2 cups broth or other liquid, using a wire whip. Place the pan back over the heat and cook, stirring constantly, until the mixture is smooth.

5. With a wooden kitchen spoon, stir in the sorrel. Add the sugar, salt, and pepper. Cover and cook over very low heat for 20 to 25 minutes.

6. Dilute the sour cream with the buttermilk or milk.

7. Just before serving, correct the seasoning, if necessary, with salt and pepper. Quickly fold in the sour cream mixture. Serve immediately.

CHEF'S SECRET: Sorrel is a spinach-like, lemon-tasting leafy vegetable. It is very popular throughout Europe. In France, turbot is often served poached, covered with sorrel, sprinkled with grated cheese, and then browned under the broiler or salamander. In Germany or Hungary, sorrel is a classic accompaniment for boiled beef, and is also served often with capon, chicken, veal, and other meats. Sorrel is also served with coddled eggs as a first course or a luncheon dish.

The sorrel season starts around the end of August and runs to the middle of October. It is readily available but must be preordered from the produce manager where you shop. You can order a half or whole bushel. You can clean and freeze the sorrel raw, packaging it so you can remove just enough for one batch. Or, you can precook the sorrel, chop it, then freeze it in cooking-size units.

Sweet-Sour German Cabbage

8 servings

1 large head white cabbage, approximately 3 lb.	½ cup sugar
4 tbsp. shortening	½ cup vinegar
1 tbsp. caraway seed	1 tsp. salt
	freshly ground black pepper to taste

1. Remove the outside leaves of the cabbage. Split the head in half and remove the core. Split the halves along the line where the core was removed. Cut the cabbage crosswise into ¼-inch slices. (See drawing.)

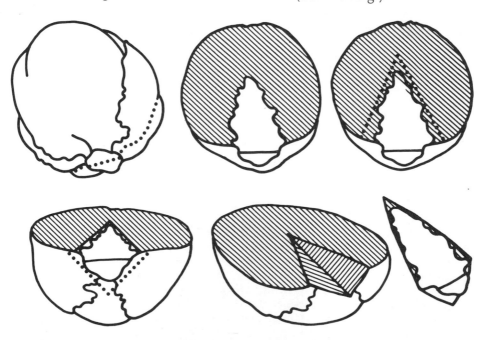

2. Place the shortening in the bottom of a very large pot. Pile the cabbage in the pot and sprinkle the top with the sugar, salt, pepper, and caraway seed. Pour the vinegar over the top.

3. Start to cook the cabbage over medium heat, without covering. Once the cabbage collapses somewhat, cover the pot and keep cooking over medium heat until the cabbage is tender, but still crisp.

4. If very much liquid accumulates in the pan, remove the cover and set the heat as high as possible. Heat, turning the cabbage and letting the liquid evaporate.

5. Serve with roast pork, fresh ham, roast picnic ham, or similar meats.

CHEF'S SECRET: The best cabbage is always the smallest head among all the heads of the same weight.

The best way to remove the core from the split cabbage is to cut a double "V" cut. One cut should come from the tip of the core down to the two sides of the outer surface, and the other should go under the half core (see drawing).

Tastes in sweetness or sourness of sweet-sour cabbage can vary widely. Adjust the amount of sugar and vinegar accordingly.

Sweet-Sour Red Cabbage

8 servings

3 heads firm red cabbage, approximately 3 lb. altogether
3 tbsp. lard, chicken fat, or duck fat
1 tbsp. finely minced onion
1 tsp. salt
1 tsp. caraway seeds

½ cup vinegar
½ cup sugar
¼ bay leaf
freshly ground black pepper to taste
very light sprinkling of nutmeg

1. Remove the outside leaves of the cabbage. Split each head in half and remove the core from each half. Split the halves into quarters. Place the quarters with a cut side flat on the cutting board and cut them into ¼-inch strips, or thinner, crosswise.

2. Quickly wash the cut cabbage in cold water. Place in a colander and shake off all the water.

3. Melt the lard, chicken fat, or duck fat in a large pot. Add the finely minced onions and let them cook until they turn glossy.

4. Add the red cabbage, salt, pepper, sugar, bay leaf, nutmeg, and caraway seeds. Pour in the vinegar. Gently toss the mixture together as you would toss a salad. Cook the cabbage over medium heat, uncovered, until it starts to steam.

5. Continue cooking over medium heat, stirring. When the liquid which develops starts to boil, reduce the heat to low and cook until tender, stirring once in a while. All the liquid must slowly evaporate; this is the only way to make the cabbage sweet-sour, tender, and a pretty purple. Pick out a few strips once in a while, let them cool a little, and taste them. You may wish to add more sugar or more vinegar, depending on your taste.

CHEF'S SECRET: Buying red cabbage is similar to buying white cabbage. Look for the firmest, hardest heads. If 3 or 4 leaves are bursting through or have burst in the same place, watch out; the cabbage is oversoaked with water, which adds additional weight.

Do not ever cover red cabbage while cooking. The odor that would develop would be unbearable, the color would fade, and the cabbage would be inedible.

Although white cabbage dishes may be easily reheated, red cabbage is hard to reheat and the result is usually unsatisfactory.

Brussels Sprouts

8 servings

2 lb. fresh brussels sprouts or 2 12-oz. packages frozen brussels sprouts
4 to 6 tbsp. melted butter

juice of ½ lemon
salt and black pepper to taste

1. Wash and clean the fresh brussels sprouts. Cook, without covering, in enough lightly salted hot water to cover plus 1 inch on top. Or cook the frozen brussels sprouts according to package directions, but cook 1 minute less than the directions specify. Let them drip and then shake or swing dry. Keep warm.

2. Just before serving, heat the butter with the lemon juice. Add salt and pepper to taste and pour the mixture over the hot brussels sprouts.

CHEF'S SECRET: Most recipes for brussels sprouts suggest that you should cut an "X" in the bottom of each before cooking. We do not feel that this is necessary, since young, tender brussels sprouts are usually available.

If you cook the fresh brussels sprouts and do not like the cabbage odor, discard the first water after 10 minutes of boiling and rinse the sprouts with cold water. Have a second pot of lightly salted water boiling and immediately place the precooked sprouts into it and finish cooking.

Brussels sprouts are also good served with a polonaise garnish. To prepare, place the precooked sprouts in a fireproof dish which has been brushed with butter. For eight people, toast 1 cup bread crumbs in ½ cup shortening, preferably butter. Spoon half of this bread crumb mixture over the sprouts and lace with a little cream or sour cream. Heat through and, just before serving, spoon the rest of the bread crumbs over the top. Sprinkle the top with finely chopped egg white, sieved egg yolk, and green parsley. Serve.

Kohlrabi

8 servings

3 lb. kohlrabi
1 cup heavy cream
3 tbsp. flour
4 tbsp. shortening (preferably half butter)

freshly ground black pepper to taste
1 tsp. salt
½ tsp. sugar
½ cup freshly chopped flat-leafed parsley

1 cup sour cream   parsley sprigs
2 cups canned chicken broth

1. Peel the kohlrabi and cut it into pieces ¼ by ½ by ¾ inch. Rinse the pieces and let the water run off, but do not shake them dry.

2. Heat a large empty pot over high heat. Sprinkle the sugar into the middle of the hot pot. As soon as it turns brown, add the shortening. Adjust the heat to medium and add the washed kohlrabi, salt, freshly ground pepper, and half the parsley. Keep stirring over medium heat for about 2 minutes.

3. Pour in the canned chicken broth, cover, and simmer for about 30 minutes or until the kohlrabi is tender.

4. Stir the flour into the cream. Stir this mixture into the kohlrabi. Add the rest of the parsley and remove from the heat. Let the kohlrabi stand in a warm place for at least 1 hour.

5. Just before serving, fold the sour cream into the kohlrabi and garnish with parsley sprigs.

CHEF'S SECRET: Buy small kohlrabi if possible. Avoid the large, light pieces, which will probably be woody and empty. The ideal size to buy is about 2 to 2½ inches in diameter.

Sometimes the root end of kohlrabi has a woody grain in the bulb itself. In this case, it is not advisable to chop the bottom part. You can save this for soup.

The little caramelized sugar in the empty pot will give an excellent taste to the kohlrabi without making it sweet.

If you wish, you may add 2 cups freshly shelled green peas or 1 package frozen peas, defrosted, to the kohlrabi about ½ hour before serving.

OTHERS

Zucchini

8 servings

4 lb. zucchini (either the small, young squash or the larger, matured variety)
½ cup chopped fresh dill weed or 1 tbsp. dried dill weed or ½ tsp. dill seed
2 tbsp. salt
½ tsp. freshly ground black pepper
1 tsp. sugar
½ cup vinegar

2 cups water
1 cup milk
1 small clove garlic
1 tsp. salt
4 tbsp. shortening (preferably half butter)
3 tbsp. flour
1 cup sour cream
paprika, finely chopped dill weed, or parsley for garnish

1. Peel the zucchini and remove the soft, seedy inside parts with a spoon. Discard. By hand or with a grater, cut the squash into strips measuring ¼ by

¼ by 4 inches. Salt the strips with the 2 tbsp. of salt and let them stand in a bowl for 2 hours.

2. Press from the squash the salty liquid which has accumulated. Quickly rinse the pieces of squash under cold water. Shake dry.

3. Crush the garlic with the 1 tsp. salt. Place the squash, dill, garlic-salt pulp, pepper, sugar, vinegar, and water into a heavy pot and cook over medium heat for 20 minutes.

4. Melt the shortening in a heavy saucepan.

5. Drain the cooking liquid from the squash. Save 2 cups of the liquid. Mix the flour with the milk and add the mixture to the 2 cups cooking liquid.

6. When the shortening is melted, slowly pour in the flour-liquid mixture, constantly stirring with a wire whip. Cook until the mixture is smooth and has thickened.

7. Pour the thickened substance over the squash, cover, and let simmer over low heat for 30 minutes.

8. Just before serving, fold in the sour cream. Sprinkle the top with paprika, fresh dill weed, or fresh, finely chopped parsley.

CHEF'S SECRET: Zucchini, in Italian, means "little gourd." However, the large, matured zucchini may be used and is probably much tastier than the smaller, younger squash.

The vinegar keeps the squash from cooking to a pulp.

Letting the squash stand with the salt removes much of the liquid from the squash, so that it will be firmer to the bite. It will not be salty if rinsed thoroughly.

Acorn Squash

8 servings

2 large (approximately 10 inches long and 8 inches in diameter) or 4 small acorn squash	8 tbsp. butter, melted
	4 to 6 tbsp. water
	salt and pepper to taste
8 tbsp. brown sugar	

1. Preheat the oven to 400 degrees.

2. Wash and split the squash in quarters or halves, depending on the size. With a very sharp knife, make fine incisions in the flesh of the acorn squash, not more than ½ inch deep.

3. Spoon the water on a cookie sheet. Set the pieces of squash on the cookie sheet.

4. Spoon 1 tbsp. of butter on each piece of squash, being careful that the butter is on the pulp or flesh of the squash rather than running off the side. Sprinkle each piece with salt and pepper, and spoon the brown sugar into the middle of each.

5. Place the squash in the preheated oven and bake for 30 minutes. Reduce the temperature to 325 to 350 degrees and continue baking until tender, but still firm. This should take approximately 1 hour to 1 hour and 20 minutes altogether.

CHEF'S SECRET: The fine slashes cut into the flesh help the acorn squash to absorb the butter and brown sugar as it melts.

Keep replacing the water on the cookie sheet or baking pan so that the acorn squash will not dry out.

Ratatouille

8 servings

2 cups sliced onion
2 cloves garlic
1 tsp. salt
6 tbsp. oil
2 cups sliced bell pepper
1 package frozen green beans or, in season, 1 lb. fresh green beans, cleaned and trimmed
1 lb. zucchini cut into 1½- by ¼- by ¼-inch pieces

2 cups eggplant, cut the same as the zucchini
1 15-oz. can tomato sauce
1 10½-oz. can tomato purée
1 lb. fresh tomatoes
salt and pepper to taste
4 to 5 tbsp. 4% white vinegar
2 tbsp. sugar

1. In a large heavy pot, over medium heat, sauté the onions in the oil until they turn glossy.

2. Mash the garlic with the salt and add to the pot with the onions. Add the bell pepper slices, zucchini, and eggplant. Add the green beans if the fresh variety is used. Sprinkle the vinegar in the pot, cover, and cook for 10 minutes, stirring once in a while. (If frozen green beans are used, add after the 10-minute cooking period.)

3. Add the tomato sauce, tomato purée, sugar, and pepper to taste. Cover and simmer over very low heat for 30 to 40 minutes, stirring occasionally to prevent the mixture from sticking to the pan.

4. Meanwhile, bring some water to a boil in a separate saucepan. One by one, drop the tomatoes into the boiling water. Leave for 2 to 3 seconds, remove, and immediately rinse under cold running water to cool.

5. Peel, core, and chop the tomatoes.

6. Add the chopped fresh tomatoes to the mixture, gently stir, then remove the pot from the heat. Let stand in a warm place for at least 1 hour.

7. Correct seasonings, if necessary, by adding more salt, pepper, or sugar. Serve hot or chilled.

CHEF'S SECRET: This famous Mediterranean dish was developed as a way for the housewife to use up the vegetables on hand which, separately, would not be enough for the family. It is more often served cold as an appetizer or first course than hot as a vegetable.

The amount of sugar needed will vary, depending on the acidity of the fresh tomatoes.

The vinegar sprinkled on the eggplant and zucchini will keep these two vegetables from turning soft during the cooking.

Frozen green beans are blanched or precooked during the manufacturing process and, therefore, do not need as much cooking time as the fresh beans.

To store Ratatouille, you must be sure that the container is airtight and that no air bubbles exist. Always be sure to cover the top of the container with oil before placing it on the Ratatouille. Then place it in the refrigerator.

If you are serving this dish as a cold appetizer, add some black olives if you wish and be sure to have plenty of freshly ground pepper, good butter, and crusty French bread on hand.

Artichokes

8 servings

8 medium- to large-sized fresh arti-
    chokes
salt
water
2 lemons, cut in half
4 tbsp. red wine vinegar

½ tsp. salt
¼ tsp. dry mustard
8 tbsp. olive oil
freshly ground pepper
½ tbsp. minced shallots

1. Break off the stem of each artichoke by bending it until it snaps. Pull off the small leaves at the base. Trim the base with a knife to flatten it so it will stand. Slice about 1 inch off the top of each and trim off the sharp points of the leaves with a kitchen scissors.

2. Bring to a rapid boil enough salted water to completely cover the artichokes. Plunge the trimmed artichokes into the water. Squeeze the juice of the lemon halves into the boiling water, then drop in the pieces of lemon.

3. Cook, uncovered, at a slow boil for 30 to 40 minutes, depending on size.

4. Immediately remove the artichokes from the water when cooked and turn upside down. Run cold water over them until they are cooled. Drain. Cover with ice cubes. When the ice has melted, drain the water.

5. With your fingers, pull out the purple center. Save. Scrape the choke (hairy center) with a spoon until all the fibers are removed from the bottom. Discard fibers. Replace the purple center by inverting it into the hollow cavity.

6. In a small bowl, blend the vinegar, salt, and dry mustard. Slowly add the oil, stirring constantly. Stir in the pepper and shallots.

7. Place the artichokes in a deep-sided serving dish and pour the dressing over them. Marinate in the refrigerator until ready to serve.

CHEF'S SECRET: While cooking the artichokes, weigh them down with a plate so they are fully immersed. The artichokes are cooked when a fork will pierce the bottom easily and when the long lower leaves can be pulled out with little effort.

If you wish to serve artichokes the Italian rather than the French way, select artichokes with at least a 3- to 3½-inch stem. Cut the top of the stem on the diagonal. Do not cut off the stems; just peel them. Discard the purple middle and put the artichokes upside down in the marinade. Serve with the stems standing up on an angle. If you wish, add 1 or 2 chopped cloves of garlic to the marinade. Remove and discard the garlic before serving.

Eggplant

8 servings

2 eggplants, 8 to 10 inches long and 6
   to 7 inches in diameter
salt and pepper to taste
2 eggs
2 tbsp. cold water

4 to 5 tbsp. flour
2 cups fine Italian or French bread
   crumbs
enough shortening to fry (preferably
   half oil)

1. Peel the eggplants with a stainless steel knife. Cut them crosswise into ½-inch slices. Sprinkle each with salt and pepper.

2. Beat the eggs with the cold water.

3. Dip the slices of eggplant in the flour, then in the egg mixture, and finally in the bread crumbs. Place the slices on an absorbent paper until all are breaded.

4. Bring the shortening to the smoking point in a large frying pan. Quickly fry the eggplant slices on both sides. Remove to an absorbent paper and keep warm until all are fried. Serve about 10 minutes after the last slice has been fried.

CHEF'S SECRET: In the Near East, each household has a wooden knife which is used only for eggplant because, with a regular knife, both the eggplant and the knife itself would turn an ugly black. Finer households have a knife carved from bone for the same purpose, but stainless steel is just as good.

Be careful when frying that you do not overload the shortening with the eggplant slices, and wait between batches so that the shortening can regain its heat. Otherwise, the slices will soak up all the oil and will be unpleasantly oily.

Beans Polonaise

8 servings

2 lb. whole, fresh green snap beans or
   yellow wax beans
1 tbsp. salt
4 oz. butter
2 to 3 oz. oil, lard, or any second
   shortening

1 cup dry Italian- or French-type bread
   crumbs
1½ cups sour cream
½ cup buttermilk or milk
1 hard-boiled egg
1 tbsp. freshly chopped parsley

1. Clean the beans by removing the strings, if any, from both sides with a bias cut.

2. Bring to a boil in a covered pan enough salted water to cover the beans plus about 1 inch. Add the beans in small bunches so that the boiling is not interrupted.

3. Adjust the heat to medium and cook the beans, uncovered, about 15 to 18 minutes or until almost done. Lift one out, dip it into cold water, and bite into it. The beans are done when they have lost their rawness but are still undercooked.

4. Remove the beans from the heat, drain the cooking liquid, and immediately submerge the beans in cold water for 1 or 2 minutes to stop the cooking. Let them drip dry.

5. Brush the inside of an ovenproof dish, large enough to hold the beans, with 1 tbsp. of the butter.

6. Melt the remaining butter with the other shortening. Add the bread crumbs and toast them until they are a pleasant walnut brown.

7. Separate the white of the hard-boiled egg from the yolk. Chop the white finely and mix it with the chopped parsley. Press the yolk through a large-holed sieve.

8. Mix the sour cream with the buttermilk or milk.

9. Place half the beans in the bottom of the buttered casserole. Spoon half the buttered bread crumbs over the beans. Lace them with 2 to 3 tbsp. of the buttermilk–sour cream mixture. Add the remaining beans, all but 2 tbsp. of the bread crumbs, and all the sour cream mixture. Bake in a preheated 350-degree oven for 30 minutes.

10. Before serving, mix the remaining bread crumbs with the egg yolks. Sprinkle the top of the casserole first with the egg white–parsley mixture, then with the egg yolk–bread crumb mixture.

CHEF'S SECRET: If you cook the green beans uncovered, they will retain their green color. Although they will lose some of it through baking, they will still appear fresher than they would if they were cooked covered.

Mixing the sour cream with the buttermilk or regular milk makes it easier to spread and helps it to penetrate the beans faster.

When the top of the casserole is finished as suggested, the bread crumbs will remain crunchy and the egg yolk will retain its vivid yellow color.

Sometimes the outside surface of the hard-boiled egg yolks have a blueish-green color. Just scrape this off and discard it. Wash the inside of the egg white with cold water and dry with a towel before chopping.

French- or Italian-type bread crumbs are simply those made from bread which contains no shortening. They will not turn rancid.

Green Peas

8 servings

2 qt. shelled, fresh peas	1 tbsp. sugar
2 cups shredded lettuce	½ tsp. salt
6 thin slices or 3 ranch-style slices bacon, cut into ¼-inch pieces	1 tsp. cornstarch
	2 tbsp. water
4 tbsp. butter	1 tbsp. chopped parsley

1. Place a heavy 12-inch frying pan over high heat. Melt the butter in it. Sprinkle the sugar in the middle of the pan and let it brown.

2. Once the sugar browns, add the peas and the salt. Stir, then push the peas around the inside rim of the frying pan, leaving the middle empty. Cover and adjust the heat to medium.

3. In another frying pan, quickly fry the bacon pieces, stirring them constantly and making sure that they do not burn.

4. As soon as the bacon pieces start to brown, remove them from the fire. Strain and save the drippings for other use. Keep the bacon bits warm.

5. After cooking the peas for 5 to 7 minutes, depending on their size, add the shredded lettuce, placing it in the middle of the pan. Cover and let the lettuce wilt for 2 minutes.

6. Add the bacon bits. Stir the mixture together, then make another ring or wreath around the inside edge of the frying pan. Cover tightly and cook for 2 more minutes over medium heat.

7. Pour the juices from the pan into a dish. Stir the cornstarch into the 2 tbsp. water, then dissolve the mixture into the pan juices. Pour this mixture back over the peas. Stir, then remove from the heat and keep covered for 10 minutes. Serve sprinkled with the chopped parsley.

CHEF'S SECRET: If you cannot get fresh shelled peas, use frozen peas. Remove them from the freezer and keep them refrigerated for several hours before cooking, or keep at room temperature for 1 hour before using. If you do not have time to do this, place the frozen peas into a sieve or colander; start rinsing with cold water and, as the peas start to separate, increase the water temperature until it is at body temperature. Shake dry and proceed as directed for fresh peas.

Peas come in many sizes, easily recognizable by comparison. The finest frozen peas are hardly bigger than the head of an old-fashioned kitchen match. The next grade compares in size to cranberries, and the common grade is even larger—about the size of a shelled hazelnut. Depending on which size you purchase or shell yourself, you can adjust the cooking time.

The caramelized sugar will not make the peas sweet, but it will enhance and emphasize the typical fresh pea taste.

The procedure of making a wreath from the peas is an oriental cooking method. The purpose is to let the heat waves and the steam circulate around the peas. The liquid collected in the middle of the pan quickly turns into steam, which condenses on the cover and drips down on the peas as they cook.

The tiny amount of cornstarch will not make the juice thick, but will thicken it just enough to make the juice adhere to the peas, enhancing the flavor.

You can substitute a small amount of finely chopped ham for the bacon bits or, if you wish, omit the meat entirely. Instead of green parsley, you can sprinkle freshly chopped mint leaves over the top.

Braised Celery Hearts

8 servings

4 celery hearts	½ cup chicken stock, or ¼ cup chicken stock and ¼ cup white wine
4 tbsp. butter	
1 tsp. salt	3 tbsp. freshly grated Parmesan cheese
1 tsp. sugar	2 tbsp. freshly chopped parsley
freshly ground black pepper to taste	

1. Wash and clean the celery hearts. Remove most of the leaves and any rough outside ribs. Split the hearts in quarters, lengthwise.

2. Heat a large, heavy frying pan. Add the sugar and let it caramelize in the bottom of the frying pan. Stirring constantly, add the butter and let it melt. Place the quarters of celery heart in the pan and lightly brown them on all sides.

3. Sprinkle over the celery hearts the salt and pepper. Pour in the liquid, cover, and simmer over low heat until the celery is tender.

4. Arrange the celery hearts in a shallow, ovenproof baking dish. Spoon a few tablespoons of the cooking liquid over them. Sprinkle the top with the freshly grated Parmesan and place the casserole under the broiler for a few minutes, just until the cheese is lightly browned.

5. Sprinkle the parsley over the top of the casserole and serve.

CHEF'S SECRET: If you do not like the pungency of the celery, first blanch the hearts by dropping them into boiling, slightly salted water for 1 to 2 minutes, then rinse with cold water. Shake dry and proceed according to the recipe.

When you are cleaning the celery hearts, before splitting, be sure that you leave on the whole white core at the root end. Start the splitting from the root end and cut toward the top.

You can make the same dish with the milder Chinese celery which is now widely available.

If you are very busy, after browning the celery hearts in the frying pan you can immediately place them in the ovenproof dish, add the liquid, and bake, covered, in a preheated 350-degree oven for 45 to 60 minutes. In this way you will not have to watch the cooking.

Braised Endive

8 servings

3 lb. Belgian endive	1 lemon
6 tbsp. butter	1 tsp. sugar
1 tsp. salt	1 cup water

1. Wash and trim the endive, removing and discarding the outside leaves.

2. In a large, heavy pot, combine the water, sugar, salt, and 2 tbsp. of the butter. Squeeze in the juice of the lemon, then drop in the pieces of lemon.

3. Bring the liquid to a boil and add the endive. Cover, bring the liquid to a boil again, and then reduce the heat and simmer for 30 to 40 minutes or until the endive is tender.

4. Immediately drain the liquid from the endive, gently pressing the endive to remove the excess moisture. Cool.

5. Just before serving, melt the remaining 4 tbsp. butter in a large frying pan and quickly brown the endive. Serve.

CHEF'S SECRET: It may seem that the amount of liquid is not enough for the amount of endive, but remember that endive is over 90 per cent water. During cooking, plenty of liquid will come out of it to supplement the original amount of water.

After the liquid comes to a boil for the second time, be sure that the simmering is done over very low heat. If you have one on hand, it is advisable to put an asbestos pad or an elevated rack between the source of heat and the pot. If you have a heavy enamel casserole or a Dutch oven, you can bake the endive in the oven.

If the 4 tbsp. of butter does not seem to be enough to brown the endive, add 1 to 2 tbsp. oil.

Asparagus

8 servings

2 bunches fresh asparagus   water
salt   butter or sauce (optional)

1. Peel each asparagus spear with a potato peeler, starting where the green part meets the white and ending at the root end. Peel to the moist layer, going completely around each spear. Cut off 1 inch from the root end.

2. Tie the spears in four small bundles with string.

3. Select a deep pot with a lid, preferably the bottom of a double boiler. Stand one bundle on the root end in the pot and fill with water until the water level reaches just below the buds on the tip of the asparagus. Remove the bundle.

4. Add approximately 1½ tsp. salt per quart of water used.

5. Bring the water to a rapid boil. Stand the bundles of asparagus in the water. When the water comes to a boil again, reduce the heat to a low boil and cover.

6. After 5 to 6 minutes, a knife should pierce the white part of the asparagus easily. Test a spear by eating it; it should have a slight resistance when you bite into the end.

7. When tender, remove from the water and place on a cloth napkin to drain. Untie the bundles. Serve from the napkin, with butter or your favorite sauce in a sauce boat on the side.

CHEF'S SECRET: When buying asparagus, try to pick spears on which the head is very firm and not too elongated and the little buds are close together. To prepare asparagus for storage, hold the bunches completely submerged in water and with a sharp knife, under water, cut approximately ⅓ to ½ inch off the bottom. Keep the bunch under water for a minute or so after cutting off the end. Remove and shake dry. Store standing on a wet cloth or wet paper towel until used. If the asparagus spears are cut under water, they will absorb enough moisture to stay fresh but will not lose their own flavor. Flavor would be lost if you stored them standing in water. Do not store for too long.

The most important thing to remember in preparing asparagus is that it must not be overcooked.

Spring Vegetable Mixture

8 servings

2 cups green peas
½ cup carrots, cut the size of the peas
1 cup kohlrabi, cut the size of the peas
1 cup turnip or rutabaga, cut the size
   of the peas
½ cup celery stalks, sliced crosswise
2 cups asparagus, cut into 1-inch pieces

4 tbsp. butter
salt and pepper to taste
sprinkling of sugar
2 cups half-and-half
1 cup chicken broth
4 tbsp. flour

1. Melt the butter in a large saucepan over medium heat. Add the carrots, rutabaga or turnip, and kohlrabi. Cover and cook for 10 minutes.

2. Add the celery, peas, salt, pepper, and sugar. Pour in the chicken broth and quickly bring the mixture to a boil. Reduce the heat, cover, and simmer for about 30 minutes.

3. Dissolve the flour in 1 cup of the half-and-half. Stir this mixture into the simmering vegetables. Add the asparagus and cook for approximately 10 more minutes. Stir once or twice so the mixture will not stick to the bottom of the pan.

4. Just before serving, add the rest of the half-and-half.

CHEF'S SECRET: This spring "medley" is very good. The secret is that no flavor should overpower the other and that the vegetables should not be overcooked. As you notice, the amounts of carrot and celery are smaller than the amounts of other vegetables used. This is because carrots and celery have a more pungent flavor, and they would overpower the rest of the vegetables if used in equal amounts.

If you wish, you can substitute sour cream for the half-and-half.

SALADS

Avocado with Crab
Russian Meat
Chicken-Waldorf
Marinated Beef—Stock Yard Inn
Fish in Tomatoes
Crab-Apple
Bibb Lettuce
Spinach-Mushroom
Mushroom-Apple
Raw Cabbage

Carrot with Lemon
Celery Remoulade
Anchovy-Celery
German Celery Root
Holiday
Cauliflower-Tomato
English Eggs
Coconut-Herring
Bean-Veal

*I*n the oldest known cookery book, Roman recipes attributed to Apicius, a big chapter contains recipes for *insalata,* which means pickled, salted, and kept in brine or vinegar. Of course, the custom of serving uncooked vegetables preserved for a long time in salt or vinegar, or prepared the same way just before eating, is much, much older than Roman times. Chinese and Korean cooks four thousand years ago discovered the art of pickling and, believe it or not, "German" or "Polish" sauerkraut is Chinese in origin.

Today's salads are a far cry from this old concept. The meaning of the word has expanded to include any raw or cooked vegetable or fruit, herbs, even meat, poultry, eggs, and cheese if they are served cold with some kind of marinade, dressing, or sauce which makes them acid or tart.

One of the oldest arguments among cooks and chefs and eaters concerns salads. When should they be served, during a meal, or before or after the main course? Some restaurants go somewhat further—they bring on the salad before the soup. I do not feel that any rule should be set. I feel that it always depends on the whole meal and on the taste of the eaters. Of course, in Europe the salad is served after the main course or with the main course. Its purpose is mainly to clean the palate and prepare it or refresh it for the joys of the next dish, which could be cheese, a "savory," or what we call dessert. To me only one thing is important: with the exception of hot German potato salad or hot Austrian cabbage salad, all salads should be served chilled (but only cooled, not ice-cold), and the dressing, whatever it may be, should be used sparingly so as not to overpower the taste of the other ingredients.

Salads

Avocado with Crab

8 servings

4 ripe avocados
2 7½-oz. cans crabmeat or, if available, 1 lb. fresh crabmeat
8 tbsp. mayonnaise (see page 214)
4 to 6 drops Worcestershire sauce
½ cup finely minced, peeled celery stalks

salt, depending on the saltiness of the crabmeat
small pinch white pepper
small pinch cayenne or 1 to 2 drops Tabasco
1 head iceberg lettuce
2 lemons

1. Split the avocados in half lengthwise and remove the pits. With a melon-ball cutter, gently enlarge the cavity toward the stem end.
2. With a fork, mash the avocado pulp which was removed.
3. Mix the pulp with 4 tbsp. of the mayonnaise, salt if needed, pepper, and cayenne or Tabasco. Gently fold in the crabmeat and the celery.
4. Divide the crab mixture among the eight avocado halves.
5. Mix the Worcestershire sauce with the remaining 4 tbsp. mayonnaise. With a pastry bag or a cone made from wax paper, pipe approximately ½ tbsp. of the mayonnaise mixture on each filled avocado half.
6. Remove the outside leaves of the iceberg lettuce. Arrange the leaves on a serving platter. Cut the inside part of the lettuce into very thin strips and make 8 small nests on the leaves lining the serving platter. Place an avocado half on each nest.
7. Cut each lemon in quarters and garnish the serving platter with the slices of lemon. Serve. If desired, offer additional mayonnaise separately.

CHEF'S SECRET: When you buy avocados, they should not be soft but, if pressed gently, should give about the same resistance as an orange. Once at home, pack each avocado in a brown paper bag and leave them at room temperature overnight. Of course, chill before serving.

If you use canned crabmeat, it is advisable to pick it over. Sometimes you may find a small piece of the shell. Definitely taste it for saltiness. Certain brands improve with a quick rinsing with water. If you have to rinse it, don't do it under the faucet. Place the meat in a sieve and dip the sieve in a small amount of water. Loosen the meat with one finger, then remove the sieve from the water and shake the meat dry. The flavor will not be destroyed, but the saltiness of the canning liquid will be gone.

Enlarging the cavity of the avocados with a melon-ball cutter has two purposes; you have the subtle taste of the pulp in the crab mixture, and it is easier to arrange the filling without making it messy.

Definitely peel the celery stalks for this dish with a potato peeler so that no strings get into the salad. The celery is needed for its crunchy texture to counterbalance the softness of the avocado and mayonnaise and the fleshy chewiness of the crabmeat. If you do not care for the taste of celery, you can substitute peeled, seeded, finely chopped cucumber.

Russian Meat

8 servings

1 lb. leftover roast meat, such as beef, pork, lamb, veal, or a mixture of these, cut into julienne strips
½ cup cooked green peas
½ cup cooked carrots, cut into ¼ -inch cubes
1 cup boiled, chilled potatoes, cut into ¼ -inch cubes
½ cup dill pickle, peeled and cut into ¼ -inch cubes
1 cup onion, sliced in julienne strips somewhat smaller than the meat strips

2 cups sour cream
2 tbsp. dill pickle juice from the jar
2 tbsp. vinegar
juice of ½ lemon
salt and pepper to taste
1 tsp. sugar
enough lettuce leaves to make a bed for the salad
dried parsley flakes or freshly chopped parsley
black olives (optional)

1. Combine the meat and vegetables in a bowl. Sprinkle them with a mixture made from the vinegar, lemon juice, pickle juice, and spices. Let marinate at room temperature for about 1 hour, turning once in a while.

2. Set aside about 1 tbsp. of the sour cream, then gently fold the remainder into the marinated meat and vegetable mixture.

3. Arrange the lettuce leaves on a serving platter and pile the salad on top. Sprinkle with dried parsley flakes or freshly chopped parsley, top with the dab of reserved sour cream, and decorate with a small sprig of parsley or with black olives. Chill and serve.

CHEF'S SECRET: This is a very elegant and easy way to use up leftover meats. Cut the meat with a sharp knife while it is very cold. Discard any fat, as it will ruin the taste.

Letting the mixture marinate at room temperature will blend the tastes, and the pickle juice will add a very nice dill flavor.

If you object to the pungency of the onion, you can use the white part only of scallion, or, after cutting the onion, put it in a colander or a sieve and quickly pour some boiling water over it and then rinse under the cold water faucet until completely cooled. The texture and taste will remain the same, but some of the pungency will be gone.

If you wish, you can add some canned beets to half of the mixture. Then, instead of one big heap, make two small ones: one with the white sour cream and one that is pink from the beets.

Chicken Waldorf

8 servings

3 to 4 cups cold, boiled, boneless white chicken meat, cut into ½-inch cubes
2 cups red apple, unpeeled, cored, and diced into ½-inch cubes
1 cup celery, peeled and diced into ¼-inch cubes

2 cups mayonnaise (see page 214)
salt
4 tbsp. chopped walnuts
1 tsp. Worcestershire sauce
lettuce leaves

1. In a bowl, combine the chicken, apple, celery, mayonnaise, and Worcestershire sauce. Add a pinch of salt if desired.
2. Line eight salad plates with the lettuce leaves.
3. Divide the salad among the plates and sprinkle the top of each with the chopped walnuts. Serve chilled.

CHEF'S SECRET: If possible, do not cut the apple and mix it into the salad until the last minute. Use a stainless steel knife when cutting the apple. Cube the apple into a mixture of water and lemon juice or water and vinegar to prevent its turning dark. If you cannot leave it to the last minute, then first mix the cut apple into the mayonnaise and be sure it is completely coated before adding the other ingredients.

Many people, for various reasons, dislike chopped walnuts. If you like, offer the nuts separately in a small dish and let the guests help themselves.

Marinated Beef—Stock Yard Inn

8 servings

1 lb. boiled, broiled, or roasted beef, cut into julienne strips
1 large onion, cut the same as the beef
juice of 1 lemon
1½ tbsp. prepared mustard
2 tbsp. sugar
¼ tsp. freshly ground black pepper

2 tsp. curry powder (or more)
2 cups commercial sour cream
½ cup white vinegar
salt to taste
lettuce leaves
paprika
chopped parsley

1. In a large bowl, mix together the beef and onion. Sprinkle with lemon juice and salt. Let stand at room temperature for 20 minutes.
2. In another bowl, mix the mustard, sugar, pepper, and curry powder until it forms a paste.
3. Gently fold the sour cream and vinegar into the spice mixture.

4. Fold this sauce into the beef and onions. Let it marinate in the refrigerator for at least 4 hours.

5. Taste for salt; add more if necessary. Serve on beds of lettuce, sprinkled with paprika and parsley.

CHEF'S SECRET: This recipe originated in Chicago at the famous Stock Yard Inn. Its secret is really in the quality of the meat used. Do not use any fat; use only the lean or marbled beef. If you feel the quality of the meat you have is not the best, cut the julienne strips very small—no bigger than matchsticks —and avoid cutting along the grain.

Marinating the beef and onions in the lemon juice and salt gives a very good taste to the beef, which will not be overpowered by the lemon. If you were to do the marinating with vinegar, the taste would be impaired.

You can make the same dish with yogurt instead of the sour cream, but be very careful while folding in the vinegar not to destroy the texture of the yogurt.

Fish in Tomatoes

8 servings

8 firm, medium-sized, ripe tomatoes, peeled and cored
8 thin 2-oz. pieces of fillet of sole or flounder
1 qt. water
1 bay leaf
1 piece lemon peel, 2 inches by 1 inch
½ tsp. black peppercorns, slightly bruised
2 to 3 sliced onions
1 cup vinegar
1 tsp. salt
2 cups mayonnaise (see page 214), or lemon, or Sauce Louis (see page 215)
1 tbsp. sugar
1 envelope gelatin
3 tbsp. water
juice of ½ lemon
capers or parsley sprigs (optional)

1. Peel and core the tomatoes. Sprinkle the inside of each with a little sugar, then turn upside down and chill.

2. Very gently flatten each fillet and sprinkle with salt. Roll jelly-roll fashion according to the drawing, and secure with a toothpick. Place the little turbans of fish into a suitable cooking dish.

3. Combine the 1 qt. water, vinegar, bay leaf, peppercorns, onions, and lemon peel and bring the mixture to the simmering point.

4. Pour the simmering (not boiling) marinade over the fish, then gently simmer the fish in the liquid for 10 minutes. Let the fish cool in the liquid.

5. Once the fish has cooled to room temperature, gently remove the turbans from the liquid. Remove the toothpicks and refrigerate the fish.

6. Strain 1 cup of the cooking liquid through a cheesecloth. Add the lemon juice and bring to a boil. Meanwhile, dissolve the gelatin in the 3 tbsp. water. Mix the gelatin into the boiling marinade, immediately remove from the heat, and cool in an ice water bath, stirring with your finger, until it becomes sticky and turns syrupy.

7. Place the fish turbans into the tomatoes. Brush the top of each lightly with the gelatin mixture. Decorate each with a rinsed caper dipped in gelatin or with a small sprig of parsley. Chill.

8. Serve with homemade mayonnaise, lemon, or Sauce Louis.

CHEF's SECRET: For instructions on peeling the tomatoes, see *Chef's Secret,* page 133. Sprinkling the inside of the tomatoes with sugar will take away the acidity and make them pleasant-tasting but not sweet.

Letting the fish cool in the liquid will keep them from drying out. If you cannot get fillets, just cook ½ lb. of fish and then heap the flakes into the tomatoes and brush with the gelatin.

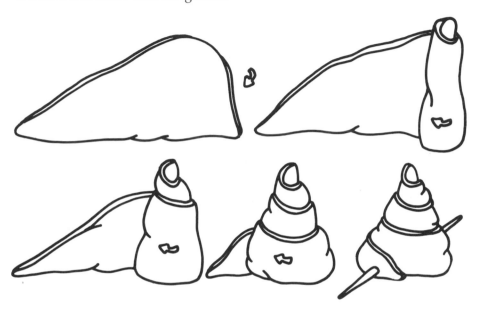

Crab-Apple

8 servings

8 large Rome Beauty apples	3 to 4 tbsp. bourbon
juice of 2 lemons	1½ tsp. prepared mustard
16 fresh pitted dates, cut into ¼-inch slices	1 tsp. Worcestershire sauce
	1 lb. Dungeness crabmeat (use claws for decoration)
2 4- to 5-inch celery stalks, peeled and cut into ⅛-inch slices	lettuce leaves
2 cups mayonnaise (see page 214)	leafy celery tops

1. Cut a slice ½ to ¾ inches thick from the top of each apple. Rub the surfaces with lemon juice. Refrigerate the tops. (See drawing, page 190.)

2. With a melon-ball cutter, scoop out 4 or 5 balls from each apple. Sprinkle with lemon juice.

3. Remove the core of each apple to enlarge the cavity. Sprinkle the inside of the apples with lemon juice. Refrigerate.

4. Combine the apple balls, dates, and celery in a small bowl.

5. Gently fold together the mayonnaise, bourbon, mustard, and Worcestershire sauce. Add half of this to the combined fruit. Chill for one hour.

6. Before serving, gently fold the crabmeat into the mayonnaise-fruit mixture and place one-fourth of the mixture into each apple.

7. Spoon the remaining mayonnaise on top of each apple. Replace tops.

8. Serve each apple on a bed of lettuce leaves and garnish each with a few crab claws and celery tops.

CHEF'S SECRET: To have nice, completely round balls from the apple, follow the drawing. It is important that you first press the whole circumference of the cutter into the apple and, turning the wrist left to right, keep pressing until you feel (or check by removing the cutter) that you have the upper half of the ball perfectly shaped. Then, with a clockwise movement, still pressing, turn the cutter 180 degrees, then remove. You can use this method for other fruit balls.

Bibb Lettuce

8 servings

4 heads Boston or 8 heads Kentucky bibb lettuce
juice of 2 lemons, diluted with a small amount of water
4 to 6 tbsp. fresh oil

1 clove garlic
freshly ground black pepper
pinch salt
pinch sugar

1. Sprinkle the bottom of a wooden salad bowl with salt. Cut the garlic in half and gently rub it on the salt; then discard the garlic.

2. Add the sugar and a little black pepper to the bowl. Pour in the oil. Then, with a fork or wire whip, dissolve the spices in the oil.

3. Pour in the lemon juice–water mixture, stirring constantly. Pour the mixture from the bowl into another container. Keep at room temperature.

4. Very quickly wash and dry the lettuce. Remove the outside leaves if necessary, then place the lettuce in the wooden bowl and chill.

5. Just before serving, vigorously stir the dressing and pour it over the salad. Toss gently and serve immediately.

CHEF'S SECRET: There are mainly two kinds of bibb lettuce available throughout the United States: Boston bibb and Kentucky bibb. Boston is tender and almost lemon yellow on the inside. Kentucky is hearty, leafy, and darker green but also very tender and tasty. It is a sin to use an overpowering dressing on either one.

If you have a wooden mortar and pestle, of course you do not have to make the dressing in the salad bowl. However, the bowl itself improves and will last longer if you keep rubbing the inside with garlic, because of the oil in the garlic.

The best way of drying the bibb lettuce or any other vegetable is to use a French wire basket which is designed for this purpose. If you do not have such a basket, just put the lettuce in a large absorbent kitchen towel which is about 20 inches by 20 inches. Fold the four corners together and, making a full circle with your arm, shake out the water.

If you chill the dressing or chill the lettuce with the dressing on it, the oil will become firm and separate and will not coat as nicely as when kept at room temperature. Of course, if you wish, you can substitute a good-quality vinegar for the lemon juice.

Spinach-Mushroom

8 servings

1 lb. fresh spinach	¼ tsp. mushroom powder
5 oz. firm, snow-white fresh mushrooms, unopened	1 scant tsp. salt
	1 scant tsp. sugar
⅔ cup white vinegar	¼ tsp. white pepper
⅔ cup oil	½ tsp. dried parsley flakes
1 cup water	

1. Carefully pick over the spinach leaves, removing the large stems. Wash and swing dry. Tear the leaves into bite-size pieces.

2. Very quickly wash the mushrooms and wipe them with a damp cloth. Slice them crosswise, using both stems and heads, into ⅛-inch slices. Mix into the spinach. Chill.

3. In a wooden bowl, dissolve all the spices in the oil, then add the water and vinegar. Let stand at room temperature.

4. Just before serving, pour the dressing over the spinach and mushrooms or toss them gently in the dressing. Serve.

CHEF'S SECRET: This is a very fine salad, simple to make and very tasty—but only if you keep strictly to the directions. Do not use the mushrooms if their heads are opened up, resembling an umbrella, and you can see the brown grooves on the underside.

See *Chef's Secret*, page 208, for instructions for washing mushrooms, but keep in mind that it is very important to work fast.

Mushroom-Apple

8 servings

4 large, tart apples, red-skinned if possible
8 oz. very firm, snow-white, large or medium mushrooms
4 tbsp. honey
4 tbsp. oil
4 tbsp. vinegar
1 cup canned apple juice
salt and freshly ground black pepper to taste
8 lettuce leaves

1. Core and split the apples in half, then thinly slice them crosswise, leaving on the skin if possible.
2. After washing the mushrooms, slice them the same thickness as the apple slices.
3. Gently toss together the apple and mushroom slices.
4. Place the lettuce leaves on individual salad plates. Spoon a portion of the apple and mushroom slices on each lettuce leaf. Chill.
5. Prepare the dressing by combining the apple juice, vinegar, honey, salt, freshly ground pepper, and oil. Keep at room temperature.
6. Just before serving, spoon the dressing over the salads.

CHEF'S SECRET: The honey in this recipe will not make the salad sweet, but will add a very desirable consistency and will help the dressing to adhere to the ingredients.

See *Chef's Secret*, page 208, for instructions on washing mushrooms.

Raw Cabbage

8 servings

1 medium-sized head white cabbage
6 tbsp. oil
1 cup vinegar
1 cup water
1 tsp. salt
¼ tsp. pepper
3 tsp. caraway seeds
3 tbsp. sugar
4 or 5 strips bacon, chopped

1. Shred the cabbage as finely as possible. Soak for several hours in ice water. Drain.
2. Prepare a marinade with all the remaining ingredients except the bacon. Pour the marinade over the cabbage and let it stand for at least 1 hour.
3. Just before serving, fry the bacon slightly. Add the bacon plus the fat to the cabbage while still hot. Toss and serve immediately.

CHEF'S SECRET: Soaking the cabbage in the ice water serves two purposes at once: it eliminates the heavy odor that would develop otherwise, and it makes the cabbage very crisp and thus easier to chew and more enjoyable.

To drain the cabbage, do not press it. Shake or swing it dry as quickly and thoroughly as possible.

If you like a more sweet-sour taste, increase the sugar to ½ cup.

Carrot with Lemon

8 servings

4 cups shredded carrots
1 cup seedless raisins
½ cup fresh lemon juice
¾ cup salad oil
2 tsp. salt

pinch white pepper
½ tsp. dry mustard
1 tsp. paprika
dash cayenne
2 cups water

1. In a small saucepan, bring the water to a boil. Add the raisins, cover, and turn off the heat. Let the raisins stand in the warm water for at least 20 minutes. Drain.

2. Place the raisins and shredded carrots in a serving bowl.

3. With a wire whip, combine the lemon juice, oil, salt, pepper, dry mustard, paprika, and cayenne.

4. Pour the dressing over the salad and refrigerate for at least 2 hours before serving.

CHEF'S SECRET: This salad has been the rage of the French gourmets for the last few years. It was always popular, but lately it has appeared on the menus in the most elegant places.

This is the type of recipe that can be modified and developed into something very uniquely your own. For instance, you can change the raisins to chopped pitted prunes, or you can substitute chopped pitted dates, figs, or any other dried fruit for a part of the raisins. If raisins or other dried fruits are too much for your diet, you can use ¼-inch cubes of a celery stalk that has been peeled before it is chopped.

Celery Remoulade

8 servings

3 to 4 large celery knobs (celeriac),
approximately 2 to 2½ lb. altogether
1 tsp. salt
⅔ cup vinegar

3 tbsp. Dijon-style mustard
¼ tsp. white pepper
⅔ cup oil
juice of ½ lemon
2 to 3 tbsp. freshly chopped parsley

1. Peel the celery knobs and cut them into thin julienne strips (⅛ by ⅛ by 2 inches). Sprinkle the strips with the salt and vinegar and let stand for 15 minutes. Drain.

2. Blend together the mustard, a little salt, and white pepper. Using a wire whip, gradually beat in the oil.

3. Add the lemon juice.

4. Toss the celery with the remoulade sauce and place it in a serving dish. Sprinkle the top with the chopped parsley.

CHEF'S SECRET: Celery knob, or celeriac, is mainly available from November through April throughout most of the United States. If you do not see it in the grocery, simply ask for it. If the produce manager does not have any on hand, he can pick up a half bushel for you. Seeds for celeriac are also readily available and easy to grow.

If you want your celery remoulade to be snow white, while you are cutting the julienne strips have on hand a plastic bowl with enough cold water mixed with vinegar to cover the celery. Keep both the peeled uncut celery and the thin julienne strips in the vinegar-water until you start to make the salad itself.

In different books, you will find many different recipes for remoulade. I am afraid no such thing as a "real" or "true" remoulade sauce exists. Whatever concoction you make with mustard, vinegar, water, and spices can be called remoulade if this is what you want to call it.

Anchovy-Celery

8 servings

8 pascal celery hearts, each large enough for 1 portion	juice of 1 lemon
4 tsp. anchovy paste	1 to 2 tbsp. white vinegar
4 tbsp. oil	1 cup mayonnaise (see page 214)
light sprinkling of sugar	8 lettuce leaves
	ice water

1. Cut the celery hearts on a very bias diagonal (see drawing). Drop the slices into the ice water and let them stay for at least 2 hours. Remove and swing dry.

2. In the bottom of a wooden salad bowl, mix the anchovy paste, sugar, oil, and lemon juice with the vinegar. Fold in the mayonnaise.

3. Gently toss the celery hearts in the dressing. Spoon the salad onto the lettuce leaves and serve.

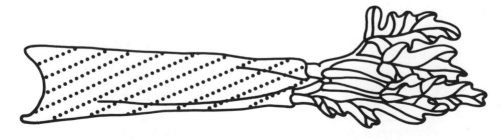

CHEF'S SECRET: This is a dish that is served in France, probably more frequently as a first course than as a salad.

The way the celery heart is cut and the blend of the dressing flavors make it a great taste surprise. It is important that the celery hearts used for this dish be fresh, crisp, and almost entirely yellow and white, with no green parts at all. Do not discard the thick bottom part of the celery heart. Thinly slice it into the salad; it is one of the tastiest parts of the celery.

German Celery Root

8 servings

4 small celery knobs (celeriac)	salt
boiling, salted water	white pepper
½ lemon	2 cups mayonnaise (see page 214)

1. Peel the celery knobs and cut them crosswise into ¼-inch slices.
2. Squeeze the ½ lemon into the boiling water, then drop the peel into the water. Place the slices of celery knob in the boiling water and cook 15 to 20 minutes or until tender. Be careful not to overcook. Drain and cool to room temperature.
3. Season with salt and white pepper.
4. Fold in the mayonnaise. Chill thoroughly in the refrigerator before serving.

CHEF'S SECRET: This is a basic recipe for the German way of serving celery root. Again, of course, you can create many variations. Many people add minced or very thinly sliced blanched onions, or thinly sliced boiled potatoes. Instead of the mayonnaise, you can make a vinaigrette using lemon juice or vinegar, or both.

Holiday

8 servings

6 cups boiled, sliced potatoes	1 cup sour cream
1 cup peeled celery stalk, sliced on the bias	juice of 1 lemon
	1 tbsp. sugar
½ cup pitted chopped black olives	3 or 4 drops Worcestershire sauce
½ cup pitted chopped green olives	3 or 4 drops Tabasco sauce
½ cup chopped onions	lettuce leaves (optional)
2 hard-boiled eggs, chopped	chopped parsley
2 cups mayonnaise (see page 214)	

1. In a large bowl, combine the potatoes with the celery, olives, and onions.
2. Stir the lemon juice, sugar, Worcestershire sauce, and Tabasco sauce into the mayonnaise, then gently fold in the sour cream.
3. Spread the dressing evenly over the potato salad mixture. Sprinkle the chopped egg on top. Gently fold the mixture together with two rubber spatulas or scrapers.

4. Pile the salad on a bed of lettuce leaves or place it in an easy-to-empty mold. Decorate it with the chopped parsley or withhold some of the chopped egg from the mixture and use it for a garnish.

5. Chill; then serve.

CHEF'S SECRET: The secret of this salad is that it should be mixed with a very light hand. Do not break the potato slices.

The addition of the sour cream and other ingredients would lift even a good commercial mayonnaise out of the ordinary.

Cauliflower-Tomato

8 servings

1 small, very firm, snow-white head cauliflower
4 large or 8 medium-sized ripe tomatoes
2 hard-boiled eggs
1½ to 2 cups sour cream
2 to 3 tbsp. vodka

salt and black pepper to taste
2 cups water
½ cup vinegar
1 bay leaf
2 tbsp. freshly chopped parsley
lettuce leaves or chopped lettuce
sugar

1. Separate the cauliflower, but do not make the segments extremely small.

2. Place the water, vinegar, and bay leaf in a saucepan and bring the mixture to a boil. Add salt and pepper. Reduce the heat to a steady simmer.

3. One by one, dip the tomatoes into the hot liquid and leave for 15 seconds. Immediately remove and rinse under cold running water until cooled. If the tomatoes are too large to be completely covered with the liquid, turn them in the liquid with a spoon.

4. Add the cauliflower to the simmering liquid and bring to a boil. As soon as the water starts to boil, remove from the heat, cover, and let cool for at least 1 hour without removing the cover. Remove the cauliflowerets from the marinade and chill.

5. Meanwhile, peel the tomatoes. Cut off the top and scoop out the inside with a melon-ball cutter or a grapefruit knife. Sprinkle the inside of each with sugar and turn upside down and chill.

6. Separate the egg whites from the yolks. Chop the whites. Press the yolks through a coarse sieve, then mix them with the chopped parsley.

7. Gently stir the vodka into the sour cream.

8. When ready to serve, place the chopped egg whites in the tomatoes. Arrange the cauliflowerets on top of the egg whites, spoon the vodka–sour cream mixture over the top of each, and then sprinkle with the egg yolk–parsley mixture and serve on a bed of lettuce leaves or on finely chopped lettuce.

CHEF'S SECRET: When the cauliflower is cooked in this way, it will absorb a lot of the spiciness of the bay leaf and the vinegar. Be careful that it is not overcooked. If you have to use a heavy pot which will retain the heat for a long time, set the pot with the cauliflowerets into a larger vessel of cold water to expedite the cooling.

The vodka folded into the sour cream will give a very mysterious but pleasant taste surprise.

English Eggs

8 servings

8 medium or 6 large hard-boiled eggs
1 cup peeled, coarsely chopped celery
   stalks
1 cup peeled, seeded, coarsely
   chopped cucumber
1 tbsp. rinsed capers

3 tbsp. French mustard
2 cups mayonnaise (see page 214)
1 tsp. Worcestershire sauce
¼ tsp. English mustard
1 tbsp. green parsley, chopped, or 1
   tsp. dried parsley flakes

1. Peel and coarsely chop the hard-boiled eggs.
2. Gently fold together the French mustard, English mustard, mayonnaise, and Worcestershire sauce.
3. Combine the chopped egg, celery, cucumber, and capers, and gently fold them into the mayonnaise mixture. Sprinkle the top with the parsley and chill. Serve.

CHEF'S SECRET: This salad is best served with cold meats such as leftover lamb, pork, beef, or poultry. However, it can also be served as a luncheon dish. Spoon on toast points and quickly heat under the broiler until it starts to bubble. A typical British vegetable such as brussels sprouts, broccoli, or asparagus spears is a fine complement.

Coconut-Herring

8 servings

4 salt herrings, or 1 1-lb. jar herring in
   wine sauce
1 cup toasted, salted coconut chips
1 cup finely minced onion
juice of 1 lemon
1 cup sour cream

2 oz. cream cheese
¼ to ½ tsp. curry powder, depending
   on taste
4 fresh coconuts, if available, or
   enough lettuce leaves to serve

1. Wash the salt herring in 3 different waters, wiping dry on paper towels after each washing.
2. Place the herring in cold water and soak overnight in the refrigerator.
3. Next day, split each herring in half. Discard the bones and as much of the skin as possible. Cut the herring crosswise into finger-thick slices.
4. In a bowl, mash the cream cheese with the curry and 1 tbsp. of the sour cream. Keep mashing and adding more sour cream until the mixture is soft enough to fold into the remaining sour cream without difficulty. Add the chopped onions and lemon juice.
5. Fold the pieces of herring into the dressing and let marinate at room temperature for 1 hour, then chill.
6. To serve, divide the mixture among the eight coconut halves or spoon onto lettuce leaves. Generously sprinkle the top of each serving with the coconut chips and, if desired, also add 1 peeled, cored, and very thinly sliced apple.

CHEF'S SECRET: It is important to dry the herring after each washing because the salt that comes out tends to stay on the surface. The reason they must be washed in three different waters is that each time the water will very quickly absorb a part of the salt and oils from the fish. Soaking overnight removes all excess salt.

The toasted, salted coconut chips are available throughout the country in better groceries. If there are none available in your location, you can prepare your own. Buy a fresh coconut and, after peeling, make chips by slicing it on a cucumber slicer. Place the chips on an aluminum foil–lined cookie sheet, sprinkle lightly with salt, and toast in a preheated 250-degree oven for 25 to 30 minutes.

Bean-Veal

8 servings

2 to 2½ lb. boneless, rolled leg of veal	black pepper
7-oz. can tuna fish in olive oil	olive oil
1 small can anchovy fillets	lemon juice
1 small onion, finely chopped	1 can white northern beans, drained
2 small carrots, finely chopped	2 hard-boiled egg yolks
2 cups dry white wine	1 tsp. capers, finely chopped
½ cup wine vinegar	2 tbsp. chopped fresh parsley
1 cup water	1 clove garlic, slightly crushed
salt	

1. Rinse the anchovy fillets quickly in lukewarm water. Chop them finely.

2. Place the veal, tuna, anchovies, onions, carrots, wine, vinegar, and water in a large, heavy saucepan with a lid. Season with salt and pepper. Bring to a boil, lower the heat, cover, and simmer very gently for 1½ hours or until the meat is tender.

3. Wash the beans with cold water. Drain. Marinate them in some olive oil with garlic, salt, and pepper.

4. Remove the veal from the pan and let it cool to room temperature, then refrigerate.

5. Strain the sauce from the vegetables and tuna. Let both cool separately.

6. Place the vegetable-tuna mixture into a blender and purée, adding strained liquid as necessary.

7. Add the egg yolks and a little more liquid to the purée.

8. Continuing to blend on low speed, slowly add enough olive oil to make a smooth sauce.

9. Stir in the capers by hand. Season with lemon juice.

10. Slice the cold veal into very thin slices. Arrange the slices of veal on a platter, slightly overlapping. Pour a little sauce over the veal.

11. Drain the beans from the olive oil. Arrange the beans on the platter and sprinkle them with the chopped parsley. Serve cold with extra sauce on the side.

CHEF'S SECRET: The veal cooked with the vegetables, tuna, and anchovies will have a very interesting, inimitable "Italian" flavor which will improve if you make the dish 1 day ahead. After removing the veal from the cooking liquid and letting it cool to room temperature, wrap it in a plastic or aluminum foil sheet, pour 2 to 3 tbsp. of the cooking liquid into the package, then place it in the refrigerator overnight.

If you have time, pierce the meat with a large cooking needle while it is cooking; even more of the flavor will penetrate the veal.

The canned beans must be washed; otherwise they will have an unpleasant taste. If possible, use Italian canned beans.

If you do not have a blender, use a food mill or sieve, or mash the vegetable-tuna mixture in a wooden salad bowl as the Italians do.

SAUCES

Beef Stock—Sauce Espagnol
Red Wine Sauce
Pan Deglazing
Gravies
Tomato Sauce
Mushroom Sauce
Chicken Stock Béchamel
Dill Sauce
Tarragon Sauce
Horseradish Sauce
Redeye Gravy
Giblet Sauce
Creole Sauce

Oxford Sauce
English Mustard Sauce
Real Mayonnaise
    Remoulade Sauce
    Green Sauce (Sauce Verte)
Sauce Louis
Vanilla Sauce
Chocolate Sauce
Cherry Glaze
Zabaglione
Whipped Cream–Orange
    Marmalade Sauce
Caramel Sauce

*S*auces are probably surrounded with more mystery and romance than anything else in the repertoire of food, with the single exception of soufflés. The greatness of a chef or cook is always measured by his ability, talent, and ingenuity with sauces. The reason for this is very old and very simple. Before refrigerators it was very difficult to keep meats, and for this reason it was important to "cover up" the taste of meats not always fresh. Later on, as times changed, sauces were not needed to "cover up" anymore. They are now served for artistic gastronomic purposes, to accompany, to enhance, to counterbalance, and to underline the taste of the food with which they are to be served. Of course, whenever sauces are made and served, this must be kept in mind: sauces should accompany, not overtake.

When you try the different sauces in this chapter, you will find their consistencies vary from thin, almost liquid, to very thick. The consistency is very important, an integral part of the success of a sauce. Some sauces should moisten, others coat; some need thickness to keep the ingredients in suspension, others do not. Of course, personal tastes can also make a difference, but for a skilled cook this causes no trouble. For thinner consistencies, the addition of a few spoonfuls of stock, milk, cream, or water is sufficient. Whenever a thicker consistency is required, one or two teaspoonfuls of cornstarch diluted with some cold water will do the trick.

Sauces

Beef Stock—Sauce Espagnol

Beef Stock

1 gallon

4 lb. beef bones
1 lb. beef shank
2 lb. veal front
8 oz. slab bacon
2 or 3 onions, depending on size, unpeeled
1 tsp. black peppercorns
1 bay leaf
4 cloves
2 cloves garlic, unpeeled

2 cups coarsely chopped carrots
2 cups coarsely chopped celery tops
1 tbsp. tomato paste
1 leek or 2 or 3 scallions
1 bunch (12 to 15 sprigs) green parsley
1 parsley root or parsnip
approximately 8 oz. turnip or rutabaga
2 to 3 tbsp. salt

1. Cut into the top surface of the slab bacon crosswise, cutting about two-thirds of the way to the rind. Put the bacon and beef bones in a large frying pan. Over medium to high heat, render the fat from the bacon.

2. When there is a layer of hot fat in the bottom of the pan, cut each onion in half, crosswise, and place, cut surface down, in the fat. Fry until deep, dark brown.

3. Remove and discard bacon and place the vegetables in the pan on top of the bones, which should be somewhat brown on the surface. Add all the spices. Stir for a couple of minutes, then let the vegetables brown slightly.

4. Place the beef shank and veal front, cut into two or three pieces, in a large soup pot. Transfer all the contents of the frying pan to the pot. Fill with enough water to cover everything and have 2 inches water above the surface. Add the tomato paste.

5. Cover pot and bring to a boil. Reduce heat to low and simmer, covered, for at least 6 hours.

6. Shut off the heat completely and let stand for 1 hour. Skim and discard all fat from the pot.

7. Pour liquid through a colander to another pot, pressing vegetables gently to remove liquid from them. Discard all bones and vegetables.

8. Chop all meat which fell off the bones, beef shank, and veal front, then grind it through a meat grinder and return it to the stock pot.

9. Again bring the stock to a boil, reduce heat, and simmer under cover for about 2 hours. Let stand for 1 hour, skim surface to remove fat, then strain through a wet kitchen towel. Correct seasoning by adding salt if necessary.

CHEF'S SECRET: This is a basic stock recipe suitable for a housewife. It may, of course, be varied by omitting certain spices or vegetables or by adding others.

If you don't want to use bacon, replace with a piece of suet.

The veal front contains a very large amount of natural gelatin which boils out, dissolves in the stock, and adds to its viscosity, or makes it syrupy. The bacon with the rind left on also helps in this regard, since a large amount of natural gelatin cooks out from the bacon rind.

If you want to store this stock for later use, the best and easiest way is as follows: Measure the amount of stock you have. If, for instance, it is 3 quarts, pour 1½ qt. water into an empty pot. Use a wooden spoon to measure the depth of the water in the pan, making a mark on the spoon. Discard water and pour the stock into the same pan. Simmer slowly, uncovered, until half of it evaporates or until the liquid level in the pan is the same as it was with the 1½ qt. water. Cool the reduced liquid, then pour into ice cube trays and freeze. Wrap each stock cube individually in plastic wrap and store in the freezer. When you need a little stock, take out one cube and dilute with an equal amount of water. You can do the same thing with any other stock or cooking liquid such as fish, chicken, veal, or ham stock.

Sauce Espagnol (Basic Brown Sauce)

1 quart

1 qt. beef stock	grinding of fresh pepper
4 tbsp. flour	4 tbsp. melted butter
1 tbsp. cornstarch	2 tbsp. lard, bacon drippings, or ren-
2 tbsp. tomato purée	dered suet
1 tsp. Worcestershire sauce	

1. Melt the butter and other shortening in a saucepan.

2. Stir the flour, cornstarch, tomato purée, Worcestershire sauce, and fresh pepper into 1 cup of the stock. Using a wire whip and stirring vigorously, blend this mixture into the melted shortening, cooking at medium heat.

3. As soon as the mixture starts to thicken, immediately begin to add the remaining 3 cups stock, pouring in a thin stream and stirring until completely incorporated.

4. Leave over medium heat for 3 to 4 minutes, stirring once in a while. Then reduce the heat to low and scrape the bottom and sides of the pan with a plastic or rubber spatula so that no thick parts adhere to the pan and the whole mixture is of an even consistency.

5. Simmer for at least 1 hour over very low heat. Correct seasoning by adding a very little sugar if too acidic or salt if too mild.

CHEF'S SECRET: In all older cook books, and even in some of today's European cook books, you will find entirely different recipes for Sauce Espagnol or Basic Brown Sauce. They will all start by making a roux, stirring the flour into the shortening and cooking until it turns brown, stirring continuously. This method was essential in the eighteenth and nineteenth centuries because of the lack of refrigeration and dry storage. If the two basic ingredients were not cooked together, the shortening would go rancid, and the flour would mildew. Therefore, the ingredients were cooked for the purpose of keeping them useful and ready for several days or even a week.

Of course, for a twentieth-century chef or for housewives with refrigeration, freezers, and good storage, it is silly to spend hours to make a concoction designed to prevent spoilage. Thus, making a Basic Brown Sauce or Sauce Espagnol is no longer the chore it used to be.

Sauce Espagnol must be simmered for a long time over low heat so that its flavors will blend. This is essential whether the sauce is to be used alone or as a base for other sauces.

Red Wine Sauce

8 servings

8 oz. sauce Espagnol (see page 204)
6 to 8 tbsp. red wine
light sprinkling of sugar

chopped or sliced mushrooms, quickly sautéed in very little butter (optional)

1. Bring the sauce almost to the boiling point (when first or second bubble appears) over medium to high heat.
2. Add the red wine and mushrooms, correct seasoning with the sugar, and serve.

CHEF'S SECRET: For variety, you can add to a basic red wine sauce 4 tbsp. melted currant jelly and 2 to 3 tbsp. red corinths (currant-like berries from the port of Corinth) or 2 oz. ham sliced into thin strips, about the size of half a matchstick, and the same amount of black truffles cut the same way, or 4 oz. beef marrow cut into small discs and poached in slightly salted water.

When you are stirring with a wire whip, the rounded end of the whip never reaches the bottom rim of the pan where the sides and bottom come together. Some imported and domestic enamel-coated pans have a rounded bottom for easy stirring, but if you use a conventional pan, buy a special wooden kitchen spoon which has one straight and one rounded side, forming a point. If you don't have this kind of spoon you can use a spatula designed for the same purpose. It is very important to scrape around the corners of the pan.

In the old days, wine used in cooking was boiled until it was reduced to one-third or one-fourth the original volume, and then incorporated into the sauce in the beginning. This was because a cheap cooking wine was used. We believe that the new method of using a good wine (the same wine which will be served with the dish) and adding it at the end of the cooking period is much more suitable for today's palate.

Pan Deglazing

4 servings

1 cup water, beef or chicken stock, canned consommé, or wine, or any combination of 2 or 3 of these	1 to 2 tsp. flour, if necessary appropriate spices to correct seasoning

1. Pour off the fat from the frying pan, leaving only a few drops in the pan.

2. Pour in the liquid and, over medium heat, scrape the bottom of the pan, loosening all particles adhering to the bottom and dissolving them in the liquid.

CHEF'S SECRET: Pan deglazing is mentioned in many of the 5,000 cookbooks I have, but I have never found any explanation of how or why deglazing is done.

When frying or sautéing meat, poultry, or fish, the recipe often calls for deglazing the pan after removing whatever was cooked in it. When you fry in shortening or sauté in a combination of shortening and liquid, the metal pan expands from the heat. When the foods you fry are placed into the pan, they are cool. The surface of the pan shrinks from the quick cooling, then expands again as the food reaches the temperature of the surrounding fat.

While the meat is frying, liquids oozing from its cut surface, as well as solids if it is dusted with flour, fine bread crumbs, or corn meal, will stick to the pan. These particles are very tasty and in most cases contain ingredients which will caramelize from the heat and will have an intense, pleasant taste and also a desirable dark color.

If you pour off all but a few drops of the fat from the pan, then nothing remains but these tasty particles. When you pour stock, wine, or water into the pan and start to scrape with the flat edge of a metal spatula, while heating the pan, all particles will loosen and will start to dissolve, transferring their flavor and fragrance to the liquid.

If you sprinkle some flour into the fat and stir until the flour starts to brown, then add the liquid, you will have a much thicker sauce-like substance instead of the pan juice. Either of these substances, spooned over the meat, poultry, or fish prepared in the pan, will enhance the taste and appearance.

There are many possible variations. Sherry, port wine, or Madeira wine may be added to the deglazed pan. Sauce prepared from the deglazed pan is the most appropriate and most natural accompaniment for the food prepared in the same pan.

Gravies

A gravy differs from a sauce in that a gravy is made from ingredients derived from the dish it accompanies. For instance, turkey gravy is made from the giblets and pan roasting liquid of the roast turkey. Chicken gravy, beef gravy for pot roast or other slowly roasted dishes, or the gravy of a stew, goulash, or fricassee are all part of the dish. On the other hand, a sauce is made from a stock turned into an Espagnol and used as a base with other ingredients, or from a white stock, fish stock, or stock from whatever dish the sauce accompanies. Therefore, with the exception of Giblet Sauce, page 211, and Redeye Gravy, page 211, we will not give gravy recipes in this chapter on sauces. You will find them as part of other recipes.

Tomato Sauce

8 servings

4 tbsp. shortening (preferably half butter)
¼ cup coarsely chopped carrots
¼ cup coarsely chopped onion
5 tbsp. flour
1 cup water or canned chicken or beef broth

2½ cups chopped fresh tomato plus 1 cup water, or 2½ cups canned tomatoes
2 to 3 tbsp. tomato purée or 1 tbsp. tomato paste
1 tbsp. sugar
½ tsp. salt
freshly-ground black pepper
garlic salt or garlic paste (optional)

1. Dissolve the flour in the water or broth.
2. Melt the shortening in a saucepan. Add the chopped onion and carrots, sprinkle in the sugar, and stir. Cook over high heat until the edges of the onion start to brown.
3. Adjust heat to medium; add the freshly chopped tomato and water or the canned tomatoes, tomato purée or tomato paste, salt and pepper, and garlic seasoning, if used. Bring to a boil. With a wooden cooking spoon, stir in the flour mixture. Again bring to a boil, then reduce heat to very low and simmer for 15 to 20 minutes.
4. Strain the sauce into a saucepan that has been rinsed with cold water. Correct seasoning by adding more sugar if too acidic or by adding salt if you used water instead of stock. Keep warm until served.

CHEF'S SECRET: The fresh tomatoes or canned tomatoes available are harvested before they get ripe. On the other hand, the tomatoes used for canned purée or sauce are harvested when perfectly ripe; the fields are generally in the back yard of the canning plant, and the tomatoes are processed immediately. This is the reason one should use some of both types. If the tomatoes you purchase are not ripe enough, put them in a brown paper bag and place the bag in a sunny place for a day or two.

If you strain the sauce into a pan rinsed with cold water, the sauce will be less likely to stick than if you use a dry saucepan.

If you want a cream of tomato sauce, stir the flour into 1 cup cream instead of water.

If you can obtain fresh herbs such as dill, tarragon, or cilantro, add 1 to 2 tablespoons, depending on taste, to the sauce before serving. Dried herbs would not have the same effect.

Mushroom Sauce

8 servings

5 oz. small, firm fresh mushrooms, thinly sliced
4 tbsp. shortening, preferably butter
1 tbsp. freshly chopped parsley
1 10½-oz. can chicken broth, or 1½ cups chicken stock or water

2 cups milk
5 tbsp. flour
½ tsp. mushroom powder
salt and pepper to taste

1. In a saucepan, melt 2 tbsp. of the shortening.
2. Dissolve the flour in the milk. When the shortening is warm, add the mixture of milk and flour together with the mushroom powder, salt, and pepper, stirring with a wire whip.
3. As the mixture starts to thicken, dilute with the chicken broth or water. Bring to a boil, then reduce heat to very low and simmer for 15 minutes.
4. Warm the remaining 2 tbsp. of shortening in a sauté pan. Add the thinly sliced mushrooms and parsley. Increase the heat and sauté the mushrooms for about 3 minutes.
5. Add the sautéed mushrooms to the sauce, scraping all the pan drippings into the sauce. Cover and let simmer for at least 30 minutes before serving.

CHEF'S SECRET: To wash the mushrooms, fill a plastic bowl half full with water. Sprinkle 2 to 3 tbsp. all-purpose flour over the top of the water, then add the mushrooms all at once. Quickly wash each mushroom with your hands, then wipe dry with a kitchen towel. I have never figured out why, but for some mysterious reason this old European secret really works.

Most recipes start by sautéing the mushrooms, then adding the other ingredients to make the sauce. Through experience, I have found that the most distinctive mushroom taste is derived through the method used in this recipe, and that the mushrooms will remain firm and will not turn rubbery.

If you prefer, you can make the sauce by substituting 1 cup white wine and 1 cup chicken broth for the 2 cups milk. In this case, sprinkle the juice of half a lemon over the mushrooms before adding them to the sauce.

Chicken Stock Béchamel

6 to 8 servings

¼ cup butter
2 tbsp. flour
1 tbsp. cornstarch
1 cup light cream

1 10½-oz. can chicken stock
salt
white pepper

1. In a medium-sized heavy-bottomed saucepan, heat the butter over medium heat until it starts to foam.
2. Dissolve the flour and cornstarch in the light cream, mixing until well blended. Pour this into the foaming butter, stirring constantly, until the sauce has thickened. Adjust heat so that it doesn't scorch.

3. Stir in the chicken stock and continue to cook over low heat for at least 5 minutes. Season with salt and pepper. Strain through a sieve. Keep warm until ready to serve.

CHEF'S SECRET: If the chicken stock is not strong enough, add half of a chicken bouillon cube and a very small amount of celery seed.

If you want an exceptional Béchamel, finish it just before serving as follows: Stiffly whip ½ to 1 cup whipping cream (depending on how rich you want it) with a pinch of salt. Tablespoonful by tablespoonful, fold some of the hot Béchamel into the whipped cream to warm it up gradually, then fold the whipped cream mixture into the sauce. Serve immediately. Don't ever use a wire whip for this folding; a rubber or plastic spatula works best.

Variations: This sauce is very versatile, and can be easily varied with the addition of small amounts of concentrated flavoring. For instance, it makes an exceptional sauce for fish, fowl, or veal with the addition of 1 tbsp. anchovy paste and 1 tbsp. rinsed capers. (Always rinse capers under running cold water to get rid of the chemical taste of the liquid from the jar.) Or you can add 1 to 2 tbsp. French mustard with 1 heaping tsp. curry powder; or 1 ripe banana mashed with a fork together with 1 tsp. curry powder; or 2 tbsp. grated Parmesan and 2 tbsp. grated Swiss cheese or 3 to 4 tbsp. processed cheese grated with 1 or 2 tbsp. Parmesan. You may experiment with other variations.

Dill Sauce

8 servings

1 cup firmly pressed, chopped, fresh young dill weed	4 tbsp. flour
	1 tsp. sugar
4 tbsp. shortening, preferably half butter	½ to 1 tsp. salt
	4 tbsp. vinegar
2 cups chicken stock or canned chicken broth	juice of ½ lemon
	¼ tsp. ground white pepper
1 cup milk	1 cup sour cream
1 cup light cream	

1. Melt the shortening in a heavy saucepan over medium heat. Add dill, sugar, and salt. Stir until the dill heats through.

2. Add the chicken stock and bring to a boil.

3. Mix the flour with the milk and half of the light cream. Pour this mixture into the boiling liquid, stirring constantly.

4. Reduce heat, add the vinegar, lemon juice, and white pepper, and simmer for at least 20 minutes, stirring once in a while.

5. Before serving, mix the other half of the light cream with the sour cream. Slowly spoon some of the hot sauce into the mixture to warm it up, then add the sour cream–light cream mixture to the sauce. Cover and keep in a warm place for about 5 minutes before serving.

CHEF'S SECRET: If you like a thicker or thinner sauce, simply increase or decrease the flour.

The dill weed required is the baby dill that is sold in bunches resembling carrot leaves. Don't confuse this with the dill weed sold in the fall for pickling; this consists of large stems and dill flower umbrellas, with a little fuzzy leaf here and there on the stem.

If you have to prepare the sauce from the pickling type of dill weed, prepare as follows: With a sharp knife, chop up enough dill for 1 cup, firmly packed. Bring 2 cups water with 3 to 4 tbsp. vinegar to a boil. Add the chopped dill stems, cover, remove from the heat, and let stand for about 1 hour. Strain; discard the liquid and add 4 to 5 tbsp. finely-chopped parsley to the prepared dill; then proceed with the recipe.

Tarragon Sauce

8 servings

¼ cup firmly packed, fresh, chopped
   tarragon leaves
4 to 5 tbsp. butter
1 cup white wine
1 cup chicken stock or broth

2 cups water
6 tbsp. cornstarch
juice of 1 lemon
salt, pepper, and sugar to taste

1. In a saucepan, melt the butter. Add the tarragon and all other ingredients except 1 cup water and the cornstarch.

2. Bring to a boil. Combine the cornstarch and the remaining water and add to the boiling mixture. Bring to a boil again, reduce heat, and let simmer for at least 30 minutes, covered, before serving.

CHEF'S SECRET: This sauce can be served with lamb, veal, or poultry. Of course, the cooking liquid from the meat can be used instead of water. The only exception is the juice from lamb, which is never used in this country.

This sauce can be frozen, but once defrosted it must be diluted with a little water and whipped with a wire whip.

Horseradish Sauce

8 servings

1 6-oz. jar prepared horseradish
4 tbsp. butter
2 cups chicken or veal stock or canned
   chicken broth
3 tbsp. flour
1 cup milk
1 cup light cream

4 to 5 tbsp. vinegar
1 tsp. prepared mustard
2 tbsp. sugar
½ tsp. salt
¼ tsp. white pepper
1 cup commercial sour cream

1. Place the prepared horseradish in a clean, wet kitchen towel. Gather the towel with one hand, forming a ball, and twist with the other hand to get rid of all the liquid in the horseradish. Then hold the ball under cold running water, gently pressing with one hand, and rinse. Squeeze dry.

2. Place the butter in a saucepan and start to heat it. When warm, add the horseradish with the sugar, vinegar, salt and pepper. Stir.

3. Slowly add the stock. Bring to a boil, then add the mustard.

4. Blend the flour into the milk and half of the light cream. Stirring constantly, add to the sauce.

5. Blend the remaining light cream into the sour cream. Once the sauce is boiling again, slowly add some of the hot mixture to the sour cream–light cream mixture to warm it up. Then add the warmed mixture to the sauce. Remove from the heat and leave with the lid on in a warm place at least 25 to 30 minutes before serving.

CHEF'S SECRET: The horseradish, when treated as suggested, will be close in flavor to fresh horseradish. If you can get fresh horseradish and if you have a special horseradish grater (which is readily available in gourmet shops or in Oriental shops), by all means use fresh horseradish.

To prevent crying while you grate fresh horseradish, try to breathe through your mouth and try not to look at the grater. Turn your head away as much as you can. If you do sniff some and have the painful sensation which can last for minutes and make one break into tears, simply press a slice of bread to your nose and breathe through the bread, exhaling first. Surprisingly, the pain from the volatile oil of the horseradish leaves immediately.

Redeye Gravy

4 servings

pan juices from frying a 1-lb. ham slice
½ cup strong black coffee

black pepper
Worcestershire sauce

1. Fry the ham slice in the usual manner.

2. Deglaze the frying pan with the coffee, scraping all bits and pieces loose from the bottom of the pan. Boil for 2 to 3 minutes, or until reduced to half.

3. Season with pepper and Worcestershire sauce. Pour over cooked ham slice.

CHEF'S SECRET: Some ham may be too dry to have any pan juices after frying. In this case, before adding the coffee, add ⅓ cup hot water; then add the coffee to do the deglazing.

The red eyes are the little specks of hot fat swimming on the top of this sauce.

Giblet Sauce

6 cups

giblets from a turkey or chicken (neck, heart, gizzard, and liver)
2 tsp. salt
1 bay leaf
1 onion
1 rib celery, coarsely chopped
water

pan drippings from the roasted fowl
½ cup flour
3 tbsp. cornstarch
salt
black pepper
Kitchen Bouquet

1. Cut the onion into four pieces. Place all giblets, except the liver, in a medium-sized saucepan. Add bay leaf, onion, salt, and celery. Cover with cold water and cook at a low boil for about 2 hours. Add liver for the last 20 minutes of cooking time.

2. Strain the stock from the giblets. Reserve the stock.

3. Remove all the meat from the neck. Finely chop the giblets and the neck meat. Discard the vegetables.

4. Place the pan drippings in a tall cylindrical container so that the fat will float to the surface. Skim off ½ cup and put it into a heavy-bottomed saucepan to heat. Discard the remaining fat. Measure the remaining fat-free drippings and add enough of the giblet stock to make 6 cups liquid. Dissolve the cornstarch in the liquid.

5. Stir the flour into the fat and cook over medium heat until bubbly and golden brown. With a wire whip, stir in the liquid and cook until thickened, stirring constantly. Add giblets and continue to cook over low heat for about 20 minutes. Stir occasionally.

6. Add enough Kitchen Bouquet to give the sauce a deep brown color. Season with salt and black pepper.

CHEF'S SECRET: If you like a more robust taste for Giblet Sauce, fry the cut-up gizzard and heart with 1 tbsp. finely chopped onions in 2 to 3 tbsp. fat, with a sprinkling of salt, over high heat until brown. Then reduce heat to low and simmer for about 10 minutes, stirring once in a while. You can add the neck meat once the heat is lowered. Then cook the giblets according to the recipe.

Creole Sauce

8 servings

6 tbsp. oil
2½ cups peeled, coarsely chopped tomatoes with 1 cup water, or 1 large can tomatoes
1 cup finely chopped celery
enough bell peppers to have 1½ cups of ½-inch squares, blanched
2 cups sliced onion
1 small can tomato sauce, preferably with peppers

1 tsp. finely minced garlic
salt and pepper to taste
4 to 10 drops Tabasco, depending on taste
2 to 3 tbsp. sugar
1 tbsp. or more Worcestershire sauce, depending on taste

1. Place the onion and the cold oil in a saucepan and heat them together, covered, for 10 minutes.

2. Add the celery and blanched bell pepper squares, cover again, and cook for an additional 10 minutes.

3. Add the tomatoes, tomato sauce, garlic, Tabasco, Worcestershire sauce, and sugar. Put the covered saucepan in a preheated 300-degree oven and bake for 2 hours. Correct seasoning before serving.

CHEF'S SECRET: If you like a hot sauce, add a small sprinkling of cayenne pepper to the vegetables while cooking. If available, add ½ cup or less thinly sliced fresh okra. It will give a typical Southern taste and consistency.

If you like a thicker sauce, dust the onions with 1 or 2 tbsp. flour sifted through a fine sieve before you add the peppers and celery, or dilute 1 or 2 tbsp. cornstarch in ¼ cup lukewarm water and stir into the sauce about 10 minutes before putting it in the oven.

If you add 2 cups brown sugar, 2 cups vinegar, and 2 tbsp. Kitchen Bouquet to the creole sauce and then press through a fine sieve, you will have the finest Southern barbecue sauce ever tasted.

If you add 1 can tiny onions rinsed under cold running water, 1 pint tiny unpeeled cocktail tomatoes that have been washed, 1 can pineapple cubes with syrup, 1 cup rice vinegar or plain vinegar, and 2 to 3 tbsp. soy sauce, the result will be a very fine Oriental sweet-sour sauce.

Oxford Sauce

2 cups

2 tsp. finely chopped shallots	1 lemon
⅔ cup port wine	water
1 tsp. sugar	1½ tbsp. cornstarch
⅔ cup red currant jelly	1 dash cayenne pepper
1 orange	1 dash ginger

1. Scald the shallots in boiling port wine for one minute in a small saucepan. Remove from the heat, add the jelly and sugar, and let them dissolve.

2. Remove the zest (outer peel) from the orange and lemon with a potato peeler. Cut the strips of zest into very fine julienne strips. Boil these for 2 minutes in enough water to cover. Drain. Discard water.

3. Squeeze the juice from the whole orange and half of the lemon. Mix it with the cornstarch in a small cup.

4. Add this juice with the julienne strips to the wine and jelly. Bring the mixture to a boil over medium heat, stirring constantly. Season with cayenne pepper and ginger. Cool at room temperature. Keep in refrigerator. Add more port wine to dilute the sauce to proper consistency, if necessary.

CHEF'S SECRET: Shallots are not available at all times or in all places. If you cannot get shallots, substitute 2 tbsp. finely chopped onion which has been boiled in 1 cup water for 2 minutes, drained, and rinsed with cold water. Or omit onion and add a light sprinkling of onion powder or onion salt.

Red currant jellies may differ in acidity or sweetness. You may have to add more or less than 1 tsp. sugar.

English Mustard Sauce

8 servings

4 hard-boiled eggs	1 tbsp. sugar
1 cup sour cream	½ tsp. salt
1 cup buttermilk or yogurt	small pinch white pepper
1 raw egg yolk	cayenne and curry powder to taste
4 tbsp. prepared French mustard	½ cup vinegar
½ tsp. English mustard powder	½ cup oil

1. Coarsely chop the hard-boiled eggs.
2. Place the oil, vinegar, French mustard, English mustard powder, sugar, salt, pepper, cayenne, curry powder, and raw egg yolk in the bowl of an electric mixer. Using a wire whip, blend on high speed for 3 minutes.
3. With a spatula, gently fold the sour cream, buttermilk, and chopped eggs into the blended mixture. Serve when chilled.

CHEF'S SECRET: This is a very popular sauce in England, where it is thickened with natural cream which is about to turn sour. Since this type of cream is not available here, the same taste is achieved by using commercial sour cream and adding the sugar.

The oil and vinegar mixed in the electric mixer with the mustard and spices will not separate if you follow the instructions. Do not try to beat the sour cream in the mixer, as it will break down and become a runny liquid.

Real Mayonnaise

approximately 1½ cups

2 egg yolks
½ tsp. salt
1 pinch white pepper
1 pinch cayenne pepper
1 tsp. sugar

2 tbsp. vinegar
1 cup corn oil
1 tbsp. lemon juice
1 to 2 tbsp. boiling water

1. Be sure your electric mixing bowl and beaters are grease-free and dry. All ingredients should be at room temperature.
2. Place the yolks, salt, white and cayenne pepper, sugar, and vinegar in the mixing bowl. Beat at high speed for approximately 2 minutes or until the mixture turns pale yellow and thin.
3. While beating at medium speed, slowly pour the oil in a thin stream into the yolk mixture.
4. When all the oil is incorporated, add the lemon juice and 1 to 2 tbsp. boiling water. Store in refrigerator.

CHEF'S SECRET: To be sure the bowl and beater are grease-free, thoroughly rinse them with a boiling mixture of 3 cups water and 1 cup vinegar, then rinse them a second time with cold water. Use a clean, completely grease-free kitchen towel or paper towel to dry them. If they are wet, the mayonnaise will not turn out properly.

Even though you are careful, it can happen that the mayonnaise will break down. If it does, pour it back into the bowl; start to beat it slowly, then raise the speed to high and slowly pour ½ cup additional oil into it in a very thin stream.

Remoulade Sauce

2 cups mayonnaise
2 to 3 tbsp. prepared mustard
1 tbsp. finely chopped sweet pickle
1 tbsp. finely chopped dill pickle
1 tbsp. capers

1 tsp. mixed dried chervil and tarragon, according to taste
1 tbsp. chopped fresh parsley
1 tsp. anchovy paste

1. Rinse the capers under cold running water.
2. Fold all the ingredients into the mayonnaise and serve with cold meats or lobster.

Green Sauce (Sauce Verte)

1 cup coarsely chopped fresh spinach
2 tbsp. finely chopped fresh parsley
1 tbsp. chopped scallion (green part only) or chopped chives
½ tsp. dried tarragon

½ tsp. chervil
2 cups mayonnaise
juice of ½ lemon
1 tbsp. vinegar

1. Place all the ingredients except the mayonnaise in an electric blender and purée them together.
2. Fold the green liquid slowly into the mayonnaise. Refrigerate. (The mixture will be somewhat runny but will become firm when refrigerated.) Serve with fish.

Sauce Louis

2½ cups

2 whole eggs
3 tbsp. prepared mustard
3 tbsp. sugar
½ tsp. salt

⅛ tsp. ground white pepper
juice of 1 lemon
1 tsp. vinegar
1 pt. sour cream

1. In a medium-sized bowl, using a wire whip, blend together the eggs, mustard, sugar, salt, pepper, lemon juice, and vinegar.
2. Slowly fold in the sour cream. Keep refrigerated.

CHEF'S SECRET: This is probably the simplest and quickest, but most elegant, sauce. It can be made in 20 seconds, without cooking or even getting near the stove.

It is very important that all the ingredients except the sour cream be mixed together vigorously by hand with a wire whip or mixed in an electric mixer at the highest speed. On the other hand, the sour cream must be gently folded into the sauce with a rubber spatula or scraper; fold the mixture over the sour cream, then fold some sour cream under the mixture. If the commercial sour cream is beaten, it will become runny and will separate, and you will not get the same silky texture and consistency.

It is possible to make this sauce using sour half-and-half or yogurt, although not every brand of yogurt will give exactly the same result.

Vanilla Sauce

approximately 4 cups

3 cups milk
⅓ cup sugar
1 tbsp. unsalted butter
3 tbsp. cornstarch

5 tbsp. water
3 egg yolks, lightly beaten
1 tsp. vanilla
1 pinch salt

1. In a heavy saucepan, bring the milk, sugar, and butter to a boil.

2. Dissolve the cornstarch in the water. Pour this mixture into the boiling liquid, stirring with a wire whip. Simmer for 2 to 3 minutes. Remove from the heat.

3. Add the lightly beaten egg yolks to the hot mixture, stirring with a wire whip until they are completely blended in.

4. Add the vanilla and salt.

5. Serve warm or cold.

CHEF'S SECRET: You will note that the recipe calls for 1 tbsp. unsalted butter and a pinch of salt. I must emphasize that it would not be the same to use salted butter and omit the salt. Salted butter presents no problem when used with salty and pungent dishes, but it definitely gives an undesirable flavor to sweet sauces.

Before placing the milk, sugar, and butter in the saucepan, rinse the pan with water and leave it wet. Once the mixture starts to form a "skin" that covers the top, start stirring and continue to stir until it boils.

Separate the yolks from the whites as carefully as possible. Be sure not to get any egg white in the sauce because it will immediately solidify and leave unpleasant lumps. The best way to avoid these lumps is to first gently beat the yolks in a small bowl with 3 to 4 tbsp. of the hot mixture and then add the warmed egg yolks to the hot sauce.

Chocolate Sauce

approximately 2 cups

¼ cup unsalted butter   1 tbsp. cornstarch
1 cup sugar   ¼ cup cold water
½ cup good-quality cocoa   ½ cup commercial chocolate syrup
1 cup milk   ¼ cup brandy

1. In a very heavy saucepan, melt the butter with the sugar and cocoa until the mixture starts to caramelize.

2. Immediately add the milk, stirring constantly. The hard lumps will dissolve as the liquid comes to a boil.

3. Dilute the cornstarch with the water. Pour this in a slow stream into the boiling syrup, stirring constantly. Remove from the fire and allow to cool to room temperature.

4. Dilute with the chocolate syrup and brandy. Refrigerate.

CHEF'S SECRET: The saucepan must be very heavy. This is necessary in order to melt the butter and chocolate with the sugar until the sugar starts to caramelize. This mixture not only browns but begins to harden. The caramelized sugar will "toast" the cocoa somewhat and the butter will get a "burned butter" taste. These are the secret flavor components of the sauce.

You can double or quadruple this recipe without changing the proportion of the ingredients, but it will take a little longer. However, if the family likes chocolate sauce, it is worthwhile. The sauce may be kept, refrigerated, up to two weeks.

Cherry Glaze

approximately 6 cups

2 large cans (6 cups) pitted sour cherries with juice
1 stick cinnamon
1 slice lemon peel, ½ by 1½ inches
2 cups red wine

½ cup sugar (or more, depending on
the wine)
7 tbsp. cornstarch
6 tbsp. cold water

1. Place half of the cherries from one can, and all of the juice from that can, in a large saucepan with the sugar, cinnamon, and lemon peel. Bring to a boil and boil for 3 minutes.

2. Add the red wine and again bring to a boil, then remove from the heat. Immediately cover and let steep for 5 minutes.

3. After 5 minutes, remove the lemon peel and cinnamon. Add the rest of the cherries from the first can.

4. Blend all the cherries from the second can with half of the juice from that can in an electric blender until smooth.

5. Bring the rest of the cherry juice from the second can to a boil and thicken it with the cornstarch, which has been diluted with the cold water. Stir until the mixture is thickened and clear. Cook over low heat for 2 to 3 additional minutes.

6. Combine the three mixtures and serve warm or cold. Correct seasoning by adding sugar and salt, if necessary.

CHEF'S SECRET: The body of the sauce will be full, with small flakes of cherry flesh. These flakes are characteristic of the sauce; however, if you want to avoid them, after liquifying the second can of cherries in the blender, strain the liquid through a fine cloth which will collect the fibers of the skin and flesh.

If you have some imitation cherry flavoring on hand, add a small drop. It also helps to add a few drops of red food coloring, very carefully, just before serving. After all, ladies wear lipstick; why shouldn't food?

If you are lucky enough to live in an area where frozen, pitted sour cherries are available, by all means use them instead of the canned variety.

Zabaglione

4 to 6 servings

4 egg yolks
¾ cup sugar
¾ cup Marsala wine

¼ tsp. grated lemon rind
¼ tsp. vanilla extract

1. With a wire whip, beat the egg yolks and sugar in the top of a double boiler, off the heat, until they are a light lemon color and very fluffy.

2. Set the water level in the bottom part of the double boiler low enough so that it doesn't touch the top pan. Place the top pan into the bottom once the water starts to boil. Reduce the heat so that the water only simmers.

3. Start whipping the mixture with a wire whip and slowly add the wine

with the lemon rind and vanilla. Continue to beat until the egg yolks are cooked to a light, fluffy, custard-like consistency. Serve immediately.

CHEF'S SECRET: These are extremely simple ingredients, but great skill is needed in using the wire whip and in the timing.

I suggest, at least for new or inexperienced housewives, the purchase of a glass double boiler. It will be a great help in watching the water level, seeing when it starts to boil, and stopping the boiling when necessary.

When the wine is added, according to the directions, you will need three hands: one to hold the top part of the double boiler, one to hold the wire whip, and one to pour the wine. Do not trust the "third hand" (or a helper) with the wire whip or the wine; let it hold the handle of the double boiler.

This sauce can be excellent served cold. In this case you will also need the 4 egg whites. Proceed as above, then stir once in a while until cool. Refrigerate. Before serving, whip the 4 egg whites, which have been kept at room temperature for at least 1 hour, with a small pinch of salt until they become shiny and soft peaks form; then slowly add 2 tbsp. granulated sugar. Remove from the electric mixer and gently fold the cold Zabaglione into the egg whites, using a rubber spatula or scraper. Serve immediately.

Whipped Cream–Orange Marmalade Sauce

8 servings

8 oz. heavy cream
1 pinch salt
3 oz. prepared horseradish

3 oz. orange marmalade
juice of ½ lemon

1. Whip the heavy cream with the pinch of salt until very stiff peaks form.
2. Combine the prepared horseradish, orange marmalade, and lemon juice.
3. Very gently fold the horseradish–marmalade–lemon juice mixture into the stiffly whipped cream. Chill until serving time.

CHEF'S SECRET: This surprising mixture sounds strange, but tastes very good.

Try to measure the horseradish with some of the liquid from the jar. If the horseradish has no liquid, increase the amount of lemon juice to 1 whole lemon. You will need a certain amount of moisture to help incorporate the orange marmalade into the horseradish. If you make the sauce ahead, in 4 or 5 hours all the orange marmalade–horseradish mixture will sink to the bottom, so gently fold the mixture together again before serving.

This sauce freezes very well. However, be sure to defrost it by leaving it in the refrigerator overnight instead of trying to defrost it at room temperature.

Caramel Sauce

approximately 1½ cups

1 cup sugar
½ cup boiling water
1 dash salt

½ tsp. vanilla extract
1 cup heavy cream

1. In a small, heavy-bottomed saucepan, heat the sugar over low heat, stirring constantly, until it melts and turns slightly brown.

2. Very slowly add the boiling water, then stir until the caramelized sugar melts.

3. Add the salt and cool slightly.

4. Slowly add the heavy cream and the vanilla, stirring continuously. Serve.

CHEF'S SECRET: Use a wooden spoon, or a spoon with a plastic or wooden handle. A metal spoon would be unbearable to hold as a result of the heat when the sugar starts to brown.

Make sure the boiling water is in a pan with a long handle. Add it slowly, drop by drop, and be careful that your hands are not over the saucepan with the sugar. A tremendously hot vapor which would burn your skin will rise from the sugar when the water is added.

Don't worry if the caramelized sugar hardens. As you keep stirring, it will all melt again. Depending on the thickness of the saucepan used, you may have to add 2 to 3 tbsp. of water.

BREADS

Quick Bread
Kugelhupf
Brioche
Savarin
Krapfen (Original European Yeast
    Donuts)
Sweet Rolls
Miniature Rolls
Biscuits

Shortcake
Cornbread
Muffins
Popovers
Ham in Rye Bread
Bread Pudding
Bread Dumplings
Breads as Serving Containers

*F*rom a purely gastronomical point of view—completely disregarding nutrition, economy, and other aspects—bread is the most sophisticated, most elegant, and most desirable building block of any meal in the Western world. Bread helps the taste buds in assorting, differentiating, and blending flavors. It helps the tongue, the gums, and the teeth to enjoy the differences in texture and chewability. It clears the palate for the wine, heightens the pleasures of the cheese, transfers the sauce from the plate to the mouth, counterbalances the salad and the soup, and stretches the joy of chewing the meat.

Real connoisseurs of good food never sit down to a table before the bread appears. Different shapes and sizes, with different proportions of the crisp rind or crust and softness of center, serve different purposes. Unfortunately, baking equipment plays a tremendous part in achieving certain textures, and the type of equipment needed is not available for a single household; but I am sure the day is coming when a bread-baking oven will be on the market so you can make crusty French bread at home. Until then, buy the best.

The recipes given here cover the types of bread which can be successfully made with regular household equipment. Three general rules should be followed very carefully. (1) It is of the utmost importance to be sure that the oven is really heated to the required temperature. Spend a few dollars on a good oven thermometer to double check the thermostatic control built into the equipment. (2) No matter who tells you different or what the label says, sift every cup of flour before measuring. (3) Be very careful with the yeast. Check the date stamp to be sure of freshness, and do not dissolve it in any liquid warmer than the temperature of your hand. As soon as too hot a liquid comes in contact with the yeast, it kills the living cells and destroys the yeast's ability to raise the dough.

Breads

Quick Bread

2 loaves

1 cup milk
2 tbsp. sugar
1 tbsp. salt
1 package dry yeast

1½ cups warm water
7 cups sifted flour
3 tbsp. melted butter

1. Scald the milk, then add the sugar and the salt. Let this cool to room temperature.
2. Dissolve the yeast in the warm water, then add it to the milk mixture.
3. In a large bowl, combine the milk-yeast mixture and 3 cups of the flour. Beat until smooth.
4. Add the melted butter and all but ½ cup of the remaining flour. Turn the mixture out onto a lightly floured pastry board and knead it until the dough is smooth and satiny.
5. Brush the inside of a large bowl with shortening. Place the dough in the bowl, cover it with a towel, and set it in a warm place for an hour or until it has doubled in size. Avoid any drafts.
6. Punch the dough down and turn it out again onto a lightly floured board. Divide it in half and let it rest for a few minutes uncovered.
7. Generously brush two loaf pans with shortening. Shape the dough to fit the pans and place it in the pans.
8. Cover the pans with a towel and let the dough rise again until double in size.
9. Preheat the oven to 400 degrees.
10. Place the loaves in the oven and bake them for 15 minutes to set the crust, then reduce the heat to 375 degrees and bake for an additional 30 minutes.
11. Let the bread stand at room temperature until cool to the touch, then remove from the pans.

CHEF'S SECRET: It is very important that you check the date stamp on the yeast to be used. If it is getting close to the end of the suggested period of usefulness, it is better to lose the price of the yeast than the product which will be made from it.

The best tool for beating the milk-yeast mixture with the flour is an ordinary wooden kitchen spoon. Buy a new one and use it only for mixing doughs. You will see how easy it is to work with once you become accustomed to it.

Before kneading the dough, wash your hands, rinse them in cold water, and dry them quickly. Do not rub your hands too much, so that you do not warm them up. This sounds like a paradox, but you must knead the dough strongly yet light-handedly. This means that the downward movement when pressing with the heel of your palm should be strong, but when you lift the dough your hands should hardly touch it, so that the dough will not stick to them. Keep turning the dough in a circular motion while kneading it. First knead on one side, then turn upside down and knead it again. Form it into a ball, press it into a tubular shape, then fold the two ends back toward the middle and keep kneading until you have one large elastic mass without any folds or creases showing. The surface should be completely smooth.

Punching the dough down means hitting it with the full palm of your hand until the air bubbles which developed during the yeast's first fermentation break, the air escapes, and the dough loses its volume. When the dough rises a second time, the air bubbles are smaller and more evenly distributed.

Kugelhupf

1 loaf

4 cups sifted flour	4 tbsp. powdered sugar
1 package active dry yeast	4 eggs, separated
½ cup warm water	1 pinch salt
½ cup black currants	1½ to 2 cups milk
½ cup white raisins	zest of 1 lemon
6 oz. butter, kept at room temperature	Kugelhupf form*

* A Kugelhupf form is a metal or enameled metal cake form (see drawing) resembling a turban and having a funnel in the middle that goes to the top of the form. Thus the Kugelhupf not only bakes from the outside but also bakes around the funnel on the inside.

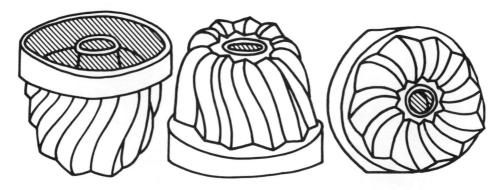

1. Activate the yeast by mixing it into the ½ cup warm water. Then bring ½ cup of the milk to a boil, let it cool to room temperature, add 2 to 3 tbsp. of the flour, and mix in the dissolved yeast. Make this into a leavening by letting it rise until it puffs and gets airy.

2. Place the butter in the bowl of an electric mixer and start to beat at high speed. One by one, add the egg yolks and the salt. Beat until the mixture is fluffy and whipped.

3. Beat the egg whites, slowly adding the sugar, until they are stiff.

4. Stirring with a spatula, add the yeast mixture to the whipped butter mixture. Fold in the beaten egg whites, zest of the lemon, and the remaining milk.

5. Sprinkle some of the flour over the top of the mixture and blend it in. Continue to sprinkle the flour on the top of the mixture and to blend it in until all of it is incorporated.

6. Sprinkle the black currants and raisins over the dough and gently fold them in.

7. Brush a Kugelhupf form with melted butter and dust it with flour. Pour the dough into the form and let it rise in a warm place until it is double in bulk.

8. Preheat the oven to 375 degrees.

9. Bake the Kugelhupf for approximately 45 to 60 minutes or until a testing needle, when inserted, comes out dry.

10. After baking, cool in the form. While still lukewarm, loosen the inner edges with a paring knife and invert to remove. Sprinkle the top generously with powdered sugar through a sieve. If possible, serve the next day.

CHEF'S SECRET: This is one of several hundred Kugelhupf recipes, each of which is claimed to be the one and only original Viennese recipe. This one is fairly easy to make, very tasty, and economical, and it can be kept in a cake container at room temperature for 3 to 4 days.

Sometimes, when the Kugelhupf is to be served as a dessert with ice cream or with a European type of cream or Chantilly Cream, it is brushed, while still warm, with a mixture of 2 tbsp. apricot marmalade and 1 tbsp. rum or brandy heated together with 1 or 2 tbsp. sugar and a little lemon juice. Then, after 10 minutes or so, when the syrup is completely absorbed, it is sprinkled with the powdered sugar.

Brioche

24 to 30 rolls

7 cups flour, sifted	1 cup half-and-half
1 cup plus 4 tbsp. butter, softened	4 tbsp. powdered sugar
1 envelope active dry yeast	1 pinch salt
½ cup warm water	1 egg yolk
½ cup milk	1 tsp. cream
3 eggs	1 tsp. sugar

1. Dissolve the yeast in the warm water. Scald the milk and cool it to room temperature, then add the yeast-water mixture to it.

2. Sift the flour into a large bowl. Add the powdered sugar, softened but-

ter, salt, and eggs. Stirring with a wooden spoon, blend in the half-and-half and the yeast mixture.

3. Turn the dough out onto a lightly floured pastry board and knead it until it is smooth and pliable.

4. Place the dough in a lightly greased bowl and let it rise until double in bulk. Meanwhile, butter and flour the muffin tins.

5. Punch the dough down and turn it out onto a lightly floured pastry board. Dust the top with a little additional flour.

6. Cut off one-fourth of the dough. Divide the remaining three-quarters of the dough into 24 to 30 parts, depending on the size of the muffin pans which you plan to use for the Brioche.

7. Dip your fingertips into flour and pick up one portion of the dough. Pull all the edges together to a point and press together, so that the dough resembles blown-up bubble gum which a child has pinched off with his lips. Put this pinched-together part in the bottom of the muffin pans. Repeat this until all the portions of dough are used.

8. Cover the pans with a towel and let them rise in a warm place for about 30 minutes.

9. Divide the remaining one-quarter of the dough into the same number of portions and make small balls of dough. Punch a hole in the middle of each Brioche with your index finger, going almost to the bottom. Insert the small balls, with the smooth side upward, in these holes. (See drawing.)

10. Let rise for another 20 to 25 minutes.

11. Preheat the oven to 375 degrees.

12. Beat the egg yolk with the cream. Stir in the sugar and keep stirring until the sugar dissolves. Brush the top of each small ball and the top of the larger ball around it.

13. Bake the Brioche in the preheated oven for about 15 minutes. Reduce the heat to 350 degrees and continue baking until an inserted testing needle comes out dry.

CHEF'S SECRET: If your Brioche is perfect the first time, it is a miracle. However, after doing this two or three times and learning from your mistakes, you will be the envy of all your friends. Therefore, be patient.

Brushing the tops of the Brioche before baking them will help them to brown and will give them a shiny appearance. If desired, they can be brushed a second time during the baking and sprinkled with sugar crystals.

It is customary, on certain occasions, to make this dough into one large Brioche. Of course, for this you will need a special large pan which is easily obtainable in many gourmet kitchenware shops. The rising and baking time would have to be somewhat longer for a single large loaf.

Savarin

1 ring

For the bread:
3 to 4 cups flour
½ cup butter
3 eggs
⅓ cup milk
1½ tsp. active dry yeast
4 tbsp. sugar
1 pinch salt

melted apricot jam
sweetened whipped cream

For the syrup:
1 cup sugar
½ cup water
2 tbsp. brandy

1. Scald the milk. Add the sugar and let the mixture cool until it is lukewarm. Dissolve the yeast in the warm mixture and keep in a warm place.

2. Sift the flour into a warmed bowl. Add the salt.

3. Place the butter in a mixing bowl. Using a paddle, add one egg and one cup of the flour and beat the mixture until it is blended. Repeat until all the eggs and 3 cups of the flour are incorporated.

4. Mix in the leavening and place the dough in a greased bowl. Cover and let rise until double in size.

5. Punch the dough down and turn it out onto a lightly floured pastry board. Knead for 4 to 5 minutes, adding as much of the fourth cup of flour as necessary to prevent the dough from sticking.

6. Generously butter and lightly flour a Savarin ring. Place the dough in the ring and let it rise again until double in size.

7. Preheat the oven to 375 degrees.

8. Bake the Savarin in the preheated oven for 20 to 30 minutes or until an inserted testing needle comes out dry.

9. Meanwhile, prepare the syrup by bringing the sugar and water to a boil. Remove from the heat and add the brandy.

10. Pour the syrup over the warm Savarin and let it stand at room temperature until it cools.

11. Turn the Savarin out onto a serving platter. Brush with the melted jam and fill the center with the whipped cream. Serve.

CHEF'S SECRET: This is one of the most elegant pastries and is a very versatile dough. It is possible to buy Savarin ring sheet pans which make miniature rings, each suitable for one serving. As a rule, six or eight individual rings are on one pan; for the amount of dough this recipe makes, you would need two such pans.

After you pour the syrup over the ring, the warm liquid will be absorbed faster and easier if you pierce the dough with a testing needle. If you see that the liquid is not absorbed within an hour, gently pour the remaining liquid off into a saucepan. Reheat the syrup, adding 1 tbsp. of water, and pour it back over the Savarin. You can also remove and turn the Savarin ring over after the first soaking.

If you do not have a Savarin ring, you can make and bake the same dough in loaf pans or in muffin pans. They will look different, but will still be delicious.

Krapfen (Original European Yeast Donuts)

approximately 24 pieces

8 cups flour, sifted	1 envelope active dry yeast
6 egg yolks	½ cup warm water
7 tbsp. melted butter	2 tbsp. sugar
4 tbsp. powdered sugar	shortening (preferably 2 parts lard
2½ cups milk	and 1 part corn oil)
1 tbsp. rum	powdered sugar for dusting

1. Scald ½ cup milk. Add the 2 tbsp. of sugar and cool to lukewarm.

2. Dissolve the yeast in the warm water. Add the scalded, cooled milk mixture.

3. Combine the egg yolks, butter, powdered sugar, and rum in the bowl of an electric mixer. Using the paddle, start to incorporate the flour, yeast mixture, and remaining milk, slowing adding some of each and beating after each addition. Keep beating until the dough turns into one lump on the paddle and none is sticking to the sides or bottom of the bowl.

4. Place the dough in another buttered bowl, dust the top with some additional flour, and cover with a kitchen towel. Place in a warm place and avoid drafts.

5. After about 45 minutes, place the dough on a fairly large pastry board and roll it out to an even ½-inch thickness.

6. Cut the dough with a round 3- to 3½-inch cutter, making the cuts as close to each other as possible.

7. Remove the pieces from between the rounds, knead them together until they form a smooth ball and let the dough rest in a warm place. Cover the rounds with a kitchen towel and let them rise until they are 1 inch high.

8. Melt enough fresh lard and corn oil (adding 2 parts lard to each part oil) to have at least 2 to 3 inches in the bottom of a heavy pot which is at least 4 to 5 inches high and has a lid.

9. As soon as the shortening reaches 360 degrees (or is almost to the smoking point), start to fry the rounds. Place the rounds in the hot shortening, cover, and fry until the bottom turns a nice rosy brown. Remove the lid, turn the Krapfen, and fry without covering until the other side is the same rosy brown.

10. Remove to an absorbent paper and keep warm.

11. Before serving, place a layer of Krapfen on a serving platter, generously dust them with powdered sugar, then add a smaller layer and again dust with powdered sugar, continuing until you have built a pyramid of the Krapfen. Serve warm with a bowl of warmed apricot marmalade diluted with 1 to 2 tbsp. rum.

CHEF'S SECRET: This is the real German Krapfen, the European great-grandfather of the donut.

It is important that you do not use the dough from between the rounds to make additional Krapfen. The dough must not be overworked. From this dough you can make walnut-sized pieces and fry them in the fat as you would fry profiteroles, then dust them all over with powdered sugar.

Krapfen freeze very well and taste excellent with warmed chocolate syrup or with a syrup made from warmed marmalade diluted with water, brandy, or rum.

Frying this pastry on one side under cover and then on the other side without the cover will give a beautiful white band around the rim. This is very desirable, and will bring compliments from the most beastly mother-in-law.

If you like to have an indentation in the middle of each Krapfen, when you lift each one up simply pinch it in the middle with your thumb and index finger until they meet.

Sweet Rolls

12 rolls

1 package active dry yeast	¾ tsp. salt
¼ cup warm water	2 large eggs
½ cup milk	2 cups flour, sifted
¼ cup soft butter	extra melted butter for brushing
1 tbsp. sugar	

1. Dissolve the yeast in the warm water.

2. Scald the milk. Stir in the butter, sugar, and salt. Cool to lukewarm.

3. Combine the eggs with the yeast and the milk. Add the flour.

4. Beat the dough vigorously until it becomes smooth. Cover and let rise in a warm place for about 1 hour or until it doubles in size. Avoid any drafts.

5. Preheat the oven to 375 degrees.

6. Stir the dough well. Spoon it into greased muffin pans, filling each about half full.

7. Let rise again in a warm place until double in size.

8. Bake the rolls in the preheated oven for approximately 20 minutes. Remove from the oven and brush each roll with melted butter.

CHEF'S SECRET: Be sure that you do not mix the yeast and egg into the milk before it cools to lukewarm. If it is too hot, it would impair the yeast's ability to rise and could partially cook the eggs.

Brushing the rolls with the melted butter while they are very hot enables the butter to seep into the rolls, making it unnecessary to serve butter with them. If you want them to be especially nice, carefully remove each one from the pans and quickly brush the bottom with melted butter before buttering the top, then place them back in the pans and brush the tops.

Miniature Rolls

approximately 48 rolls

8 cups flour, sifted	2 tbsp. sugar
1 package active dry yeast	6 egg yolks
½ cup warm water	8 tbsp. (1 stick) butter
2 cups milk	grated zest of ½ lemon

1. Scald ¾ cup of the milk. Add the sugar to the scalded milk, then cool to lukewarm.
2. Dissolve the yeast in the warm water. Add the milk mixture and one-third of the flour; mix into a soft leavening. Sprinkle the top with some additional flour and let rise in a warm place.
3. When double in bulk, incorporate all the other ingredients except the butter.
4. Knead with your hands until the dough starts to come off your hands by itself.
5. Now, break the butter into small pieces and work it into the dough. When all the butter is incorporated and the dough no longer sticks to your fingers or the bowl, sprinkle the top with a little flour, cover with a towel, and let rise in a warm place until double in bulk.
6. Gently and lightly roll the dough out on a floured pastry board to ½-inch thickness.
7. With a pastry wheel, cut tiny rectangles, 1 by 1½ inches or 1 by 2½ inches.
8. After the rectangles are cut, form each into a little ball by pinching the 4 corners together; or make little ovals by pinching 2 corners together; or, if you wish, brush the tops with additional melted butter and fold them in half like Parker House rolls.
9. Place the little rolls on a lightly greased cookie sheet and let them rest in a warm place for 10 minutes.
10. Preheat the oven to 375 degrees.
11. Bake the rolls in the preheated oven for 10 to 12 minutes, depending on their size.

CHEF'S SECRET: This dough produces excellent dinner rolls which are very suitable for freezing. However, if you plan to freeze the rolls, underbake them somewhat so they will not become hard when you reheat them to serve.

You can make these rolls for a party two days ahead and store them in a well-sealed plastic bag at room temperature. Just reheat them in the oven for 3 to 4 minutes before serving.

If you want the rolls to be shiny, mix 1 egg yolk with a little powdered sugar and lightly brush the top of each before baking. If you like, melt some butter and brush the rolls with the melted butter as soon as you remove them from the oven.

If you prefer a variety, brush the tops of each with the egg yolk mixture and sprinkle poppy seeds on the ovals, sprinkle caraway seeds and coarse salt on the rounds, and press a half almond into the Parker House–style or sprinkle this style with chopped almonds.

If you plan to make them ahead, do not brush the top with the egg. Instead, butter the rolls as soon as you remove them from the oven after reheating them, immediately before serving them.

Biscuits

14 biscuits

2 cups sifted all-purpose flour   ⅓ cup shortening
2½ tsp. baking powder   ¾ cup milk
1 tsp. salt

1. Sift together the flour, baking powder, and salt.
2. Cut the shortening into the dry ingredients.
3. Add the milk and stir with a fork until a soft dough is formed.
4. Turn the dough out onto a lightly floured board and knead it about twenty turns.
5. Pat or lightly roll the dough to a ½-inch thickness.
6. Preheat the oven to 450 degrees.
7. Cut the dough with a floured 2-inch cutter or with a glass.
8. Bake the biscuits on an ungreased cookie sheet for 12 to 15 minutes.

CHEF'S SECRET: Biscuit dough should never be overmixed. While you are giving the so-called twenty turns, just use the tips of your fingers and the heels of your palms. The term "turn" means that you push the dough away from yourself, lightly touching the part closest to you with the heels of your palms and pushing away until the heels of your palms are at the other end of the dough. Then you quickly gather the dough with your fingertips from either the right or left side (depending on whether you are right- or left-handed), put it in front of you, and start to push it away again. Do this twenty times.

If you like flaky biscuits, brush the surface of the dough with water after rolling it lightly to the ½-inch thickness. Then fold the dough in half, roll it again, brush with water, fold, roll, and cut it with the cutter.

Shortcake

8 servings

1 cup flour   1½ tsp. baking powder
2 eggs   1 tbsp. melted butter
½ cup sugar   ½ cup scalded milk
sprinkling of salt

1. Beat the eggs in an electric mixer on high speed until they turn light and fluffy.

2. Add the sugar, pouring in a slow stream. Keep beating until the mixture turns lemon colored and is fluffy.

3. Sift together the flour, baking powder, and salt.

4. With a rubber or plastic spatula, gently fold the dry ingredients into the egg mixture.

5. Start to beat again on low speed. Add the hot milk and the melted butter. Continue to beat until all the ingredients are incorporated.

6. Pour the batter into a lightly greased and floured square pan or an 8-inch cake pan.

7. Place in a preheated 375-degree oven and bake for approximately 30 minutes, or until a testing needle, when inserted, comes out dry. Cool before serving.

CHEF'S SECRET: You can use a wire whip for this dough, because it is very light.

Besides being used for the customary strawberry or peach shortcake, this shortcake can be used with many other fruits—for instance, sliced fresh banana marinated in a little sherry with sugar added, sliced oranges marinated in an orange liqueur, or any ripe yellow or green melon coarsely grated and marinated in rum, brandy, or other liqueur with a little sugar added.

Cornbread

8 servings

½ cup sifted flour	3 eggs, lightly beaten
1½ cups yellow cornmeal	1 cup milk
1 tsp. salt	¼ cup heavy cream
1 tsp. sugar	⅓ cup melted butter
3 tsp. baking powder	bacon fat

1. Preheat the oven to 400 degrees.

2. Combine the flour, cornmeal, salt, sugar, and baking powder.

3. Mix the eggs into the milk.

4. Add the dry ingredients to the egg-milk mixture. Beat the batter with a wooden spoon until it is thoroughly blended.

5. Stir in the cream and the butter.

6. Grease a small iron skillet with bacon fat, place it over high heat, and heat it until it starts to smoke.

7. Remove the skillet from the heat and spread the batter evenly in it.

8. Place in the oven and bake for 30 minutes or until the cornbread is well browned.

CHEF'S SECRET: This cornbread is an old original Southern recipe. The bacon fat gives it an especially good flavor.

For success, it is very important that the heavy iron skillet is heated; however, if you do not have an iron skillet and you use a glass baking dish, the dish cannot be preheated in the same way. In this case, pour about 2 to 3 tbsp. bacon fat into the dish and place it on a cookie sheet in the oven as you start to heat the oven. Let it stay in the oven until the temperature gets to about 400 degrees. Then pour the batter slowly into the heated dish, adding about 1 to 2 tbsp. at a time so the temperature of the dish itself will not go down.

Muffins

about 12 muffins

2 cups all-purpose flour
2 tsp. baking powder
½ tsp. salt
2 tbsp. sugar

1 cup milk
1 egg, well beaten
¼ cup melted butter

1. Preheat the oven to 400 degrees.
2. Combine the flour, baking powder, salt, and sugar.
3. Add the milk, egg, and melted butter to the dry ingredients. Stir, but do not beat.
4. Pour the batter into well-buttered muffin pans, filling each about two-thirds full.
5. Bake for 20 to 25 minutes.

CHEF'S SECRET: The secret of muffins is in the method of combining the ingredients. The batter should not be overmixed and should never be beaten, but just stirred. As soon as the batter is stirred together, it should be immediately poured into the well-buttered pans.

If you wish to use paper muffin cups, still brush the pans with butter and brush the insides of the paper cups after inserting them in the pans.

This basic recipe can be altered by adding some soaked, dried, and blanched raisins or black currants, or some chopped pecans or other nuts. In case you are adding as much as ½ cup of any of these ingredients, add an additional 2 to 3 tbsp. milk and ¼ tsp. baking powder.

Popovers

8 medium-sized popovers

2 eggs
1 cup milk
1 cup sifted all-purpose flour

¼ tsp. salt
oil

1. Preheat the oven to 425 degrees.
2. Beat the eggs slightly. Add the milk, flour, and salt.
3. Beat the mixture vigorously for 2 minutes.
4. Oil eight iron popover pans. Place them in the oven until they are very hot.
5. Fill each cup two-thirds full with batter.
6. Bake for 40 minutes or until puffed and browned. Serve at once.

CHEF'S SECRET: If you do not have any iron popover pans, do not attempt this recipe. It is very important that you heat the oiled pans in the oven until the oil starts to smoke.

Use asbestos gloves to handle the pans to make sure you do not burn your hands.

You can beat the ingredients together in an electric mixer if you have a paddle, but do not beat it for 2 minutes—1½ minutes will do.

Ham in Rye Bread

8 servings

6 cups all-purpose flour, sifted
3 cups rye flour
2 packages dry yeast
½ cup warm water
2½ cups boiling water
½ cup melted butter

1½ tbsp. salt
1 pinch sugar
1 3- to 3½-lb. piece, cut from a semi-boned, smoked, ready-to-eat ham
1 egg, slightly beaten

1. Dissolve the yeast in the warm water. Add the pinch of sugar.

2. In a metal bowl, mix the rye flour with the melted butter and the salt. Pour in the boiling water and mix with a wooden spoon. Let this mixture cool until it reaches the temperature of your hand.

3. When cooled, add the activated yeast.

4. Add all but ½ cup of the all-purpose flour, stirring it into the liquid slowly.

5. Dust a pastry board with some of the leftover flour. Place the dough on the pastry board and dust the top of it with some flour. Cover with a towel and let the dough rest for 10 to 15 minutes.

6. Start to knead the dough with both hands, gently but vigorously, as described in the directions for Quick Bread (see page 223). Knead the dough until it becomes smooth—about 10 minutes.

7. Brush the inside of a bowl with a little butter and place the dough in it. Brush the top of the dough with more butter or turn it in the bowl. Cover with a towel and set in a warm place which is draft free until it rises to double its bulk.

8. Punch the dough down, cover, and let rise again until double in bulk.

9. Lightly grease a cookie sheet. Place it next to the pastry board.

10. Roll out the dough until it is large enough to completely encase the ham.

11. Place the dough half on and half off the cookie sheet.

12. Set the ham (which must be at room temperature) on the dough on the cookie sheet. Fold the other side over the top of the ham and press the edges together, completely sealing in the ham. Tuck all the sealed edges under the ham.

13. Cover with a kitchen towel and let rise in a warm place for approximately 30 minutes.

14. Meanwhile, preheat the oven to 350 degrees.

15. Brush the top of the crust with the slightly beaten egg. Bake in the oven for 30 minutes, then reduce the heat to 325 degrees and bake for another 15 to 20 minutes or until a testing needle, inserted in the dough only, comes out clean and not sticky.

CHEF'S SECRET: This is a 200-year-old Hungarian recipe which, traditionally, is made only twice a year—for Christmas and Easter.

Be sure the ham which is used is the fully cooked, ready-to-eat type. If anything, it should be warmer—not colder—than room temperature. Some brands have a piece of skin toward the shank end which should be removed. If you wish, you can even cut off the shank end. Some chefs, and even housewives, leave the shank out and use the extra dough to make a braid or leaf and flower decoration for the top.

When you remove the ham baked in bread from the oven, make 2 or 3 deep gashes on each side, close to the bottom, so that the juices coming out of the ham can run out. Otherwise the bread will be soggy.

If you plan to eat the bread cold (which is delicious), rub the surface of the ham with 2 envelopes unflavored gelatin before encasing it. This will coagulate the juices around the ham and keep the slices from falling apart.

If desired, about 1 tbsp. caraway seeds may be added to the dough before kneading it.

Bread Pudding

8 servings

10 to 12 thin slices bread
½ cup raisins
1 cup water
1 cup sugar
4 cups half-and-half
4 eggs
½ tsp. salt

1 tsp. vanilla extract
¼ tsp. cinnamon
⅛ tsp. grated nutmeg
1 tbsp. currant or raspberry jelly (optional)
softened butter

1. Bring the water to a boil and pour it over the raisins. Cover and let stand for about 5 minutes to plump the raisins. Drain.

2. Generously brush the inside of a shallow casserole with butter.

3. Remove the crusts from the bread. Lightly butter one side of each slice of bread. Cut each slice of buttered bread into four strips.

4. Place a layer of the bread strips in the bottom of the casserole, buttered side up. Sprinkle some raisins and about 1 tbsp. sugar over the bread. Repeat, layering until all the bread is in the dish. If you wish, spread currant jelly over the layer which is in the center.

5. Rinse a saucepan with cold water. Do not dry it.

6. Combine the half-and-half, remaining sugar, salt, cinnamon, and nutmeg in the saucepan and bring the mixture to a boil, stirring constantly.

7. Beat the eggs. Stir some of the hot half-and-half mixture into the beaten eggs to warm them, then pour the egg mixture into the saucepan. Remove from the heat.

8. Add the vanilla, then strain the mixture into the casserole. Let stand at room temperature for at least 30 minutes before baking.

9. Preheat the oven to 325 degrees. Set the casserole in a larger pan or dish with about ½ inch water in the bottom. Bake for approximately 1 hour, or until a knife, when inserted, comes out clean. Serve warm or cold, garnished with whipped cream if desired.

CHEF's SECRET: For ordinary bread, it is advisable to remove the crusts, but if you have a real French "flute" or a good-quality Italian or Vienna bread, you can leave the crusts on because the baking process makes this crust different from that of conventional American bread.

If you have only soft bread on hand, first toast it lightly and then butter it.

It is important to let the bread pudding stand at room temperature for 30 minutes so the liquid has a chance to soak into the bread. Otherwise, all the butter would come to the top and the bread would stay dry and chewy.

Bread Dumplings

8 servings

1 qt. ½-inch bread cubes made from day-old French, Italian, or Vienna bread	3 cups flour
	3 eggs
	1 cup scalded milk
3 tbsp. butter	1 tsp. salt
2 tbsp. bacon drippings or lard	fresh black pepper (optional)

1. Place 2 tbsp. of the butter and the bacon drippings or lard in a large skillet. Toast the bread cubes in this shortening.

2. Mix the flour with the salt in a deep bowl.

3. To the hot milk add the remaining butter. Pour this mixture slowly into the bowl with the dry ingredients, stirring constantly.

4. As the mixture starts to cool, break in the eggs. Keep stirring until all ingredients are incorporated.

5. Beat with a wooden spoon, adding a little warm water if necessary, until the mixture turns into a smooth dough somewhat stiffer than ordinary pancake dough.

6. Fold in the bread cubes. Sprinkle with a little pepper if desired.

7. With wet palms, form 16 dumplings and drop them into a pot filled two-thirds full with slightly salted boiling water. Cook for approximately 10 minutes after you drop the last dumpling into the water.

8. Remove the pot from the heat and let the dumplings steam for another 3 to 5 minutes. Remove the dumplings with a slotted spoon and sprinkle them with melted butter or lard, or spoon some sour cream over them, depending on what they will be served with.

CHEF's SECRET: The recipe given is a very basic one. You can vary this recipe by adding 2 tbsp. finely chopped onion sautéed in the shortening before adding the bread cubes, or 2 tbsp. finely chopped onion and 1 tbsp. chopped fresh parsley sautéed in the same way. Instead of using 3 tbsp. butter and 2 tbsp. bacon drippings or lard, cut 4 to 6 slices of bacon into ¼-inch bits and fry the bacon bits with 2 tbsp. butter, then toast the bread cubes with the bacon bits.

Be sure the pot you use is large enough to allow the dumplings to move about freely; if it is not, cook only half the dumplings at a time.

Breads as Serving Containers

One of the simplest solutions to the housewife's question "What shall I serve it in?" is to buy a round or football-shaped rye, Italian, or Viennese bread, cut off the top, remove all of the soft inside or as much as necessary, and use the bread itself as a container. For instance, remove the inside from a 2-lb. rye carefully, cutting around and then separating it from the bottom by first inserting a grapefruit knife and then by putting all ten fingers in the part farthest away from you and moving your fingers and pressing toward your stomach, removing the inside in one piece if possible. Fill the bread with a cheese mixture or a thick cheese spread or dip. Cut small finger-sized pieces or triangles from the bread which was removed from the center and arrange them around the filled bread.

You can also fill a bread with barbecued hot-dog tidbits, meatballs, or liver pâté. Or it can be used instead of the usual patty shell as a container for Chicken à la King or creamed chicken.

The bread container will always be unique and elegant, and there will be no dish washing. However, do not attempt to fill the bread with dishes that contain too much liquid, as seepage may result.

Round rolls, Kaiser rolls, or oblong, ready-to-bake or bake-yourself rolls are ideal for individual edible containers. For breakfast, bake an egg or two surrounded with partially cooked bacon inside a well-buttered, hollowed-out roll. Or remove the inside of a roll, brush it with butter and toast it under the broiler, and then heap scrambled eggs in it. For dessert, remove the inside of Kaiser rolls, brush the hollow generously with butter, sprinkle with cinnamon sugar, and bake until crisp. Just before serving, place a baked apple in each, fill each with a scoop of vanilla ice cream sprinkled with some cinnamon, or spoon some applesauce into each and top with a scoop of lemon sherbet.

Better yet, devise your own combinations.

DESSERTS

Short Paste
   Fresh Strawberry Tarts
   Pecan Tartlets
1-2-3 Dough
   Linzer Torte
Pâté à Choux
   Fresh Banana Eclairs
   Mocha Cream Puffs
Spongecake
   Viennese Chocolate Strawberry
     Spongecake
Basic Soufflé
   Lemon Crêpe Soufflé
Fruits in Chemise
Basic Vanilla Cream
   Chocolate Cream
   Coffee Cream
   Strawberry Cream
   Chantilly Cream

Pears Helene
Apple Bertchy
Fast, Easy Napoleon
Stuffed Pineapple (Baby's Dream)
Pears in Burgundy
Fruits in Vermouth
Gâteau Allard
Crêpes
   Crêpes Suzette
Quick Parfait Bombe
Watermelon Ice
Baked Alaska
Apples Stuffed with Pistachio Ice
   Cream
Parfait Fürst Pückler

*T*he human mind works in a very peculiar way. When we think back to an event, what we always remember first is what happened last. This explains the great importance of carefully chosen and prepared desserts on the end of a meal.

The dessert should be the finishing touch of the meal, adding the color, texture, taste, and fragrance which were not supplied in the other courses. For instance, if the meal started with fruit, or if fruit was in the salad which accompanied the main course, the dessert should be something different. On the other hand, if no fruit was served during the meal, the dessert should emphasize it. If the main course included a velvety cream sauce, no sauce-y dessert should follow it. And so forth and so on.

According to many researchers, the preferred colors for food are browns and reds; according to some others, reds and browns. This is also something to be kept in mind. Chocolate, strawberries, some melons, cherries, ice creams, creams, or gelatins fulfill the color requirement. As far as tastes go, in my opinion there is only one general rule—do not make anything "icky"—oversweet.

Desserts

Short Paste

3 cups all-purpose flour	1 tsp. salt
1 cup butter	3 tsp. sugar
1 large egg	½ to ¾ cup cold water

1. Sift the flour into the middle of a pastry board or onto a clean, even-surfaced kitchen table so that the flour looks like a wide-based cone.

2. With three fingers, make a hole in the middle of the flour and sprinkle in the salt and sugar.

3. Break the egg, add 2 to 3 tbsp. of the cold water, and beat the mixture slightly with a fork. Pour it into the well.

4. Pour the remaining water into the well, using only ½ cup to begin with and adding more as needed. Using all fingertips, start to incorporate the flour with the liquid. Start on top, bringing the flour into the egg mixture. Do not wet your fingers.

5. With floury fingers, break the butter in small pieces, about the size of almonds. Never touch the butter with your skin; always use floured fingertips.

6. Place the butter in the middle of the flour mixture and start kneading. Be careful to always bring the flour from the sides and incorporate it into the moist and buttery middle. Continue to knead until all the flour is incorporated, but work fast, touching the butter as little as possible. Depending on the flour and on your skill, you will probably need an additional 3 to 4 tbsp. of the cold water.

7. With the back of a knife, scrape off your fingers and add the scrapings to the dough. Dust your palms with a little flour and press the dough out to a square approximately 8 inches by 8 inches. Fold the dough into the middle, folding one-third from the left, one-third from the right, one-third from the bottom, and one-third from the top.

8. Turn the dough upside down and quickly press it out again into a 5-by-5 square. Quickly roll this square into a ball. Wrap it in a plastic bag and place it in the refrigerator.

CHEF'S SECRET: This pastry is the basic dough for lining tarts and tartlets. It is the base of petit fours, and can be used for fancy butter cookies, cake bottoms, and so forth.

Wash your hands very thoroughly, dry them, and clean your fingernails. Then, rub your hands with a little cornstarch before starting, because when you make this dough as much as a third of it will be lumping on your fingers before you are through. You would not want to scrape the dough back and use it if you were not sure that your hands were as clean as possible.

The only equipment I have found that could replace your hands when making this dough is the dough hook on a heavy-duty home electric mixer. No wire whip or paddle would do, and you need a powerful motor. The result will still not be the same; the dough hook will not feel the right time to stop and it will be harder to work with the dough.

Flouring the hands when handling the butter is very important. If the naked hand worked with the butter, it would heat up the surface and the melted butter would soak into the flour. This would make the dough heavy and greasy, since the aim is to have small particles of butter surrounded with flour.

If you have never made this type of dough, or never worked with dough at all, it is advisable to add to this dough a scant ½ tsp. baking powder. Mix it into the flour. The leavening effect will counteract the beginner's imperfect workmanship. Of course, after you master making the dough this can be omitted.

Fresh Strawberry Tarts

8 servings

½ portion basic short paste
1 pint fresh strawberries
3 tbsp. strawberry jam
1 tbsp. water
1 tbsp. lemon juice

½ package strawberry gelatin
1 to 2 cups heavy cream, depending on taste
8 3-inch tart forms

1. To line each tart form, roll a piece of short paste to a round somewhat bigger than the form. Loosen each piece of dough with a spatula and press it into the little tart forms with your fingers. When all 8 are ready, refrigerate them.

2. Preheat the oven to 375 to 400 degrees.

3. Place an empty cookie sheet in the oven and heat it for about 10 minutes.

4. Remove the tart pans from the refrigerator and place them on the hot cookie sheet. Bake for 10 minutes. With a fork, quickly pierce little holes in the bottom of each shell, then bake for another 6 to 8 minutes, or until the edges turn brown. Remove from the oven and cool. Remove the tart shells from the pans.

5. Place the strawberry jam, water, and lemon juice in a small saucepan. Melt the mixture together, then cool.

6. Brush the bottom of the tart shells with the strawberry jam mixture. Pile the cleaned and hulled fresh strawberries in the shells and refrigerate them.

7. Prepare the strawberry gelatin, using one-third less water than the package directions require. Place the gelatin in an ice-water bath to cool. As it starts to get syrupy, brush some over the strawberries.

8. Whip the cream and pipe small stars of it between the strawberries or around the edge. Serve.

Pecan Tartlets

16 to 24, depending on size

½ portion short paste
8 oz. chopped pecans
2 eggs

½ cup firmly packed brown sugar
¼ tsp. vanilla
16 to 24 tartlet forms

1. Line each tart form by rolling each piece of short paste to a round somewhat bigger than the form, loosening it with a spatula, and pressing it into the little tart form with your fingers. When all are ready, refrigerate them.
2. Preheat the oven to 350 degrees.
3. Place an empty cookie sheet in the oven and heat it for about 10 minutes.
4. Separate the eggs. Beat the egg yolks with the brown sugar until the mixture is fluffy and light in color.
5. With a spatula, fold the chopped pecans and the vanilla into the egg yolk mixture.
6. Place the tart forms on the hot cookie sheet and bake them for about 8 minutes.
7. Beat the egg whites until they form soft peaks.
8. Gently fold the egg yolk mixture into the egg whites, using a spatula.
9. Divide the mixture among the half-baked tartlets and bake for another 8 to 10 minutes.
10. Remove from the oven and dust each with powdered sugar or decorate each with a small piece of candied cherry. Serve.

1-2-3 Dough

For the basic dough:
2½ cups flour
1¾ cups butter
1 cup sugar

1 large egg
½ tsp. baking powder
grated zest of ½ lemon*

* The *zest* means the outside yellow part of the skin, without the white pulpy part. The best way to remove it is to use a lemon-zester. This is a small, triangular-shaped metal tool mounted on a wooden or plastic handle. The tip of the triangle is attached to the handle; the base has a row of four or five holes, which take off the zest perfectly. If you do not have this tool or cannot obtain it in a shop, you can use a grater—very carefully so as not to grate the bitter pulp along with the skin.

1. Sift the flour into the middle of a pastry board or on a clean, even-surfaced kitchen table so that the flour looks like a wide-based cone.
2. Make a well in the middle and add the sugar, the baking powder, egg, and grated lemon rind.
3. Dust the surface of the butter with flour and start breaking the butter into small pieces, dipping your fingers into the flour before breaking each

piece. Continue until all the pieces of butter are about the size of an almond or smaller.

4. Quickly mix the dough together with your fingertips, incorporating the flour from the outside into the middle.

Variations:

(a) Instead of the flour, use half flour and half very finely ground almonds. Add ¼ tsp. almond extract.

(b) Substitute ground walnuts or pecans for half the flour. Add ½ tsp. nutmeg, ½ tsp. cinnamon, a pinch of ground cloves, a pinch of mace, and ¼ tsp. black walnut extract.

CHEF's SECRET: Basically, all the chef's secrets of Short Paste (page 241) pertain to this dough. This is the famous so-called Linzer dough that comes from the Austrian city of Linz. If it is rolled thin and baked into cookies, the result is nice crisp cookies. If baked in cake form, it produces a somewhat moist dough which is between a cookie dough and a cake.

All pastries made from this dough improve with proper storage after baking.

Linzer Torte

2 tortes

1 portion 1-2-3 Dough, variation *b*	1 drop green food coloring
2 8-inch cake pans	1 egg white
1 cup red currant jelly	4 tbsp. powdered sugar
1 cup seedless black raspberry jam	2 or 3 drops red food coloring
2 tbsp. chopped almonds	

1. Line the bottom of each cake pan with a piece of wax paper.

2. Preheat the oven to 375 degrees.

3. Divide the dough into three equal portions. Press 1 portion of dough into the bottom of each pan.

4. In a small saucepan, melt the raspberry jam and the red currant jelly together, over medium heat, until the mixture comes to a boil. Keep stirring and cook for 5 to 6 minutes. Remove the mixture from the heat and stir until it cools to lukewarm. Chill in the refrigerator, stirring once in a while.

5. Once the mixture has chilled, divide it in half. Reserve half, and spread the other half over the top of the dough in the two pans, dividing the mixture evenly.

6. Divide the third portion of dough in half. From each half, form strips ½ inch wide. Lay a diamond-shaped lace on the top of each pan with the ½-inch strips of dough. (See drawing.)

7. Place the tortes in the preheated oven and bake for 15 minutes. Reduce the heat to 325 degrees and bake for an additional 15 minutes.

8. Remove the tortes from the oven and let them cool. Cut around the edge of the tortes with a knife to loosen them from the pan, then remove.

9. Place the remaining jelly-jam mixture into a pastry bag fitted with a small star tube. Press some of the mixture into the diamond shapes, starting in the middle of both cakes and going in circles toward the edges, making sure you have some of the mixture for each diamond.

10. In a small bowl, with a spoon, stir the 4 tbsp. of powdered sugar and the egg white with a few drops of the red coloring until it turns into a smooth pink substance. Pipe this substance all around the rims of the Linzer Tortes. Place them back in a 200-degree oven for 15 minutes to dry.

11. With your fingertips, mix the chopped almonds with 1 drop of green food coloring so that all the pieces of almond become somewhat greenish. Sprinkle the almonds over the top of each torte. Store the tortes at least 2 days before serving.

CHEF'S SECRET: If you wish, 2 to 3 tbsp. of good brandy or bourbon may be added to the dough.

Work very fast with this dough to avoid "burning" it with your fingertips. Professional pastry chefs roll the dough into rope-like pieces by hand, but this is difficult. It will be easier to roll out the dough on a pastry board dusted with a little flour, then cut the strips with a knife or with a round-bladed pastry or crinkle cutter.

If you have pistachio nuts on hand, use them instead of making the almonds green. To avoid having green fingertips from coloring the almonds, smear some cold butter on your fingertips before starting. Or, drop the food coloring into 1 tsp. of the powdered sugar and stir it until the powdered sugar is evenly green, then rub it into the almonds.

If you like a very moist Linzer Torte, increase the baking powder to 1 tsp. and reduce the baking time by 5 to 8 minutes.

Pâté à Choux

1 cup sifted flour
7 tbsp. butter
1 tbsp. sugar

1 cup water
4 eggs

1. Place the water, sugar, and butter in a medium-sized saucepan. Bring the mixture to a boil, over medium heat, stirring until the butter is melted.

2. As soon as the butter is melted and the mixture begins to boil, remove from the heat. Add the flour all at once. Stir vigorously with a wooden kitchen spoon until the mixture turns into a ball.

3. Place back over the heat and keep stirring vigorously with the spoon until all the dough will form a ball around the spoon, without sticking to the spoon or the pan.

4. Immediately place the dough in an electric mixer bowl. Start to beat, using a paddle or, if available, a dough hook. (If neither is available, do it by hand. Do not attempt to use a wire whip, as it will not work.)

5. Break each egg separately into a cup. Incorporate the eggs one by one, stirring or beating constantly after each addition until the dough turns shiny and no trace of the egg is visible before adding another egg. This is very important.

6. The way in which the dough is baked depends upon what you wish to make from it. Recipes for two desserts using Pâté à Choux are given below.

CHEF'S SECRET: If you master this dough, you will be able to make a great number of very elegant French and continental pastries, appetizers, and main-course dishes.

Timing is very important. It is also important that you always clear the sides and bottom of the container you use while incorporating the eggs.

Fresh Banana Eclairs

8 to 12 servings

1 portion Pâté à Choux
4 ripe bananas
1 pint heavy cream
½ cup plus 3 tbsp. water
2 envelopes unflavored gelatin
6 to 8 tbsp. granulated sugar

2 to 3 tbsp. rum or few drops rum extract
3 oz. semisweet chocolate
2 tbsp. sliced, toasted almonds
Chocolate Sauce (see page 216)

1. Preheat the oven to 425 degrees.

2. Spoon the dough into 2 long giant éclairs, the length of a cookie sheet (approximately 12 inches long).

3. Bake the éclairs in the preheated oven, without opening the door, for 20 to 25 minutes. Reduce the heat to 350 degrees and bake for 20 minutes. Reduce the heat again to 325 degrees and bake an additional 10 minutes.

4. Dissolve the gelatin in the 3 tbsp. water. Bring the ½ cup water to a boil and stir in the gelatin mixture. Cool in an ice-water bath until it starts to gel.

5. Meanwhile, whip the heavy cream with half the sugar until it forms stiff peaks. Gently fold the rum or rum extract into the cooled gelatin. Pour the gelatin all over the surface of the whipped cream and gently fold it in.

6. Press the bananas with a fork until they turn into a pulp. Stir in the remaining sugar. Fold this banana-sugar mixture into the whipped cream, using a spatula. Chill.

7. When the éclairs have cooled, split them in half lengthwise, parallel with the bottom. Remove and discard the soft inside parts.

8. With a pastry bag fitted with a star tube, fill the bottom of the éclairs with the banana-cream mixture. Chill in the freezer for at least 1 hour.

9. Melt the chocolate in a small saucepan and brush the top parts of the éclairs with the melted chocolate. Sprinkle the almonds over the chocolate while it is still warm. Let dry.

10. With a sharp knife, cut the top half of each éclair into serving-sized pieces. Place the top pieces on the banana-cream-filled bottom half and finish cutting through. Serve with Chocolate Sauce.

CHEF'S SECRET: This pastry is good only when it is made from fresh bananas which are so ripe that the skin is almost brown (or at least more than half brown), thin, and soft. Do not try to make it from light lemon-colored, firm-skinned bananas. It will not have any taste at all. If you cannot get any ripe bananas, store unripened ones in a brown paper bag for 2 to 3 days to allow them to ripen before trying to use them.

Do not try to run the bananas through a food mill, as they will turn into a liquid and will not serve the purpose. If gently pressed with a fork, they will retain their consistency.

Mocha Cream Puffs

12 to 16 puffs

1 portion Pâté à Choux	1 egg
1 pint heavy cream	2½ to 3 tbsp. instant coffee
4 to 6 tbsp. fine granulated sugar	3 to 4 tbsp. powdered sugar

1. With a pastry bag, press the dough onto a cookie sheet in portions the size of a walnut or, if desired, the size of a small egg.

2. Beat the egg yolk slightly.

3. With a fine pastry brush, coat the top of each puff with the egg yolk.

4. Bake the puffs in a preheated 425-degree oven for 25 minutes. Reduce the heat to 350 degrees and bake for an additional 20 to 25 minutes or until a testing needle, when inserted, comes out almost dry.

5. Cool and split in half.

6. Whip the heavy cream slowly, adding all the granulated sugar except 1 tbsp., until it forms stiff peaks. Combine the remaining 1 tbsp. sugar with 1½ to 2 tbsp. of the instant coffee. Sprinkle this sugar-coffee mixture over the top of the whipped cream, distributing as evenly as possible. Gently fold together.

7. With a pastry bag fitted with a star tube, divide the whipped cream among the puffs. Refrigerate.

8. In a small bowl or a round-bottomed coffee cup, mix the egg white, powdered sugar, and the remaining 1 tbsp. instant coffee until it turns into a light brown, shiny "royal" sugar icing.

9. Dribble the icing over the top halves of the puffs. Let it dry at room temperature. Place the tops on the refrigerated cream-filled bottoms. Serve.

CHEF'S SECRET: This is the classic way of serving cream puffs. Of course, if you wish, you can omit the icing and sprinkle powdered sugar or a mixture of powdered sugar and instant coffee over the tops.

Sometimes, with certain brands of instant coffee, there may be little dark specks in the whipped cream. I am afraid there is not too much you can do to prevent this. It is best, as a precaution, to dilute the instant coffee in a few teaspoons of brandy. This will, of course, improve the quality of the dessert.

Spongecake

8 tbsp. all-purpose flour
½ tsp. baking powder
5 tbsp. granulated sugar
5 medium eggs

2 oz. melted butter or other shortening
1 tsp. vanilla or ½ tsp. almond, lemon, or orange extract

1. Preheat the oven to 375 degrees.

2. Separate the eggs.

3. In an electric mixer, start to beat the egg yolks and the sugar at medium speed. Increase the speed to high and continue beating them until the mixture becomes very light, lemon colored, and fluffy. If you stop beating, large air bubbles should come to the top and burst.

4. Whip the egg whites in a separate bowl until they form stiff, but not dry, peaks.

5. Combine the flour and baking powder and sprinkle some of the mixture through a sieve over the top of the egg yolk–sugar mixture. Fold in with a spatula. Continue sprinkling some of the flour–baking powder mixture over the egg yolk mixture, and then folding it in, until all but 1 tbsp. of the flour is mixed in. Add the flavoring.

6. Sprinkle the last 1 tbsp. flour over the beaten egg whites. Gently fold it in with a wire whip.

7. With a spatula, add one-third of the egg white mixture to the egg yolk mixture and gently fold the two together. Pour the egg yolk mixture slowly over the top of the remaining egg whites and quickly, but gently, fold the mixtures together until not too much of the whites show. Do not mix completely, since overmixing must be avoided, but do not leave large pieces of the egg white either.

8. Brush the inside of an 8-inch cake pan with the melted butter or other shortening and dust it with flour. Place a round of wax paper in the bottom, butter the paper, and dust it with flour.

9. Pour the batter into the cake pan and bake in the preheated oven for approximately 20 to 25 minutes or until a needle, when inserted, comes out dry.

10. Cool the cake on a rack, in the pan. Then invert the pan and remove the cake.

CHEF'S SECRET: The ingredients of this dough are simple, but the preparation is not easy. Do not lose your confidence if it does not work the first time. Success is again dependent on the timing, speed of movement, light-handedness, and, of course, correct temperature. The latter is probably the most important. Depending on your oven and the accuracy of its thermostat, you will probably have to make the spongecake two or three times before perfec-
 is reached.

Possible mistakes are: mixing the egg yolk–sugar mixture too little, which will result in a heavy-bottomed cake that will collapse in the middle; over-beating the egg whites, which will cause a flat, heavy cake without a good aerated texture; too hot an oven, which will cause the top to burn and the cake to rise quickly and collapse early; and too cold an oven, which will cause liquifying and hardening on the bottom and an empty, too-spongy top that will collapse.

Viennese Chocolate Strawberry Spongecake

1 spongecake layer	1 egg
1 pint fresh strawberries	2 tbsp. boiling milk
1 pint heavy cream	sprinkling of salt
3 to 4 tbsp. granulated sugar	1 envelope unflavored gelatin
6 oz. sweet butter	3 tbsp. cold water
½ cup pure unsweetened cocoa	½ cup boiling water
1 cup powdered sugar	

1. Beat the heavy cream with a light sprinkling of salt and 2 to 3 tbsp. of the granulated sugar. Soften the gelatin in the cold water, then add it to the boiling water. Cool in an ice water bath until syrupy, then fold into the whipped cream. Chill the mixture.

2. Quickly wash and hull the strawberries, leaving about 12 of the nicest unhulled. Slice the rest into ¼-inch slices.

3. Put the sliced strawberries on a board and, with a sharp knife, gently chop them, being careful not to press out too much liquid.

4. Sprinkle the chopped strawberries with the remaining 1 tbsp. sugar.

5. Place half the butter, broken into small pieces, half the cocoa, half the powdered sugar and the egg, slightly beaten, in a mixing bowl. Start to blend on low; as soon as the dry ingredients are incorporated enough so that they will not fly, increase the speed to high and beat until the mixture becomes smooth.

6. While still beating on high speed, add the remaining butter, bit by bit. Stop the mixer and add the rest of the cocoa and powdered sugar. With a spatula, scrape down the sides and try to incorporate the dry ingredients as much as possible. Scrape any ingredients adhering to the spatula back into the mixing bowl and start to beat the mixture again at low speed. Then in-crease the speed to high and beat until the mixture is light and fluffy.

7. Add the boiling milk and let it cool to room temperature.

8. Split the cake into 3 layers.

9. Spread a little of the chocolate cream on the bottom layer. With a pastry bag fitted with a star tube, pipe some chocolate cream around the edge to form a rim.

10. With a slotted spoon, spoon the chopped strawberries on the layer. Reserve any juice that has accumulated. Place a second layer on top.

11. Fold two-thirds of the whipped cream together with the juice from the chopped strawberries. Pile this light pink whipped cream on top of the sec-ond layer. Place the third layer on top and chill for at least 1 hour.

12. After the assembled layers have chilled, coat the sides of the cake with the chocolate butter cream. Pipe the remaining one-third of the whipped

cream over the top and decorate with the reserved unhulled strawberries. Chill and serve.

CHEF's SECRET: If you first hull the strawberries and then wash them, they will soak up the water and lose their taste. Be sure to use a very thin-bladed knife for chopping the strawberries, so that as little as possible of the juice oozes during the chopping.

The fluffiness of the Viennese Chocolate Strawberry Spongecake depends on your patience in beating the whipped cream and preparing the butter cream; only through spending the proper amount of time can you achieve the highest volume.

When mixing the strawberry juice and the whipped cream, use your judgment; if too much liquid oozed, use only part of it or stir it into a little strawberry jam or jelly to thicken it before folding it into the cream.

Basic Soufflé

4 servings

1 cup milk	1 tsp. vanilla or other desired flavoring
½ cup granulated sugar	8 egg whites
3 tbsp. flour	2 tbsp. powdered sugar
2 tbsp. butter	additional powdered sugar for dusting
3 egg yolks	after baking

1. In a small saucepan, bring half the milk to a boil with 2 tbsp. of the granulated sugar and 1 tbsp. of the butter.

2. Dissolve the flour in the remaining ½ cup milk. Add the milk-flour mixture to the boiling milk, stirring constantly, and cook over medium heat until the mixture turns into a medium-thick cream sauce.

3. Remove the cream sauce from the heat and let it cool at room temperature. It will become somewhat stiff.

4. Approximately 1 hour before serving, preheat the oven to 425 degrees.

5. Add the egg yolks and the vanilla or other flavoring to the cream sauce.

6. Start to beat all but 2 of the egg whites in an electric mixer. Slowly add the remaining sugar and continue to beat until the egg whites form soft peaks. Pour in the remaining 2 egg whites and beat until they become firm and are shiny.

7. Prepare a 2-qt. soufflé dish by brushing the inside of it with the remaining 1 tbsp. butter and generously dust it with the 2 tbsp. powdered sugar.

8. Fold one-third of the egg whites into the egg yolk–cream sauce mixture, then pour this mixture evenly over the top of the remaining beaten egg whites. Gently fold the mixtures together with the use of a spatula, folding in one direction, 10 to 12 times. Don't worry if some pieces of egg white are still showing; it is important not to over-mix.

9. Pour the batter into the prepared soufflé dish and place it in the preheated oven. Bake it without opening the door for at least 15 minutes.

10. Then, slowly open the door and turn the soufflé a half turn so that the front will then be in the back of the oven. Close the door and bake for another 15 to 20 minutes.

11. Reduce the heat to 250 degrees and leave the soufflé in the oven for 3 to 4 more minutes. Remove from the oven and dust the top with powdered sugar. Serve immediately.

CHEF'S SECRET: It is no mystery to make a soufflé. I do not believe it requires all the rigmarole some people think.

In old times, the thick white sauce with sugar used to be called "panda," but this expression is no longer used. It is possible to make the cream sauce in the morning and let it stand at room temperature all day (except, of course, in extremely hot weather).

If you wish, you can incorporate many other ingredients into a basic soufflé. You can soak leftover spongecake in brandy or sherry and then add small chunks or crumbs to the batter. Pour about one-third of the batter in the bottom of the soufflé dish, add some of the spongecake chunks or crumbs, add another third of the batter, more chunks or crumbs, and then pour the remaining batter on the top and bake it. You can add candied or fresh fruits, or, for a coffee royal soufflé, add instant coffee to the white sauce before adding the eggs.

Any imitation flavors and food colorings can be added, but it is important that you add these to the white sauce before adding or while adding the egg yolks.

Remember, a soufflé should not be overcooked to the point of becoming dry. Good soufflés are almost runny in the center when served. They practically finish cooking on the plate of the people who enjoy them. (See drawing.)

Another very easy to prepare and elegant soufflé is the Lemon Crêpe Soufflé that follows.

Lemon Crêpe Soufflé

8 crêpes (see page 262)

1 portion basic soufflé mixture with juice and grated zest of 1 lemon mixed with the egg yolks into the cream sauce and with 1 or 2 drops

lemon oil, lemon extract, or liquid lemon flavoring added to the egg whites while incorporating sugar

butter

1. Rub the inside of two 8- or 9-inch glass pie dishes with some butter.
2. Preheat the oven to 425 degrees.
3. Quickly place one-eighth of the soufflé mixture in the center of a crêpe. Fold the crêpe almost in half, but not entirely. Fold the two corners together, forming a triangle. Place in the pie dish. Quickly fill and fold the remaining crêpes, and place four crêpes in each dish.
4. Bake the crêpes in the preheated oven for 8 to 12 minutes. Remove, dust with powdered sugar, and serve immediately. If you wish, decorate each with a thin slice of peeled, seeded lemon.

Fruits in Chemise

For the batter:
2 eggs
4 to 8 tbsp. flour, depending on type of fruit
2 tbsp. granulated sugar
½ tsp. baking powder
sprinkling of salt
small amount liquid—milk, water, club soda, white wine, sherry, or beer
shortening

Suggested fruits:
sliced apple, peeled and cored
whole strawberries, hulled
wedges of pear, peeled and cored
peach halves, peeled
whole, pitted Italian plums (replace pit with a small cube sugar and a pinch cinnamon)
pitted prunes, stuffed with a pecan or almond
pitted dates
whole figs
banana, peeled and thickly sliced or in chunks
pineapple cubes

1. Separate the eggs. In a bowl, mix the egg yolks with all the dry ingredients. If the mixture seems too stiff, add some liquid, 1 tablespoon at a time.
2. Beat the egg whites until they form soft peaks. Fold a part of the beaten egg whites into the egg yolk mixture, then fold the egg yolk mixture into the remaining egg whites.
3. Test the batter by dipping a piece of the fruit to be used into it. If it is too thick, too much will stick to the fruit; if it is too thin, the batter will run off, leaving uncoated fruit exposed.
4. Heat enough shortening to submerge the batter-dipped fruits. Once the shortening is hot, dip the fruit into the batter, one by one, and immediately fry in the hot fat for 2 to 3 minutes. Remove and drain on an absorbent paper. Serve as quickly as possible.

CHEF'S SECRET: This is a very elegant dessert when prepared at the table. Prepare the fruits in advance and deep-fry them at the dining table in a fondue dish. Serve the dessert with a fruit sauce, vanilla sauce, or ice cream.

As mentioned before, almost every fruit will need a batter of a different consistency. Therefore, you will have to experiment with the batter beforehand. It is best to keep a piece of the fresh fruit on hand while preparing the batter, so that you can dip it in to see how much time it takes for the batter to run off. Some flour will turn the batter thin after it stands for a while; with other flour it will thicken. This, too, is something you will have to judge and correct by adding a small amount of additional flour or liquid.

The best shortening to use is fresh oil, which will be heated for the first time. Be sure the shortening is hot before attempting to fry the fruit.

Basic Vanilla Cream

approximately 1 quart

1 qt. milk	3 egg yolks
½ cup sugar	8 tbsp. cornstarch
½ tsp. salt	3 oz. butter
1 tsp. vanilla	

1. Dissolve the cornstarch in 1 cup of the milk.
2. Beat the egg yolks slightly with a fork and add them to the milk-cornstarch mixture.
3. Place the remaining 3 cups milk in a medium-sized saucepan. Add the sugar, salt, vanilla, and butter. Start to heat this mixture, stirring to dissolve the sugar.
4. Once the mixture begins to boil, start to stir with a wire whip and pour in the milk–cornstarch–egg yolk mixture. You will have to beat this mixture very vigorously with the wire whip as it will become very stiff. It will not be necessary to cook more than 5 minutes; the mixture will thicken almost immediately.
5. Remove from the heat as soon as the cream is smooth and thick. Let cool.

CHEF'S SECRET: Once you master this basic cream, which is not too difficult, you will be able to make many variations and combinations. You can divide the amount in half and make two different flavors to be served together—chocolate and vanilla, coffee and raspberry, chocolate and strawberry, and so forth. The following are some of the variations which can be made from the Basic Vanilla Cream.

Chocolate Cream

Mix 4 tbsp. cocoa with 1 additional tbsp. sugar into 1 cup of the milk along with the cornstarch, then proceed according to the recipe.

Coffee Cream

Mix 1 to 1½ tbsp. instant coffee with 1 additional tbsp. sugar into 1 cup of the milk along with the cornstarch, then proceed according to the recipe. (Depending on the brand and the consistency of the instant coffee, you may have to add more or less.)

Strawberry Cream

Prepare the cream according to the recipe, using only 3 cups milk altogether. Mash enough strawberries to have 1 cup fresh strawberry pulp. Add 1 to 2 tbsp. sugar to the pulp, depending on the sweetness of the berries. After the basic cream has cooled, stir in the strawberry pulp and add 1 or 2 drops strawberry essence.

All other fruit creams can be made by following the directions for the Strawberry Cream.

Chantilly Cream

Prepare the Basic Vanilla Cream according to the recipe. Beat 1 pt. heavy cream with 2 tbsp. sugar and a pinch of salt until it is very stiff. When the Basic Vanilla Cream has cooled, fold in the whipped cream.

Pears Helene

8 servings

8 firm pears (preferably d'Anjou or Wilhelm)
1 qt. water, or enough to cover
6 whole cloves
1 2-inch piece cinnamon stick
1 cup sugar
juice of 1 lemon

4 tsp. tart jelly, such as red currant
8 small pieces spongecake or any other leftover cake
1 recipe Basic Vanilla Cream (see page 253)
Chocolate Sauce (see page 216)

1. Peel the pears, leaving the stem on. Cut a slice from the bottom of each, so that the pears will stand on a flat surface. Remove the core from the bottom, leaving a hole big enough to turn a teaspoon in.

2. Combine the water, cloves, cinnamon stick, sugar, and lemon juice and bring the mixture to a boil.

3. Add the pears to the liquid, bring the mixture to a boil again, then reduce the heat to low. Simmer under cover until the pears are fork tender, approximately 1 hour.

4. Remove the pan from the heat and let the pears cool in the liquid until lukewarm. Then remove them with a slotted spoon, place on a tray, and chill in the refrigerator.

5. When the pears have chilled, stuff each with ½ tsp. of the jelly and a piece of the cake.

6. Place each pear in an individual glass dish with about ½ cup of the Basic Vanilla Cream. Spoon some Chocolate Sauce over each and serve.

CHEF'S SECRET: If you try to make this dessert from overripe, soft pears, they will fall apart before they finish cooking.

To speed the cooking of the pears, with a small paring knife gently make small incisions about ½ inch deep on the inside of the cavity, but be careful not to cut though the pears. To test for doneness, pierce the pears with a cooking needle, above the cavity. If the needle goes in easily, the pears are ready. It is most important not to cook the pears over high heat.

If the Basic Vanilla Cream is too stiff, dilute it with a few tablespoonfuls of the cooking syrup from the pears.

Do not throw out the cooking syrup from the pears. Add the peelings, cores, and the pieces which were cut from the bottom and continue to cook it over low heat until it turns into a thick, gelatin-like substance. This very pleasant pear glaze can be used to glaze fresh or cooked fruit or pastry. It can be stored in a jar with a tight-fitting lid, in the refrigerator, for 2 to 3 months.

Apple Bertchy

8 servings

4 large, tart, firm apples
1 qt. water, or enough to cover
6 whole cloves
1 2-inch piece cinnamon stick
juice of 1 lemon
1 cup plus 3 tbsp. sugar
8 tsp. red fruit jelly, such as red currant, red raspberry, or strawberry

1 pint heavy cream
1 pinch salt
½ tsp. vanilla
2 to 3 tbsp. toasted, sliced almonds
1 portion Basic Vanilla Cream (see page 253)

1. Split the apples in half crosswise. Remove the core with a melon ball cutter, being careful not to break through the apples. Peel the cored halves.

2. Combine the water, cloves, cinnamon stick, lemon juice, and 1 cup of the sugar in a pot large enough to hold the apples.

3. Bring the liquid to a boil and add the apples. Slowly bring the liquid to a boil again, then turn off the heat immediately and leave the apple halves in the syrup for about 5 to 10 minutes, depending on the firmness of the apples.

4. Remove the apples with a slotted spoon and let them cool to room temperature.

5. Place the Basic Vanilla Cream in a round serving dish which is large enough to hold the eight apple halves.

6. Imbed the halves in the cream, cut side up. Fill the holes with the red fruit jelly.

7. Whip the heavy cream with the remaining 3 tbsp. sugar and the salt until stiff peaks form, but do not overbeat. Add the vanilla.

8. With a pastry bag fitted with a star tube, pipe the whipped cream around the jelly with a circular motion, covering the whole cut surface of each apple half. Sprinkle with the almonds and chill. Serve.

CHEF'S SECRET: If you were to peel the apples first and then try to core them, you would probably damage their texture or even break the halves. They are much easier to handle if you core them first and then peel them.

It is very hard to give a valid, exact cooking time for apples because of the great variance even between apples of the same family.

If the Basic Vanilla Cream is too stiff, add a small amount of the cooking syrup.

Fast, Easy Napoleon

10 to 12 servings

1 package frozen filo leaves or strudel
   leaves
1 cup melted butter
½ cup very fine white bread crumbs
½ cup granulated sugar
1 recipe Basic Vanilla Cream (see
   page 253)
3 eggs

1 pint heavy cream
3 tbsp. sugar
1 pinch salt
1 envelope unflavored gelatin
3 tbsp. cold water
½ cup water
powdered sugar

1. Defrost and handle the filo or strudel leaves according to the package directions.

2. Lightly brush 2 cookie sheets (each large enough to hold a piece of dough approximately 12 by 16 inches) with some of the melted butter.

3. Mix the bread crumbs with the ½ cup sugar. Lay two filo or strudel leaves on each cookie sheet. With a pastry brush, generously sprinkle the leaves with some of the melted butter, then evenly sprinkle each with some of the bread crumb–sugar mixture. Repeat this process four times on each sheet, so that you have eight leaves on each.

4. With a small paring knife, gently cut fine incisions in the pastry and bake it in a preheated 375- to 400-degree oven for 4 to 5 minutes. Remove and let the pastry cool.

5. Separate the eggs. In a large bowl, combine the Basic Vanilla Cream with the 3 egg yolks, which have been slightly beaten with a fork.

6. Beat the egg whites until they are stiff but not dry.

7. Dissolve the gelatin in the 3 tbsp. water. Bring the ½ cup water to a boil and dissolve the softened gelatin in the boiling water. Cool by setting the pan in an ice-water bath until the gelatin is syrupy.

8. Whip the heavy cream, adding the pinch of salt and the sugar.

9. Fold the beaten egg whites into the stiffly beaten cream. Add the cooled, syrupy gelatin and fold in with a spatula, distributing the gelatin throughout the mixture. Fold into the Vanilla Cream mixture.

10. Evenly pile this mixture on one of the pastry sheets. Place in the freezer to chill until firm.

11. With a wet, sharp knife, cut the filling and bottom pastry into serving-sized pieces. Cut the other baked pastry sheet into pieces of the same size and place these pieces on top of the precut filling and bottom layer. Chill in the refrigerator.

12. Just before serving, dust the top of the Napoleon slices with powdered sugar.

CHEF'S SECRET: If filo leaves are not available in your area, they are available through mail order houses such as H. Roth & Son in New York, Hungarian Enterprises in Cleveland, and The Gourmet Market at the Cannery in San Francisco.

To make your work easier, cut four pieces of cardboard, making two of them 12¼ inches long and two 16¼ inches long. Tape the four pieces together with scotch tape, then cover them with aluminum foil and tape the foil on the outside. Place this foil frame around the bottom strudel pastry sheet after baking it, before you pour the filling over it. The filling will not run and will be evenly distributed over the surface. When you want to remove the frame, simply heat a dull knife in hot water, run the knife around the inner edge of the frame, and lift it off.

If you cannot get the filo leaves anywhere, make one portion of the dough which is given in the recipe for Saucisson en Croûte (see page 20). Divide the dough in half. Roll out one-half of the dough on a very lightly floured pastry board, as thin as possible. Fold the dough one-third from the top, one-third from the bottom, one-third from the left, and one-third from the right so that you have a square. Place this in the refrigerator and let it rest for 30 minutes. Roll out again, making it as long as you can, this time being careful that it remains a straight-sided oblong. Fold one-third from each direction as before, and place it in the refrigerator for another 30 minutes. Roll out again to an oblong 12 by 16 inches, place on a cookie sheet, and chill in the refrigerator. Follow this procedure with the other half of the dough. To bake, preheat the oven to 425 degrees. Make small incisions in the dough with a small paring knife. Bake in the preheated oven for 8 to 12 minutes.

This dough will be different from the filo leaves, but it will make a very fine Napoleon and it requires very little skill. In France, I ate millefeuille or Napoleon slices made from this type of dough in many places, and it is preferred by many.

If you master this dough, you will be able to prepare numerous desserts with it. The most important secret is that little flour is used when rolling out the dough; however, the rolling pin should be floured and kept cold so that it does not get sticky.

To keep the dough square while you are rolling it, follow the drawing and the following instructions: (a) Place the square of dough in front of you. Holding the handles of the rolling pin, hit the dough strongly on a diagonal from the lower left corner to the upper right corner. Turn the rolling pin and hit the dough on a diagonal in the opposite direction, from the upper left to the lower right corners. You should see a strong indentation resembling an "X." (b) Now start to roll the dough. Press the rolling pin only in the middle of the dough, easing the pressure as you get to the edges. Always go straight, so that the rolling pin is parallel with the lower and upper edges and on a 90-degree angle to the left and right sides; then turn the pin and roll from left to right and right to left, parallel to the sides and on a 90-degree angle to the top and bottom. If one of the corners start to extend further than another, give a few extra rollings while holding the pin diagonally. If both of the upper or lower corners start to become ear-shaped, then roll the middle part until the edge is straight again. If possible, avoid touching the roller of the pin to prevent it from getting warm and greasy from your hands.

Although wood is a very poor conductor of heat, it is still advisable to chill the rolling pin before starting to roll the dough. Keep in mind the fact that the dough has 4 oz. more shortening than flour. You do not want to melt the butter or cream cheese which is in it, because the flour will absorb the shortening.

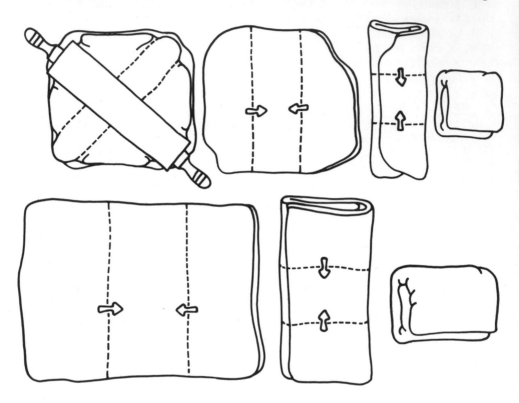

Stuffed Pineapple (Baby's Dream)

8 servings

1 large pineapple, approximately 12 inches long	8 slices poundcake or spongecake
1 qt. large, firm strawberries	1 qt. heavy cream
1 cup kirsch or orange liqueur, such as Cointreau or Triple Sec	5 to 6 tbsp. sugar
	1 pinch salt
	red food coloring

1. Split the pineapple in half, from top to bottom, leaving on the leafy parts. From the outside of each half, cut a slice parallel with the cut surface so the halves will stand firmly.

2. With a sharp knife, remove the inside of the pineapple as follows: About ½ inch from the top, cut across the flesh, being careful to avoid cutting into the skin and to stay at least ½ inch from the sides. Make a similar cut across the bottom. Now remove the hard core by cutting first on one side and then on the other side, holding the knife so that the tip runs under the core. After removing the core, there should be a "V"-shaped groove inside the pineapple. Now cut parallel to the sides of the "V", approximately ½ inch in from the skin and almost down to the bottom. Then cut from the bottom of the "V" toward the sides and remove the fleshy parts. (See drawing.)

3. Cube the flesh of the pineapple into pieces about the size of the strawberries.

4. Quickly wash, shake dry, and hull the strawberries. Set the eight nicest berries aside to be used for decoration.

5. Combine the pineapple cubes and the strawberries and marinate them in the kirsch or other liqueur.

6. Whip the cream with the salt and sugar until it is firm and holds its shape, but do not overbeat it.

7. Remove about 2 cups of the whipped cream and fold a few drops of the red food coloring into it. Coat the top of each piece of spongecake or poundcake with this pink whipped cream.

8. Place the two pineapple halves on a large serving platter so that the bottom ends are together and the leafy tops are at the two ends of the platter. Secure the ends together with toothpicks or bamboo skewers.

9. Arrange the pieces of cake on both sides of the pineapple halves.

10. Pour the marinade from the fruits. Divide the remaining whipped cream in half and gently fold the marinade into half the cream. Now fold the fruits into the whipped cream–marinade mixture.

11. Heap the fruit–whipped cream mixture into the two pineapple halves.

12. With a pastry bag fitted with a star tube, pipe the remaining whipped

cream over and around the filled pineapple halves. Decorate each half with four of the reserved strawberries.

13. Chill for about 1 hour before serving.

CHEF'S SECRET: The original of this recipe was devised by August Escoffier and called "Dream of a Baby." The main difference is that we do not suggest that you make a pink frosting–coated spongecake base for the two pineapple halves and then discard it after the dinner. We feel the dessert is just as pretty when served as suggested here.

Pears in Burgundy

8 servings

8 small-sized Bartlett pears (approximately 2 to 2½ lbs.)
2 cups Burgundy red wine
3 cups water, or enough to cover
2 to 3 cups sugar

1 2-inch cinnamon stick
4 whole cloves
lemon juice–water or white vinegar–water mixture (at least 1 qt. water and juice of 1 lemon)

1. Peel the pears, leaving the stems attached. Remove a slice from the bottom of each, then core from the bottom side, using a potato peeler. Keep pears in the lemon-water or white vinegar–water mixture so they will not darken.

2. In a large saucepan, combine the wine, water, sugar, and spices and bring the mixture to a boil.

3. Add the pears, one by one, and poach them gently until they are tender.

4. Let them cool in the syrup, then remove. Serve lukewarm or cold.

CHEF'S SECRET: This is one of the favorite recipes of Frenchmen. It is hard to imagine a French restaurant, especially in Paris or other large cities, that does not have this dessert on the menu, at least from August to February.

Be careful when selecting the Burgundy red wine. It is not true that cooking wine should be inferior. Of course, you do not have to use a great vintage wine; a good California Burgundy-type red wine will be fine.

In many restaurants, the Pears in Burgundy have an extremely vivid red coloring which is, of course, from red food coloring. If you wish to add food coloring, use it in moderation.

If you wish, you can make this same dessert using a good white wine. In this case, call it "Pears in Chablis."

For this dish, be sure you get Bartlett pears or, if they are not available, Gusset pears. These are the two best choices for Pears in Burgundy.

Fruits in Vermouth

about 2 quarts

½ bottle Riccadonna Torina Red Bitter vermouth

½ bottle Riccadonna Torina Golden Bittersweet vermouth

2 cups sugar
1 package pitted California dates
1 package pitted California prunes
1 package California mixed dried fruits
1 package California figs

1 package dried apricots
1 package large white raisins
1 package dried apple slices
1 slice fresh orange rind (optional)

1. Mix all the fruits together in a large bowl.
2. Place one-fourth of them in the bottom of a large container which has a tight-fitting lid. Add ½ cup sugar and another layer of fruit; continue until all the fruit and sugar are used.
3. Fill the container with the two vermouths. Add the orange rind if desired.
4. Store the mixture at room temperature for 4 to 5 days, then refrigerate at least one week before using.

CHEF'S SECRET: A two-quart jar of these Fruits in Vermouth can be stored in your refrigerator for as long as 3 to 4 years without spoiling. I am afraid however, that you will have to keep refilling it, because it will be very popular.

It can be eaten "as is" or chopped and spooned over any kind of cake or ice cream. It is a very good accompaniment for gamebirds, or you can mix 1 cup chopped Fruits in Vermouth with 2 cups whole cranberries and serve it with poultry. It is a good topping for yogurt or for broiled grapefruit. With melon balls, it makes a festive dessert, and it can turn a plain vanilla soufflé into an exotic masterpiece.

Gâteau Allard

8 servings

For the gâteau:
1 1-lb. loaf heavy-crusted white bread
(Italian, Vienna, French, or a round white bread), at least 1 day old
2 qt. fresh raspberries
2 cups sugar
1 cup soft butter

For the sauce:
2 cups sour cream
1 cup half-and-half
4 tbsp. brown sugar

1. Remove all the crusts from the loaf of bread, being sure to leave only the white inside part.
2. Slice the bread into ⅓- to ½-inch slices.
3. With about ½ cup of the butter, generously brush the inside of a straight-sided casserole or two-quart soufflé dish.
4. Pour the sugar into the buttered dish and keep shaking and turning the dish until about half the sugar adheres to the bottom and sides. Pour out the remaining sugar and reserve.
5. Using the smaller slices of bread, line the bottom and sides of the dish.
6. Quickly wash the raspberries and shake very dry in a towel. Reserve a few of the nicest for garnish.
7. Divide the raspberries into thirds. Put one-third on the bread in the bottom of the dish. Sprinkle in some of the sugar, then cover with another layer

of bread. Repeat this two more times, leaving the largest slices of bread for the top.

8. Generously spread the remaining butter on one side of the slices of bread which will cover the top. Place the buttered bread on the top, buttered side down.

9. Press the Gâteau gently with a plate somewhat smaller than the soufflé dish. Refrigerate for at least 6 hours.

10. To unmold, dip the casserole in enough very hot water to come almost to the rim. Run a wet knife around the inside edge and immediately unmold onto a large platter. Chill again.

11. Decorate the top with a few nice fresh raspberries and, if available, a few green leaves. Serve very cold with the sauce made by gently stirring together the sour cream, half-and-half, and brown sugar.

CHEF'S SECRET: For the last decade Allard has been the most famous luncheon place in Paris. It is among the very few Parisian restaurants where the chef and cooks are all female. The Gâteau Allard is simple but extremely delicious. It is so famous that during the raspberry season people come all the way from Brussels to Allard just to eat it.

Utmost care should be taken that the raspberries are not watery. You must wash them, but wash them quickly by just sprinkling some cold water over them; then immediately place the berries into an absorbent kitchen towel and swing them dry. Do not shake them, because the berries will break in the towel. Of course, the bread, when pressed down, will break the berries, but the juice will be absorbed in the bread.

If you feel the raspberries are not sweet enough, add more sugar.

The bread must be at least a day old; two-day-old bread is even better.

Crêpes

approximately 24 8-inch crêpes

2 cups flour	2 to 2½ cups milk
1 tbsp. sugar	1 cup butter
¼ tsp. salt	1 cup other shortening, such as lard or
4 eggs	oil

1. Separate the eggs. Beat the egg yolks slightly and then stir them into 2 cups of the milk.

2. Combine the flour, sugar, and salt.

3. Slowly stir the milk–egg yolk mixture into the dry ingredients, until you have a batter with a consistency similar to that of buttermilk or cold syrup. You may need to add a little more of the milk.

4. Beat the egg whites until they form soft peaks.

5. Gently fold the beaten egg whites into the batter. Let the batter stand in the refrigerator for at least 1 hour.

6. Melt the butter with the other shortening.

7. To fry the crêpes, heat a heavy, well-balanced, 8-inch frying pan over medium heat. Brush the skillet with 1 tbsp. of the melted shortening. Stir the

crêpe batter with a 2-oz. ladle, then fill the ladle with batter and pour it into the pan, tilting the pan at the same time in all directions so that the batter is quickly distributed and covers the bottom. Place the pan back over the heat and run around the edges of the crêpe that is frying with a spoon filled with about ½ tbsp. of shortening, holding the spoon so the shortening runs between the edge of the batter and the pan. As soon as the edges start to brown and the top looks somewhat dry, loosen the edges with a spatula. Gently ease the spatula underneath the crêpe and, with a quick turn, turn the crêpe over.

8. When the crêpes are cooked on both sides, stack them on a warm platter, on top of each other, and keep warm.

CHEF'S SECRET: If the egg yolk–flour mixture is lumpy, you can strain it through a sieve, dissolving the lumps with the extra milk. The fastest and best method of frying crêpes is as follows: Use two heavy-duty, 8-inch frying pans, which are well balanced so that the handle will not cause the pan to tip over. If possible, purchase two new pans and keep them only for crêpes, eggs, and omelets. Do not wash them in water; just wipe them dry.

Heat the two pans over medium heat with 1 generous tbsp. of the melted shortening. Put the first pan over the heat about a minute before you start to heat the second one. Stir the crêpe batter; then pour two ounces of the batter into the first pan, tilting the pan as suggested to distribute the batter. Place the pan back over the heat and run around the edge with the spoonful of shortening. The second pan will heat while you are doing the previous two steps; while the first side of the first crêpe is browning, you can repeat these steps, starting a second crêpe in the second pan. When you have finished repeating these steps, the first crêpe will be ready to be turned. Continue to alternate steps between the two skillets.

Do not give up too quickly. If you learn the little easy-to-learn trick discussed above, it will not be difficult to make the crêpes. The reasons we suggest doing two at a time are (a) it takes half the time, and (b) all your attention will be required, so that there will be no chance of your forgetting about a frying crêpe.

Pouring the shortening around the edge of the crêpe along the wall of the pan will give enough shortening to the pan, so that you will not have to add more when turning. It will also help make the edges crisp and brown and will cook the crêpe faster.

The quality of the flour and the way in which it was stored will determine its moisture content, and the moisture content determines the amount of milk you will have to use.

You can substitute club soda for a part of the milk; this will help to keep the batter light.

If you plan to make a large number of crêpes, you can double or triple this recipe.

Crêpes Suzette

8 crêpes

4 tbsp. butter	juice of 1 orange
4 tbsp. sugar	juice of ½ lemon

grated zest of orange and lemon   8 crêpes
½ to 1 cup orange liqueur
2 oz. brandy, cognac, or a good-quality
   bourbon

1. Fold the crêpes in half, then in half again so they resemble a slice of pie. Keep them warm.

2. In a heavy pan, melt the butter and the sugar together with the orange and lemon juice. Add the grated zest of the orange and lemon and continue to heat.

3. Add the orange liqueur; as soon as the mixture starts to bubble, add the folded crêpes. Allow the crêpes to heat through, turning once.

4. In a separate small saucepan, heat the brandy, cognac, or bourbon.

5. Ignite the crêpes as follows: remove 1 tsp. of the hot liquor and light it with a match. Gently pour the flaming teaspoonful back into the pan to ignite the whole amount. Then pour all the flaming brandy (or whatever liquor is used) over the crêpes and serve as soon as the flames burn out.

If you wish to flame the crêpes in front of a group of guests, first try to ignite a small amount of the spirit which you plan to use in the kitchen. You will avoid embarrassment; sometimes, for some reason, even the best brandy will not light.

Quick Parfait Bombe

1 qt. vanilla ice cream in a round plas-   1 pt. raspberry sherbet in a round plastic container   tic container

1. Soften the vanilla ice cream by placing it in the refrigerator.

2. With a spoon dipped in hot water, carefully scoop about a pint of ice cream from the center of the container. The hole in the center of the ice cream should be about the size of the pint container. (See drawing.)

3. Keep the sherbet as frozen as possible. Dip the container of sherbet into very hot water and leave for about 10 seconds. Loosen it from the container by running a thin-bladed knife which has been dipped into the hot water around the inside edge of the container. Press the bottom of the container to release the sherbet.

4. Quickly press the sherbet into the center of the vanilla ice cream. Replace the cover and refreeze the mold.

5. To serve the bombe, remove it from its container by again dipping it into hot water for a short time and running a hot knife around the edge to loosen it. Invert onto a serving platter. Cut it with a heated knife.

CHEF'S SECRET: Work as quickly as possible. Have the hot water always on hand, but do not work close to the stove, as you do not want the ice cream to melt.

If you do not have a suitable container for the hot water, heat a coffee pot filled with water. This will be good for keeping the tools hot.

If you want to be extremely successful with this dessert, make it a day or two ahead and keep it in the coldest part of the freezer. Be sure to place some solidly-frozen food on top of it, since cold travels downward.

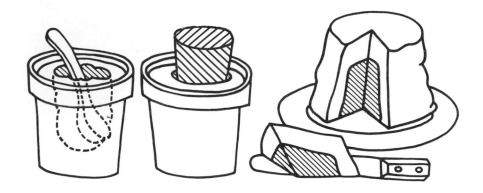

Watermelon Ice

10 to 12 servings

2 10-oz. packages frozen cranberry-orange relish
1 pt. heavy cream
1 pinch salt
2 to 3 tbsp. granulated sugar

½ gallon vanilla ice cream, brick style
1 pt. lime sherbet
1 piece cardboard, 12 by 12 inches
masking tape
aluminum foil

1. Prepare the mold: Fold the cardboard in half to form a "V"-shaped opening with 6-inch sides. Reinforce the fold on the outside with masking tape. Secure the opening of this "V" by placing tape on each side from top to bottom. Line the "V" with aluminum foil. (See drawing, page 266.)

2. Whip the cream until it forms stiff peaks, adding the salt and the sugar.

3. Chop the frozen relish and fold it into the whipped cream. Chill. Pile this mixture into the foil-lined mold, forming a half-moon shape to resemble the inside of a watermelon.

4. Cut a ¾-inch-thick slice from the long side of the ice cream. Cut it diagonally to make two triangles. Place these triangles, with their large ends together, around the cranberry mixture. Pat them into place. Place the mold in the freezer and let it freeze until it is firm.

5. Smooth the lime sherbet over the ice cream to resemble a watermelon rind. Freeze again.

6. To serve, remove the cardboard-foil frame. Place the mold on a serving platter and slice it crosswise into 10 to 12 pieces.

CHEF'S SECRET: This is one way to make a very festive-looking, elegant, but easy-to-do dessert without a fancy mold or special equipment. If you do not intend to use it right away, pack it in plastic wrap and then in aluminum foil and keep frozen until later.

If you want to be very fancy, press some chocolate chips into the red cranberry portion of the mold to resemble seeds of a watermelon.

Instead of the lime sherbet, you can use crème de menthe or pistachio ice cream.

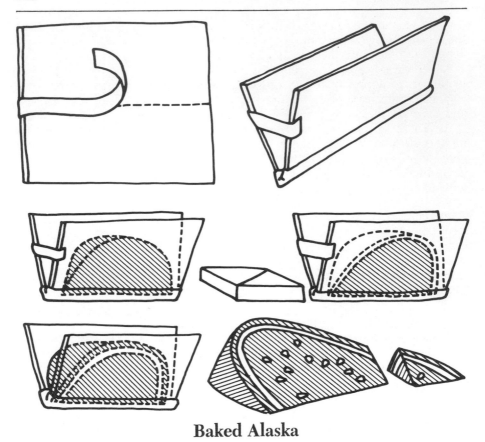

Baked Alaska

8 servings

1   1-lb. spongecake or poundcake (homemade or commercial)
10 egg whites
1 cup granulated sugar

1 cup powdered sugar
1 pint vanilla ice cream (preferably brick style)
1 pint raspberry sherbet

1. Select the plate or platter you will use to serve the Baked Alaska.

2. Cover the serving dish with a piece of paper and draw a line around the inner edges of it. Cut this out and copy it onto a piece of strong cardboard. Test to be sure the piece of cardboard will fit on the serving plate, then cover it with aluminum foil and place it in the freezer.

3. Cut enough ½-inch slices of the cake to cover a surface approximately 6 by 8 inches. Arrange on the foil-covered cardboard and freeze.

4. Cut the vanilla ice cream into slices and cover the cake, leaving a ½-inch rim around the edges uncovered. Refreeze.

5. Mound the sherbet over the vanilla ice cream, rounding and smoothing the top. Freeze again.

6. Put about seven of the egg whites into a mixing bowl. Add a little of the granulated sugar and start to beat them. As they get frothy, slowly add the rest of the granulated sugar and about two-thirds of the powdered sugar.

7. As soon as the egg whites are stiff and start to get dry, stop beating. Add the remaining egg whites and the rest of the powdered sugar and start to beat again. Continue until they are stiff and shiny.

8. With a wide rubber spatula, cover the ice cream and the cake completely, using approximately three-fourths of the meringue.

9. Place the remaining meringue in a pastry bag fitted with a star tube and decorate the top with swirls, curls, and stars. Freeze until ready to use.

10. To serve, preheat the oven to 500 degrees. Sprinkle the top of the meringue with powdered sugar, through a sieve, and place in the oven for about 1 minute. Check the Baked Alaska and turn it around if the front is not as brown as the back; leave for another minute. Serve immediately, slicing with a knife dipped in hot water.

CHEF'S SECRET: It is very important to refreeze the Baked Alaska after every step, especially when you make it for the first time. Later, when you feel you have mastered the task, you will probably not have to refreeze it after each step.

If you follow the steps for making the meringue, you will have the stiffest and easiest-to-use meringue ever. Dusting the top of the meringue with powdered sugar before baking it will hasten the browning of the top and improve the looks of the dish.

If you wish, you can use the egg yolks to make a special sauce to be served with the Baked Alaska. In an electric blender or mixer, mix the 10 egg yolks with 10 tbsp. sugar until the mixture turns lemon colored and fluffy. Add 1 cup cognac, brandy, or other liqueur, starting drop by drop and then increasing the amount to a thin stream, beating continuously. Spoon the sauce over the Baked Alaska after the portions are served or spoon some on each serving plate before laying a slice of the Baked Alaska on the plate.

Apples Stuffed with Pistachio Ice Cream

8 servings

8 firm medium-sized apples, unpeeled
1 pint pistachio ice cream

lemon juice–water, or white vinegar–
water mixture

1. Select apples which have stems, if possible. Cut a ½-inch slice from the top of each apple. Save this slice.

2. With a small paring knife and a melon-ball cutter, carefully remove the cores from the apples.

3. Carefully remove the inside pulp from the apples with the melon-ball cutter or with a spoon. Save the pulp. Hold in water mixture to prevent darkening.

4. After all 8 apples are hollowed out, quickly mix the ice cream (which should be semisoft) with the chopped apple flesh and spoon the mixture into the apples. Replace the tops and serve.

CHEF'S SECRET: Speed is the most important secret of this recipe. Before you start to pare the apples, be sure you have on hand some water mixed with lemon juice or white vinegar. Dip the apples into the acidulated liquid so they will not turn brown. Always cut the apples with a stainless steel knife; this will also help keep them from turning brown.

If you must put the ice cream–filled apples in the freezer, instead of serving them immediately, do not leave them in the freezer for longer than a couple of hours; if you do, the apples will become inedible. But this dish is worth the bother. The taste and texture contrast is in beautiful harmony.

Parfait Fürst Pückler

8 servings

For the first mixture:
1 pt. heavy cream
pinch salt
2 eggs, separated
1 tsp. vanilla
4 tsp. sugar
4 tbsp. powdered sugar

For the second mixture:
1 pt. heavy cream
8 tbsp. sugar
4 tbsp. cocoa

1 egg
2 tbsp. brandy
1 pinch salt

For the third mixture:
1 pt. heavy cream
1 envelope unflavored gelatin
3 tbsp. water
½ cup water
1 cup fresh purée of strawberries
6 tbsp. sugar
1 pinch salt

1. Line a three-quart oblong container with aluminum foil as follows: First place in the bottom a strip as wide as the bottom but long enough to come up the two ends with 4 additional inches of foil on each end. Then, line the dish with another piece of foil covering the width and coming up the two sides with 4 additional inches on each side.

2. Prepare the first mixture by beating the heavy cream with the salt and the sugar until it forms stiff peaks. Lightly beat the egg yolks with the vanilla and gently stir this mixture into the whipped cream. Beat the egg whites with the powdered sugar until they are stiff, but not dry. Gently fold the cream–egg yolk mixture into the beaten egg whites. Pour this mixture into the foil-lined dish and place it in the freezer until firm.

3. Prepare the second mixture by beating the heavy cream until it is stiff, adding the sugar gradually. Beat the egg with the cocoa, brandy, and salt until the mixture is frothy. Gently fold the egg-cocoa-brandy mixture into the heavy cream. Pour over the first mixture and place in the freezer again until firm.

4. Prepare the strawberry purée by first cutting the strawberries in small pieces while holding them in your hand, then gently pressing them with a silver or stainless steel fork in a sieve and collecting the liquid as it runs off. Add the sugar to the liquid. Dissolve the gelatin in the 3 tbsp. of water. Bring the ½ cup water to a boil and add the dissolved gelatin. Cool in an ice-water bath. Beat the heavy cream until stiff, adding the salt. Pour the gelatin over the surface of the cream and gently fold it in. Add the strawberry purée, folding all ingredients together. Pour this mixture over the top of the chocolate

mixture. Place in the freezer. As soon as the top mixture is firm, fold the aluminum foil from all four sides over the parfait and keep it frozen.

5. To serve, cut very thin slices from the parfait with a hot, wet knife.

CHEF'S SECRET: This original ice cream recipe was named after a German prince or Fürst who was a great gourmet. As you can see, besides the flavorings, only one ingredient—whipped cream—is used.

This is the finest ice cream dish imaginable, but do not serve too much because it is so rich.

Index

Louis Szathmáry was educated as a journalist and psychologist in his native Hungary. He has, in a much traveled life, been actor, soldier, marriage counselor, prisoner of war, lecturer, and chef. In recent years, as a man for all seasonings, he has been a food consultant for industry and government and now conducts The Bakery, a unique restaurant on Chicago's Near North Side.